SCATOLOGY AND CIVILITY
IN THE ENGLISH-CANADIAN NOVEL

THEORY/CULTURE

General editors:
Linda Hutcheon, Gary Leonard, Jill Matus,
Janet Paterson, and Paul Perron

REINHOLD KRAMER

Scatology and Civility in the English-Canadian Novel

UNIVERSITY OF TORONTO PRESS
Toronto Buffalo London

© University of Toronto Press Incorporated 1997
Toronto Buffalo London
Printed in Canada

ISBN 0-8020-0746-5 (cloth)

Printed on acid-free paper

Canadian Cataloguing in Publication Data

Kramer, Reinhold, 1959–
  Scatology and civility in the English-Canadian novel

  (Theory/culture)
  Includes bibliographical references and index.
  ISBN 0-8020-0746-5

  1. Canadian fiction (English) – 19th century – History
and criticism.* 2. Canadian fiction (English) – 20th
century – History and criticism.* 3. Scatology in
literature. I. Title. II. Series.

  PS8191.S32K73 1997   C813.009'353   C96-931894-4
  PR9192.6.S32K73 1997

This book has been published with the help of a grant from the Humanities
and Social Sciences Federation of Canada, using funds provided by the
Social Sciences and Humanities Research Council of Canada.

University of Toronto Press acknowledges the assistance to its publishing
program of the Canada Council and the Ontario Arts Council.

Contents

ACKNOWLEDGMENTS   vii

A Graphic Introduction to the Civilized Self   3

Part I: Manners and the English-Canadian Novel
1. 'It Never Was Mine': Bodily Disgust in Personal and Social Histories   17
2. Country and Town: 'The Size of Sheep's Dung' and Other Metaphors   25
3. Doubling Back: The Rhetorical Recovery of the Body   30
4. Extreme Scepticism: Parodies of the Civilized Self   34

Part II: The Social Body: Scatology and Ideological Hierarchy in the English-Canadian Novel
5. Immigrants, Foul Ghettos, and Social Climbers: Marking Fictional Class Structures   41
6. 'This Is the British Fucking Empire': Race   53
7. Allegories and Sites of Power: Politics and Economics   71
8. Hygiene Guidelines for Virtual Bodies: Science and Technology   85
9. Polluted Women   99
10. 'The Hind Parts of God': Materialist Epistemologies and the Mimesis of Religion   115

Part III: Two Studies in Scatology and Literary Genre
   Introduction   143
11. 'Wen I de Small Man Sometime I Used to Eat Goat Shit': The Base and Written Self in Fictional Autobiography   147

12 Post-Modern Decomposition: Guaranteeing the World of an Indeterminate Text   162

Epilogue: New Detours to the Symbolic   181

NOTES   189
WORKS CITED   225
INDEX   245

Acknowledgments

I owe a great debt to David Williams and Robert Kroetsch, whose fictional and scholarly experiments greatly influenced this study, and who allowed me many civil liberties. Thanks also to Judith Weil, Evelyn Hinz, Wolfgang Kloos, David Arnason, and Gerry Friesen for many extremely helpful suggestions and corrections. Most of all I thank my wife, Rita.

This book is dedicated to Madeline, Stephanie, and Michelle – architects of disorder – and to Rita, who civilized us all.

Humani nil a me alienum puto

SCATOLOGY AND CIVILITY
IN THE ENGLISH-CANADIAN NOVEL

A Graphic Introduction to the Civilized Self

To all who carve their love on a picnic table
or scratch it on smoked glass panes of a public toilet,
I send my thanks for each plain and perfect fable
of how the three pains of the body, surfeit,
hunger, and chill (or loneliness), create
a furniture and art of their own easing.

– Mona Van Duyn, 'Open Letter from a Constant Reader'

The body must educate itself.

– Gamaliel Harding in *The New Ancestors*

Circa 1555 in *Galateo*, Giovanni Della Casa offered some advice: 'It is not a proper habit when, as sometimes happens, one sees something disgusting on the road to turn to one's companions and point it out to them. Even less so should one offer something unpleasant to smell, as some insist on doing, placing it even under a companion's nose saying: "Now Sir, please smell how this stinks," when instead he should be saying: "Don't smell this because it stinks"' (Della Casa 5–6). Between the implied reader for whom such an admonition would be necessary and Mordecai Richler's possible self in *St Urbain's Horseman*, Jake Hersh, who cannot pick up his own stool, lie several hundred years in which Western attitudes towards the body and bodily excretions changed so much that what once evidently aroused

4 Scatology and Civility in the English-Canadian Novel

sensate curiosity now evokes disgust. Not that either the admonition or the disgust would be impossible in the other century, but the satiric effect of Richler's scene depends upon the reader's momentary, civilized implication in Jake's dilemma.

In 1939 Norbert Elias – rooted in Freud's comments in *Das Umbehagen in der Kultur* (1930) about a revised history which would cover the history of bodily repression – surveyed manners books from the twelfth to the eighteenth century, showing how courtesy and manners arose as a substitute for feudal action (9) during the time when European monarchies became centralized.[1] After the Middle Ages[2] coercion in regard to manners increased on several fronts, all of which Elias connects to the repression of the appearance of animality: carving tends to move behind the scenes so that the whole animal rarely reaches the table (120), the bedroom is privatized (163), and proscriptions about bodily excretions greatly multiply so that to urinate in public (130), to look into one's used handkerchief (147), or even to speak about certain body parts becomes bad manners. These changes create a different emotional life because they increase bodily separation between people (69), enlarging the sphere of the 'civilized' individual. For Elias, the mannered 'I' cannot be understood as the result of incipient bacteriology, since the changes predate Pasteur by centuries; nor are manners attributable to inner or familial processes (228, 259). 'Nichts an der Verhaltensweisen bei Tisch ist schlechthin selbstverständlich, gleichsam als Produkt eines "natürlichen" Peinlichkeitsgefühls' (144; 'Nothing in table manners is self-evident, as it were, or the product of a "natural" feeling of delicacy' 107): the socialization of the child recapitulates a social history (306). 'Gerade weil das gesellschaftliche Gebot, sich nicht entblösst oder bei natürlichen Verrichtungen zu zeigen, nun gegenüber allen Menschen gilt und in dieser Form dem Kinde eingeprägt wird, erscheint es dem Erwachsenen als Gebot seines eigenen Innern und erhält die Form eines mehr oder weniger totalen und automatisch wirkenden Selbstzwanges' (189; 'Precisely because the social command not to show oneself exposed or performing natural functions now operates with regards to everyone and is imprinted in this form on the child, it seems to the adult a command of his own inner self and takes on the form of a more or less automatic self-restraint' 139). The adult's invitation, then, to smell a piece of excrement would appear as 'ein "Überbleibsel" aus der Kinderzeit' (193; 'a "remnant" from childhood' 142).[3]

Elias's work is difficult to verify, since to put together a history of the body he must rely on textual transmission at a time when the belief that a text can represent the body is under question. Historical novels such as Patrick Süskind's celebrated *Das Parfüm* (1985) now rely heavily on a notion of history very similar to Elias's, and theorize an aesthetic shift corresponding to the suppression of the senses. Several critiques have been levelled at Elias – that he ignores other variables such as architecture, gender, medicine, technical change (Bullough 444), that manners implicate only the surface and not the real historical self (Adams 1015), that writers on manners borrowed extensively from one another, and that manners books are biased towards the court (Seigal 125).[4] These commentators indicate that the process is more complex than Elias thought, but do not deny the magnitude of his contribution, in particular his sociological revision of psychoanalysis. Like *Surveiller et punir*, Michel Foucault's later study of penal architecture and the *disciplines* in public buildings, on the job, and in the home, Elias shows how the cultural authorities 'qualifient et répriment un ensemble de conduites' (Foucault 1975, 180; 'defined and repressed a mass of behaviour') that the criminal justice systems ignored (1984, 193), but Elias does so without Foucault's (disavowed) nostalgia.

One of the bases of this study is Foucault's description in *Folie et déraison* of how post-Enlightenment societies constitute themselves on precisely that liminal madness which, newly rationalized, has been banished to the geographical boundaries of the society; filth likewise appears as a subject of prohibition at the civil boundaries of the manners book. Foucault's project is not merely academic, since for him the appropriate response to the boundary is transgression, via, for example, LSD or bondage, whereby the body apocalyptically escapes its docile habit. According to James Miller, Foucault's biographer, the main interest of these experimental trangressions was Foucault's wish 'to become someone else' (Foucault interview quoted in Miller 328), a wish that Miller uses as a central trope in *The Passion of Michel Foucault*. My purposes are much more docile and depend much less upon a notion of the law and repression as an *alien* surveillance. Following Niklas Luhmann, I would situate the law at the point where differing behavioural expectations (between individuals or groups) need to be coordinated, especially in a complex society (17). Instead of allowing the fully variant expectations of two individuals in a situation, we evolve a mass of daily behavioural controls and a legal code

6   Scatology and Civility in the English-Canadian Novel

to limit this double contingency. While Luhmann perhaps underemphasizes the incarcerating effects of manners, especially where certain classes and races control manners, he is able to show how manners operate not simply either to permit and repress behaviours, but also to allow individuals to anticipate what is expected of them (26), and how, at the more explicit level of law, 'an orientation towards the rule makes the orientation towards expectations unnecessary' (30), simplifying social interactions. Conscious that the law is both coercive and enabling, Elias calls Foucault's 'panopticon' by its more traditional, if no less political, names: socialization, the process of civilization.

Contemporary manners books suggest the continuing validity of this approach. Elias comments on the lack of embarrassment with which Erasmus discusses, in *De civilitate morum puerilium*, the questions of urinating and farting in public (130).[5] We might compare this to recent guides such as *The Amy Vanderbilt Complete Book of Etiquette*, where the only hint at urination avoids direct reference, enjoining boys to put the toilet seat down when leaving the bathroom (Vanderbilt 30): filth here looks like (still) the domain of the child, not of the adult. In *Charlotte Ford's Book of Modern Manners*, which is advertised as willing to address questions that other manners books ignore, the only references to toilet behaviour have been transferred a stage further – to dogs. It is the responsibility of the civilized owner to clean up the animal's mess (Ford 482).[6] *Emily Post's Etiquette* emphasizes that bathrooms must be left immaculate, but refers mainly to tub, basin (679), and paper on the floor (90). When she does mention the toilet, it is only to say that toilet seats and lids ought to be left down (737). Llewellyn Miller (*The Encyclopedia of Etiquette*), who does speak of urination – 'Only a spoiled child or an irresponsible adult leaves a basin messy, a tub ringed, or a toilet seat splashed' (36) – curiously insists that even the noisiest toilet must be flushed (36), as if it is *over-fastidiousness* about liquid noise, not a *lack* of fastidiousness about urine, which postpones flushing. Silence, of course, is even more effective in the creation of a taboo than the aforementioned cues: thus Vanderbilt will not explain the difference between a '"slightly naughty" story' and a 'dirty story' because 'everyone knows the difference' (746); thus these writers on manners speak of burping and scatological language, but are silent on farting.[7] Peter Stallybrass and Allon White, following Pierre Bordieau, suggest that in the cultural production of a 'new man,' the abbreviation of manners into details of dress and bearing puts them 'beyond the grasp of consciousness' (Stallybrass 88).

By the time of *Miss Manners' Guide to Rearing Perfect Children* (1984), it is as if the compulsion of the manners book to exhibit and to speak has finally collided with its own inhibitions. Since the writer on manners must, of course, have good manners, she is under her 'own' prohibition and so ought not to mention the bathroom in the formal context of a book. The result is the creation of Miss Manners's (Judith Martin's) ironic voice, taking manners very seriously even as she affects to play with them: 'In vain does Miss Manners cry that she doesn't care what people do in the bathroom – she doesn't want to think about it' (52). A series of civilized censorships follow: do not ask where people are going, do not ask how long they will be gone, do not ask if you can get in soon (52), do not mention the pills or cosmetic devices in a host's bathroom, do not speak through a closed bathroom door (53). To the gentleman who turns the water on so that people will not hear his bathroom sounds and to the lady who wonders if she should ask a guest not to leave a toilet lid up, Miss Manners replies that no gentleman or woman would listen to what goes on behind a bathroom door and that 'a true lady does not acknowledge that there is such a thing as a toilet' (54). In this way Judith Martin's irony splits off her own voice from the voices that ask embarrassing questions. The crisis that the self-conscious humour masks is that to justify her book Martin must speak of filth at the same time as she wants to inaugurate silence.

Although Miss Manners might complicate the details of Elias's history, his thesis of a growth in Western civilized repression not only fits manners books, but also the history of the self in a number of postwar Canadian novels. The selves in manners books are created and allegorical, tracing imagined, repressed, and wished histories which both create new historical events and originate in lived histories. The novelistic version of the self too is an abstraction (shortened, coded through the technology of the alphabet and past texts) of a potential historical self. If, as Jacques Lacan convincingly suggests, 'le sujet est décentré par rapport à l'individu' (17; 'the subject is decentered in relation to the individual' 9) and relocated in discourse, then literature becomes an important scene for the operation of an unconscious. This conception of the ego as a linguistic construct loses something of Freud's bodily determinism, but it gains what was missing in Freud – a social context mediated by a theory of language. And if the relation between books on manners to actual social practice is debatable, the books at least encode a set of European and North American social ideals that the novelist, like any other member of the culture, is heir to: 'The novel ... has become the zoo of everyday practices since the establishment of modern science' (de Certeau 78). Both manners book and novel often put implicit culture, that mnemonic culture coded through the body, under the eye of consciousness, and I confess that I am one of those readers (identified in Havelock Ellis's *Studies in the Psychology of Sex*) who want to hear about the hero's digestion and excretion (67).

Robertson Davies lets the reader in on privacies, and yet his hyperbolic abstractions in *World of Wonders* 'outmanner' the manners book: Paul Dempster knows that he ought not to 'go' anywhere except at home (32), and that his sodomy thus appears to be invited. The hospital in Audrey Thomas's *Mrs Blood* rebroadcasts the privatization taking place in the surrounding culture – urination and the stripping of bloody sheets take place behind curtains (15).

In Gabrielle Roy's *La petite poule d'eau* the teachers like Mlle Côté who come to the Water Hen introduce hygiene. The Tousignant children learn the symbolization of animality during a dance in which they stick their buttocks into the air like the water hens, and they also (to follow Roy's pun) learn *all* the *signs* of a mannered body, so that when their mother Luzina questions them, her near-explicitness about snot – 'T'as pas mis tes doigts dans le nez?' (88; 'You didn't stick your fingers in your nose?' 54) – already marks her as a past for the children. Roy approaches the silent nature of manners prohibitions in her narrative style. Instead of reporting a direct reply, she edges the children's voices into that of the narrator: 'On ne parlait pas de doigts dans le nez devant la fine et belle demoiselle, voyons!' (88; 'You didn't even talk about fingers in the nose before nice, pretty Mademoiselle!' 54). Silent on the mimetic level, but spoken on the diegetic, the exclamation retains not only the scientizing force of impersonal address ('On ne parlait pas') as opposed to Luzina's familiar and colloquial 'T'as pas mis' (87), but also the authority of a narrator who stands above the represented world of the Water Hen.

In Part I of this study I will show how this creation of the civilized self takes several forms in the Canadian novel, including personal histories, implied social histories, and images of a rural/urban shift. As the instance from Roy indicates, the 'origins' of the unclean self are generally placed, *mise en abîme*, in a past or on a farm, from which the self rises to manners and urbanity, before becoming nostalgic for the body or sceptical about civilized values.

Part II of my study covers a similar terrain, but from a very different, at times contradictory, perspective. Anthropologist Mary Douglas argues that hygiene, taboos, and pollution rites, whatever their psychological origins or effects, serve to order such cultural systems as cosmology, class hierarchy, and gender relations. The very difficulty about the *transcription* of the body that Elias encounters suggests the potency of Douglas's model: she follows the linguistic model in which the sign is not directly related to its referent but is conventional and interpretable only within a system. Thus she explains pollution rites as a culture-specific *language*. In any speech act 'I am, in fact, constantly expressing a plenitude of meanings, some intended, others of which I am unaware' (Holquist xx). This allows us to address the civilizing process not just as a monolith – 'the conquest of nature by technology had to include our own bodies' (G. Grant 185) – but as a set of specifications, some of which have been of incalculable value and some of which have not.

Looking at language, we must allow for metonymic expansion and interdisciplinary leaps. Metonymically the sign 'feces' links with 'the lower body' – anus, vagina, penis – and thus with the erotic, the animal (whose lower body is not usually covered), and, on the other hand, with underwear; as a medico-scientific term, with levels of formality in language; as 'manure,' with 'dirt,' but also with 'earth,' 'fertility,' and 'life'; as a 'by-product,' to 'digestion' and other industrial processes which create 'garbage' and 'pollution'; as 'bodily ejectus,' to other, advertent and inadvertent ejecta such as 'saliva' and 'blood'; as 'waste,' to the process of 'decay' ending in 'dead matter' and 'corpse.' Clearly significations can be diametrically opposed, so the attempt to find a single meaning apart from the cultural and discursive contexts would be misguided.

At times it will appear that I am addressing what is marginal in a text. According to Derrida, however, it is exactly upon the margins that a text is constituted: his carefully reasoned blindness – 'I do not know what is essential and what is accessory in a work' (Derrida 1987, 63) – allows us to notice that every mark in a text can be interpreted as a deictic mark. This does not mean that the part becomes a substitute for the whole, genetically bearing the code for the entire organism, but that each part (and especially the repressed part) can tell us something important about the speech act. That the ejected is often a trope for the marginal in gender, class, and race leads us to a second corollary: we have no choice but to cross disciplines because, for example, scatology has been used as a social register to differentiate classes from one another. In Part II, then, I investigate the ideological uses to which filth has been put in the Canadian novel vis-à-vis class, race, politics and economics, science and technology, gender, and religion.[8]

If in Part II I reduce texts to examples of social systems, I hope that in Part III (discussing fictional autobiography and post-modernism) I return what is owed to chaos. Benjamin Walker's *Encyclopedia of Esoteric Man*, a not always reliable but always interesting reference guide, identifies thirty-nine types of solids, liquids, and gases that the body is in the habit of ejecting. These we might call the repressed in Descartes's *reductio*: 'Je ne suis donc, précisément parlant, qu'une chose qui pense, c'est-à-dire un esprit, un entendement ou une raison' (II, 277; 'To speak accurately I am not more than a thing which thinks, that is to say a mind or a soul, or an understanding, or a reason' II, 173). Walker's list does not even include inorganic 'wastes' such as heat and electrical impulses, but under the rubric of scatology these substances (especially those expelled through the anus or the urethra) take us into a very narrow range of human experience which is further narrowed if we look for filth as the explicit object of textual discourse.

On the other hand, as satirists and psychoanalysts never tire of noticing, excretion is a biological and therefore psychological universal among primates: 'le déchet comme le cadavre *m'indiquent* ce que j'écarte en permanence pour vivre. Ces humeurs, cette souillure, cette merde sont ce que la vie supporte à peine et avec peine de la mort' (Kristeva 1980, 11; 'refuse and corpses *show me* what I permanently thrust aside in order to live. These bodily fluids, this defilement, this shit are what life withstands, hardly and with difficulty, on the part of death' 1982, 3). Although Eric Partridge puzzled over the fact that so much information on the word 'shit' for his *Dictionary of Slang and Unconventional English* seemed to come from Canadian academics (Partridge, Vol. 2, 1269), scatological invective too is hardly parochial: St Thomas More called the Lutheran heresy a 'foule fylthy dunghyll' (quoted in Manuel 136); Washoe, one of the first apes to learn bits of American Sign Language, called a threatening rhesus macaque 'dirty monkey,' improvising upon a sign which she had been taught to apply to soiled objects or feces (Fleming 100). If figurative language 'distinguishes us from the beasts' as Augustine claimed in

De Doctrina Christiana (3.84), what are we to make of Washoe's trope?[9]

Throughout this study, but especially in Part III, I want to focus concerns about the materiality and historicity of literary texts (Erich Auerbach, Fredric Jameson, Edward Said, Elaine Scarry) as well as about the role of the body in the text (Mikhail Bakhtin, Francis Barker).[10] In Auerbach's estimation, Tacitus's avoidance of slang when reporting the speech of the common soldier and rebel ringleader Percennius means that Tacitus has transformed the language that would have been spoken into rhetoric (34). Auerbach may be right, but in many quarters (not just among realists and autobiographers) this means that colloquial language laced with bodily references is not rhetorical but a more direct transcription of reality, a notion that Salman Rushdie plays with in *Midnight's Children* by means of Padma, Saleem Sinai's 'dung goddess' and reader who makes the demands of matter upon word-spinners. In an age of 'scratch 'n sniff' books on the one hand and deconstruction on the other, it is worth analysing how 'language both absorbs the material world and empties itself of material content. To get "things" into words will be the project of some, to get 'things' out of words the project of others. Materialist criticism simply observes the ways in which this may be done (as well as the costs in each direction) and avoids collapsing into a generalized state of scepticism each time an instance of emptying, or referential slipperiness, is encountered' (Scarry 1988, xx). Scarry's balanced notion of mimesis is crucial to my study: 'A materialist conception of language ordinarily has two companion assumptions: first, that language is capable of registering in its own contours the contours and weight of the material world; second, that language itself may enter, act on, and alter the material world' (1988, xi).[11]

My study will focus mainly on what I hope is a broad selection of postwar English-Canadian novels: by major Canadian novelists and minor, male and female, patriot and ex-patriate; novels from various Canadian regions; a variety of genres from the naturalistic to the experimental, the best seller to the academic. I include *The Collected Works of Billy the Kid: Left Handed Poems* since it, like *Coming through Slaughter*, uses prose narrative and historical photographs even as it calls the term 'novel' into question.

Compared to nineteenth-century texts, the work of Lawrence and Joyce, of Jarry and Beckett, and, after 1960, of Canadian writers displays scatology much more visibly and in greater material specificity.

12   Scatology and Civility in the English-Canadian Novel

Alongside the increased privatization of excretory functions – even nudists insist on private elimination facilities (Kira 107) – we find such an explosion of references to scatology that some have begun to call post-modern culture 'excremental' (Kroker 7). Metaphors of reticence and speech (or repression and expression) are notoriously difficult to substantiate, but nevertheless we may remark on the differences between a society which in 1934 banned *Such Is My Beloved* from open library shelves, and a society which in the 1960s eventually gave its blessing to *Lady Chatterley's Lover* with its hints at anal sexuality.¹² In comparison to almost any post-1960s novel, Frances Brooke's *The History of Emily Montague*, James De Mille's *A Strange Manuscript Found in a Copper Cylinder*, and Susanna Moodie's *Mark Hurdlestone* seem empty of scatology. Brooke mocks the 'curled, powdered, perfumed' self in Sir George Clayton (100), but she does it without recourse to scatology, and manners in her novel are primarily used for governing the relations between the sexes. In *Mark Hurdlestone*, the civilizing process is clearly important in differentiating characters – 'the one was all soul, the other a mere animal' (157) – but decay is described very generally (76, 79, 168), and Moodie's nearest approach to scatology is in 'soiled mattresses' (185). Judging by later Canadian literary productions, Donnaconna was not pulling Jacques Cartier's leg: 'Donnaconna ... nous a certifié avoir été à la terre du Saguenay, où il y a infini or, rubis et autres richesses, et y sont les hommes blancs comme en France, et accoutrés de draps de laine. Plus, dit avoir vu autres pays, où les gens ne mangent point et n'ont point de fondement' (Cartier 79–80; 'Donnaconna assured us that he had been in the country of the Saguenay, where there was plentiful gold, rubies, and other riches, and where there were white men as in France, dressed in woollen clothing. Moreover, he had seen another country where the people ate nothing and had no anuses'). Some of the differences, to be sure, can be ascribed to genre. There are more scatological references in an autobiographical account such as *Roughing It in the Bush* and many more in Thomas Haliburton's satire. However, if we compare *The Clockmaker* to Mordecai Richler's work, Martha Ostenso's realism to that of Margaret Laurence, the mythic recurrences in *Such Is My Beloved* or *Tay John* to those in *The River Horsemen*, A.E. van Vogt's science fiction to William Gibson's, or even Richler's novels in the 1950s to his later novels, the vast increase in scatology again seems overwhelming.¹³

Alice Munro's Ada Morrison, who fashioned her literary persona upon Tennyson's Princess Ida, and whose notion of 'classic' literary history is somewhat foreshortened, complains and prophesies: 'I never expected to see such a use made of the printed word ... Next day they will be telling about how they go to the toilet, why do they leave that out? There isn't any of that in *Silas Marner*. There isn't in the classic writers' (*Lives of Girls and Women* 145).

More sinisterly in David Pownall's *Masterclass*, Andrey Zhdanov plays the piano with his bum to parody, he thinks, Shostakovich's style of music. My purpose is neither to praise the liberties won by modernist or post-modernist art, nor to lament the loss of some innocent form of discourse. To say that 'the most proscribed literary forms – like the most persecuted social deviants – must reveal unsettling truths about society that it does not want to hear' (Davis xx) is too simple a notion of social repression. Yet scatology does (as Wolfgang Kayser says of the grotesque) challenge the principle of 'Kunst als Nachbildung der schönen Natur bzw. als ihre idealisierende Steigerung' (31; 'art as an imitation of beautiful nature or as its idealization' 30). More damaging to Zhdanov, we shall see in Part III that scatology offends against mimesis itself.[14] Although I will argue that filth never completely decomposes representation, the authors of manners books may be guarding more than just daintiness. 'Whatever causes offence when revealed to men's sight likewise offends when forced upon their hearing. If the conversation requires one to mention some private part of the body, it should be referred to by the way of polite circumlocution. Again if something should come up that might physically upset a listener, for example, if someone should mention vomiting or a latrine or a stench, he should preface it by saying, "by your leave"' (Erasmus 287). By your leave, then.

PART I

MANNERS AND THE
ENGLISH-CANADIAN NOVEL

1
'It Never Was Mine': Bodily Disgust in Personal and Social Histories

Dégoût d'une nourriture, d'une saleté, d'un déchet, d'une ordure. Spasmes et vomissements qui me protègent.
(Loathing an item of food, a piece of filth, waste, or dung. The spasms and vomiting that protect me.)

– Julia Kristeva, *Pouvoirs de l'horreur*

Is it still me? ... It never was mine.

– Christian Enzensberger, *Grosserer Versuch über den Schmutz*

One of the chapters by her husband that Susanna Moodie allowed into *Roughing It in the Bush* tells the story of the 'Ould Dhragoon,' a halfpay officer, indeed something of an *alter ego* to J.W.D. Moodie except that the dragoon enters pioneer life more wholeheartedly than the author. The dragoon plasters his chimney with a mixture of clay and cow-dung; he writes poems:

> And I've made me an illigant pig-sty
> Well littered wid straw and wid hay
> And it's there, free from noise of the chilther,
> I sleep in the heat of the day. (350)

Even if his dialect did not clash so significantly with the voices of the Moodies, especially with the stifling voice in Susanna's poetry, his too-easy familiarity with excrement dissociates him from them – making him quaint at best, at worst a sign for the loss of culture, the loss that Susanna fears in the new country. The Moodies, despite their insufficient patrimonies, were not about to herd swine in the old country; yet from the distance of Canada, English pigsties hardly seemed defiling. Susanna condemns the dealers in wild lands for misrepresentations; they neglected to mention the 'dens of dirt and misery, which would, in many instances be shamed by an English pig-sty' (13).

Georges Vigarello suggests that cleanliness in Europe and North America is closely connected to the rise of democratic individualism, because individual cleanliness creates a self-sufficient sphere (225). Christian Enzensberger calls hygiene a way of separating oneself from other people (88) and as a strategic move in the creation of an 'isolated, untouchable, homogeneous, structured, unique' individual (32). In De Mille's *A Strange Manuscript Found in a Copper Cylinder*, Agnew's lack of repugnance for the savages costs him his life. De Mille's closest approaches to scatology are 'filth, squalor, and unutterable foulness' (231) and 'foul fiends' (234) – vague, embracing terms, the latter more allusive than olfactory – yet the implied scatology nevertheless sharply separates civilized and primitive.

One hundred and twenty-five years later, Alice Munro still represents the history of Rose's identity-formation in *Who Do You Think You Are?* as a repression of excremental functions, of the place in which those functions take place (the bathroom, and more broadly West Hanratty), and of the person who most often calls attention to filth (her adoptive mother, Flo, who is pleased 'to see people brought down to earth' 24). In Rose's home the bathroom is next to the kitchen: 'They were all familiar with each other's nether voices, not only in their explosive moments but in their intimate sighs and growls and pleas and statements. And they were all most prudish people. So no one ever seemed to hear, or be listening, and no reference was made. The person creating the noises in the bathroom was not connected with the person who walked out' (*Who Do You Think You Are?* 4). The social shift in Europe from communal conveniences to private (Corbin 159, Elias 130–1), concomitant with the notions that the repulsion of waste can autonomize the self (Kristeva 82) and that the communal sphere transgresses against the individual (Vigarello 225), are thus replayed in Rose's personal history, both at home (where nether voices are managed by civilized consensus) and in the even more public domain of the school, where the outhouse gives way to a more easily supervised indoor flush toilet. The half-door latrines in public buildings (which Foucault cites as instances of 'panopticism') allow a much more benign exposure than that experienced by Munro's women under the old architecture. Del Jordan, in *Lives of Girls and Women*, too young to understand the degradation of Mary Agnes as rape, nevertheless recognizes, as Rose does, a threat against the private individual in the exposure of Mary Agnes's buttocks, 'the most shameful, helpless-looking part of anyone's body' (36).

Though less immediate, similar dangers in the communal sphere are hinted at in Atwood's *The Edible Woman*. Marian feels embarrassed that Duncan, whom she has just met, might attribute Ainsley's lacy underwear to herself. Duncan refers more aggressively to communal bodily transgressions: 'The only thing about laundromats ... is that you're always finding other people's pubic hairs in the washers. Not that I mind particularly' (102). The scatological markings not only separate the main culture (in Marian) from the counter-culture (in Duncan), but also contrast (and here the positions of power are reversed) the tenuousness of female access to the male-dominated sphere of the individual. Since she is a woman, Marian cannot seem to invite transgression against the civilized sphere because any ensuing suffering will likely be hers.

In Laurence's *The Stone Angel*, Bram Shipley (blowing his nose with his fingers, using language like 'puke' 79) is scatologically presented as a less dangerous rural and Western assault on Hagar's town- and Eastern-manufactured sensibility.[1] Laurence makes Bram explicitly excremental in wordplay – 'Bramble Shitley' (131) – and in his final illness (172). When Bram relieves himself against the steps of Hagar's father's store, only Bram himself can interpret the event as accidental; Hagar certainly understands it as the displaced aggression which, structurally, it is. Since she is also the novel's consciousness, narration and 'literature' are predicated upon a repressed self. For Morag Gunn in *The Diviners* the conflict is essentially the same, but Laurence achieves greater complexity in the processes of civilization: Morag, aided by her adoptive father Christie Logan, creates a family romance in which the 'real' father, Colin Gunn, 'smells clean, not of manure or of horseshit, even though he is a farmer' (8). Furthermore, although Morag is 'delicate-minded' (35), she will not let on. As a result the civilized self in *The Diviners* is more hypothetical (above all a narrated self) than in *The Stone Angel*, and therefore more secure, especially because Morag hides her imagined delicacy, a delicacy which includes her early attempts at writing. In Morag's binary self the terms repressed in her psyche, not just hidden from public scrutiny, are the adoptive parents, who stand under the scatological sign of the real; Christie, the town scavenger, stinks of urine and excrement (6, 205, 248) and his wife Prin, prematurely senile, soon requires a bedpan (208).[2] Laurence's protagonists, even Hagar who is herself incontinent, dissociate themselves from the ill and the aged, who in Laurence's novels helplessly transgress against the privatization of eliminative functions.

Leah Adler in Richler's *Son of a Smaller Hero*, Maggie Kyle in Hodgins's *Invention of the World*, and Martin Gare in Ostenso's *Wild Geese* similarly try to create individual spheres by repressing filth. Leah isolates herself from her husband, Wolf, because he offends her sensibilities. He smells his hand after scratching his armpit (61), and uses the word 'pisher' (90) in front of guests. Since smell in wolves and other mammals seems to be an extension of the self (differentiating the home territory from other territories), excretion and urination (which often include musk) become 'secondary social gestures' (Guthrie 20, 39, 192).[3] Leah's uneasiness with this separates her from animal styles of individuation and fits her aspirations to culture. Maggie cleans her house with lye in an attempt to erase the signs of the past inhabitants who threaten to impinge upon her present community, and who thus threaten her attempts to trade her past role as loggers' whore for independence.[4] Near the end of the novel, she rises high enough to get epiphanies and to see Vancouver Island from the air. In a sense she agonizes for the entire island, which is accused of being an uncivilized place because it lacks public washrooms (235).

If that is the case, the inarticulate Martin Gare who builds washrooms in the Manitoba Interlake must be the agent of culture. And so he is. His father, Caleb, constricts the marginal form of culture Martin aspires to; even once the family has enough money, Caleb will still not allow Martin to build a new house. But the power of the civilizing process is such that it is only diverted, and Martin transfers his energy tangentially, building ornate outhouses instead (Ostenso 110, 127). Ostenso does not simply represent a history of origins (an escape from the farm and its manure), but paradoxically has the architecture surrounding excrement register the *distance* from abject origins.

In contrast to these variations on the civilizing process, those characters who represent uncoalesced personalities tend not to have privatized their eliminative functions. Mate in Mitchell's *The Vanishing Point* can pass wind on demand and in a variety of styles, making him 'the most sophisticated boy in North America' (317) to Carlyle Sinclair, but perhaps not to the reader. The same boy who insists that he bears some part of his mother's insanity leads the boys in their excremental games and claims responsibility even for feces which is not his own. In Audrey Thomas's *Mrs Blood*, Mrs Maté, 'child of nature' (40), farts unselfconsciously, while the title character in Moore's *The Luck of Ginger Coffey* is arrested for urinating in public, unintentionally focusing the accountability that he, like any proto-individual Trickster, has evaded. Herky, the toilet salesman in Richler's *St Urbain's Horseman*, pushes his idea for 'a toilet with a mind' (369), a toilet which releases only as much water as is necessary. Herky grasps something about ecology,[5] but underestimates the civilizing process, which insists upon an exorbitant amount of clean water to overwhelm the filthy evidence. He comes under the satiric sign of the incomplete person, caricature, because Richler does not allow him to become conscious of his own anal fascinations that are expressed in his photographs of Harrods' toilets: 'Not many people see the London I'm seeing' (218), he says. Harold Sonny Ladoo creates a whole society of excremental caricatures who continuously transgress against the privatization of the body in *Yesterdays*. He represents Poonwa's personal origins scatologically: 'Never forget boy dat you pee and shit fust touch dis earth in Karan Settlement' (108). Writing in Toronto about a rural Trinidadian past, Ladoo also gives a scatological version of cultural origins, confirming the version rhetorically in the contrast between characters' dialect and the third person narrator's Standard English.

Cultural 'origins' are also present in the social constructions of Thomas's *Latakia*, Hine's *The Prince of Darkness and Co.*, Davies's *The Rebel Angels*, and Mitchell's *The Vanishing Point*. Near the beginning of *Latakia* when Heleni milks facing the goat's rump, the narrator Rachel's desire and nostalgia for Michael's body is nearly parallel to her nostalgia for the Greek peasant life. Thomas, however, sets up a growing disenchantment. Rachel theorizes that for the Greek peasants 'the landscape as something to sit and admire, to be "kept up," is probably an alien concept'; in a bathing-suit changing shelter, she discovers 'shit everywhere and tampax and sodden paper diapers'; when she sees even the spotless Heleni's unconscious role in the mess, Rachel finally applies an explicit, civilized critique: '[Heleni] lets her little grandson shit under the big tree ... And the flies come and land on her food or mine perhaps. Surely she understands the connection' (111). In Herakleion Rachel discovers people who live underground, taking care of toilets: 'the guardians of the underworld have become an old man and an old woman sitting in a public lavatory beneath the city' (112–13). Rachel goes even further back than epic cosmography when she arrives in Latakia (Al-Lādhiqiyāh) the alien city in Syria marked by a bathroom so filthy that neither Rachel nor Michael will touch it (165–6).

Through Philip Sparrow, who wants to be a warlock (but only in theory), Hine's The *Prince of Darkness and Co.* parodies Robert Graves's myth-ritual fixation; both Sparrow and William Bruce, an effete, overcivilized poet, have forgotten exactly what it was that Apollonian civilization repressed. Sick and squatting to excrete in the primitive toilet at the bullring, William returns with misgivings to an abject prehistory.[6] Both Hine and Thomas implicitly valorize the civilizing process by presenting a careful loathing of cultural origins. Davies and Mitchell, on the other hand, attempt to symbolically recuperate lost origins. Simon Darcourt recognizes himself in *The Lyre of Orpheus* as the tarot deck's Fool, whose arse is being sniffed by a dog. Dogs 'have to be trained not to do it, but they forget because they have the great gift of scent, which wise, thinking Man has almost murdered' (287–8). Professor Hitzig in *The Rebel Angels* insists that civilization depends upon 'the voluntary ability to inhibit defecation.' Stromwell adds that 'when Man ate the fruit from the Tree of Knowledge he became aware of himself as something other than a portion of his surroundings and he dropped his last carefree turd, as he, with wandering steps and slow, from Eden took his solitary way' (177). Mitchell's mythical history is very similar: 'She gave Adam a bite or two and right then they clearly knew – they weren't any osprey or rainbow or fungus ... sure blew the ass off the Garden of Eden' (*The Vanishing Point* 185). The latter-day Mate's farting takes Carlyle Sinclair back from the existential 'vanishing point' to a time before the detonation at the end of innocence. Despite Davies's scatological parody of Miltonic origins, a certain amount of nostalgia surrounds the paradigmatic shift in both novels. Davies's highly stylized and sympathetically treated 'gypsies,' like Mitchell's Mate, retain many scatological signs of the implied past. Mamusia advertises a way to break up a dogfight – you 'lick the long finger good ... and you shove your finger up the arse-hole of one dog' (221) – a cure that Uncle Yerko approximates when he kicks Maria in the rear to stop her fight with Mamusia (231). More important, Mamusia represents 'the voice of the ages' (156) to the novel's scholars because she has retained an ancient filth cure, the bomari, which, depending upon the need, either rejuvenates or ages violins in a bath of horse manure.[7] Although Davies doubles back against the process that Thomas and Hine imply, the recuperation is mainly compensatory; Davies gives his scatological characters emotional force, predictive ability, and curative powers in order to counter the Cartesian splits in philosophers like John Parlabane; nevertheless, the narrating voices are always civilized academics – in this case Simon Darcourt and Maria Theotoky – who mediate between origins and the civilized self.

This discourse of unclean origins ties the Canadian novel to what might almost be classified as a paradigm shift in other disciplines. Social histories such as Barrington Moore Jr's *Privacy: Studies in Social and Cultural History* and Lawrence Wright's *Clean and Decent: The Fascinating History of the Bathroom and Water Closet* signal a shift in historiographic foci from public to bodily spheres.[8] For Moore and Wright, as for Elias, the progress of civilization is gradually, though unevenly, towards a 'clean and decent' body. Moore knows of no society where adults are permitted to defecate in the cooking area (61). Wright implicitly equates the origins of civilization with the latrines at Knossos (7), while advances are associated with demands for cleanliness.[9] A popular science account such as Theodor Rosebury's *Life on Man*, looking back further than Wright to neolithic privies (95–6), claims that feces is handled with less restraint in less technologically advanced nations, and that the infant recapitulates the progress of society. Likewise, in an early attempt at sexology, *Love in the Machine Age* (1930), the shift in primates towards permanent habitations is believed to create a necessity for 'a socially inculcated disgust at excrement,' while ceremonial handlings of filth among primitive tribes and scatological humour among the civilized are seen as symbolic expressions of 'infantile interests' (Dell 87). The Freudian commonplaces behind these filiations are that the child's greatest cultural achievement is instinctual renunciation (*BPP* 15), which turns out mostly to be the repression of genital and anal functions.

For an anti-philosopher like Georges Bataille, the evolution of repression is already axiomatic: 'L'anus humain s'est profondément retiré à l'intérieur des chairs, dans la fente des fesses, et il ne forme plus saillie que dans l'accroupissement et l'excrétion' ('The human anus secluded itself deep within the flesh, in the crack of the buttocks, and it now forms a projection only in squatting and excretion'). The anus therefore has, he claims, 'le potentiel d'épanouissement' ('the potential for blossoming'); transferring to the face its explosive energies, it may explode from the pineal eye at the top of the head in 'les cris d'une éjaculation grandiose mais puante' ('Le Jesuve' II, 18–19; 'the screams of a magnificent but stinking ejaculation' 77).[10]

The limit to such approaches, Mary Douglas argues, is that they depend upon the nineteenth-century anthropology of Sir James Frazer and Robertson Smith (Douglas 13) for an evolutionary understanding of scatological rites as survivals from archaic religion. Douglas's critique is important, because a more recent approach such as Claude Lévi-Strauss's *La pensée sauvage* reinterprets totemism so that what was once understood as a manifestation of archaic religion becomes a proto-Linnaean system of biological classification. The effect of this reinterpretation of 'origins' is to move 'marriage with the animals' and chthonic origins into an ever more distant past. This growing distance perhaps explains why the scatological return to the animal is such a resonant myth for Lévi-Strauss in *Tristes tropiques*.[11] Douglas reverses Lévi-Strauss's method by showing how modern secular culture transfers the idea of purity from religion to hygiene (11). For Douglas, the body in all cultures is a model for the social structure (115) and there is no reason to treat bodily margins psychologically, as separate from other margins (121). Like Norbert Elias, Douglas makes the crucial connection between the body and the social system. She has been criticized by Julia Kristeva who wonders what the desire is that is required to uphold the social system (67): 'Pourquoi est-ce un *déchet corporel*, le sang menstruel et l'excrément, ou tout ce qui leur est assimilé, des ongles à la pourriture, qui représente – telle une metaphore qui se serait incarnée – cette fragilité objective de l'ordre symbolique?' (1980, 85; 'Why does *corporeal waste*, menstrual blood and excrement, or everything that is assimilated to them, from nail-parings to decay, represent – like a metaphor that would become incarnate – the objective frailty of the symbolic order?' 70). Nevertheless, with Douglas and Elias it becomes possible to see how scatology codifies past and present, country and town – without being led into a too-literal equation of represented origins and actual origins.

2

Country and Town: 'The Size of Sheep's Dung' and Other Metaphors

We are creatures of air.

– Gibreel Farishta in *The Satanic Verses*

'What do you know, city boy?' she cried ... 'In my village there is no shame in being named for the Dung Goddess. Write at once that you are wrong completely.' In accordance with my lotus's wishes, I insert, forthwith, a brief paean to Dung.

– Saleem Sinai in *Midnight's Children*

On 1 January 1967, the first day of Centennial celebrations in Canada, politicians in Ottawa lit a perpetual flame to symbolize the life of the nation, and the *Winnipeg Free Press* carried a picture of the Golden Boy, another palladium, on its cover. Lower on the same page, however, people at the periphery of the country were celebrating another event – the *Free Press* carried pictures of the burning of the outhouses in Bowsman, Manitoba. United Church minister Jim Liles eulogized them as 'good enough for the first 100 years of Canada, but not the second ... The time has come to destroy friends who held up their ends through the years ... They have provided shelter from stormy blasts.' The hinterland both mocked its own past and yet also parodied Canada's dominant culture as Bowsman erased a sign of its marginality (to use the language of Harold Innis's margin/centre tension in Canada's staples economy). In the completion of a $350,000 sewer project, Bowsman assimilated itself to urban standards of hygiene, but the communal parodic inversion of the Centennial flame marks an artistic production that does not grant Ottawa all of its assumed seriousness. While the new technology diminished the consciousness of one's waste, scatology reappeared as political satire in the prairie scatological mockery of an Ontario-centric symbol, as religious satire in the parody of 'Rock of Ages,' and as social satire in the country-town's self-mocking progress to urban centre.

Who Has Seen the Wind is only the most famous case in which the civilizing process is coded, nostalgically yet definitely, through the categories of 'country' and 'town,' with 'country' signifying fecal origins, 'town' the negation of those origins, and the movement from 'country' to 'town' a weightless migration into the air. The fecal role of the country can be seen in the disingenuous metaphors of *The Clockmaker*, where Haliburton has Sam Slick scrape the bottom of a pot until he gets to 'a sight of little forced meat balls, of the size of sheep's dung' (56). A more naïve scatological denigration occurs when in *The Apprenticeship of Duddy Kravitz* Max Kravitz insists that the country means 'ants and mosquitoes and skunks and – if you've got the appetite – bull-pies all over' (307). The narrator of Davies's *World of Wonders* compares poorly done snow in a theatre to turkey diarrhoea, a particularly telling simile given the cultural contrast between tenor and vehicle. The manure-spreader that Madmother Thomas drags all over the island in Hodgins's *The Invention of the World* signifies the disillusionment that she projects, while Henry Burke's project to demythologize Lily Hayworth in the same novel is rooted in his rural past – raising 'shitty chickens.' He transports the scatological terms from that past for his critique: 'She wasn't so goddam Queen-like, I tell you, with her skirt hoisted up around her waist taking a crap out behind a tree' (178).[1]

Throughout the symbolic structure of *Wild Geese*, 'manure' repeatedly stands for the farm, both substantially as fertilizer and etymologically as the hand-labour at that time involved in the fertilizing process.[2] Other early references to the manuring process in *The Clockmaker, Roughing It in the Bush,* and *The History of Emily Montague* generally show a respect for labour and an unconsciousness of manure as shameful.[3] By the time of Ostenso, manure has become more problematic. Judith Gare's individuating impulse in *Wild Geese* involves leaving her farm origins for the town; that departure is already implicit when she moves her cow to the extremity of the pen where it is 'a little prettier' (22). This scatological relativity (like the relativity signalled by her brother Martin's outhouses) is touching, despite the obvious potential for satire, because Ostenso is not quite ready to give in to the perceived effeminacy of the town; thus she doubles language in her description of the animal who is at times a surrogate for Judith: 'The cow's flanks were satiny, her tail clotted with manure' (22). In fact, the technological lag between country and town, town and city (in the shift towards flush toilets) elsewhere allows characters from the peripheries to claim a superiority in breadth of experience: 'I have cleaned out chamber pots to get my education' (Munro, *Lives of Girls and Women* 66). Yet it is the consciousness of Lynd Archer, the *city* woman in *Wild Geese*, which structures the frame that surrounds the shifting narrative points of view, and Ostenso eventually has Judith leave fertilizer and labour, which have been too closely associated with Caleb's control over Judith's individual sphere.

The social negation of country origins is more explicit and satirized in Buckler's *The Mountain and the Valley*, where David Canaan's impulse, like Maggie Kyle's, is to rise. David is ashamed of the old outhouse when showing it to his town visitor, Toby Richmond, and defends Toby's prudishness about urinating in company against Chris's jokes.[4] Instead, David creates a hypothetical civilized self and redirects the jokes against the outhouse: '"Take a coarse sight, and curb your trajectory." He spoke as if he were really a visitor in the place, denying any part of its crudity except as the basis for a joke' (139). In this he goes one better on Toby's euphemizing: he scientizes language, a technique compatible with the abstracted artist-self that he, as a recipient of Emerson's romantic individualism, is heir to.[5] Jud Spinney, not fully conscious of what he is doing, attacks David's individual artistic sphere by using a crude sexual comment to undercut David's princely role in the school operetta. David afterwards responds in kind, but only mentally: 'He'd just take him by the collar and turn him around and kick his ass and walk away' (83). Both the demythologizing moment and the response to the demythologizing moment are signalled by the lower bodily level, but in the 'civilized' response nothing is actually *said*. More important, Buckler signals David's attempt to arrange ideal scenes and his inability to accept the critiques that occur once art is presented to the community.[6]

Like Buckler, Ethel Wilson and Margaret Atwood retain the country/town pattern of the civilizing process without idealizing the disembodied town. Wilson's protagonist in *Swamp Angel*, Maggie Lloyd, leaves her husband and Vancouver, and goes to a fishing camp near Kamloops to regain her body. This is stressed mostly by her swimming, but also by the toilet arrangements: '"The privies is back behind the cabins"' (34). Maggie's archaeological search (too many symbols destroy reality, she thinks; 79) uncovers not only a less sophisticated language, but also a more primitive life in which 'her avatar tells her that she is one with her brothers the seal and the porpoise' (99). The coding does not mean that Wilson herself is nostalgic for the country: '[Maggie's] avatar had better warn her that she is not really a seal or a porpoise' (99). Neither does Wilson commit to the town: Nell Severance, city woman and symbolist, makes too few concessions when she cancels her visit to the lodge where Maggie lives because it has 'no plumbing, just privies' (128).

Atwood too uses the code without trusting it. In *Bodily Harm* Elva prescribes a filth-cure, urination, to ease the swelling caused by stepping on a sea-urchin, but the filth, associated with the primitive conditions in the Third World prison, is still horrifying. In *Cat's Eye* Elaine Risley is fascinated with flush toilets when she first gets to the city. Atwood represents a gradation between the country where there are not even any outhouses, the intermediate motels that have outhouses or 'smelly' toilets (29), and their cheap home in the city, which has a toilet with a ring around the bowl (33). The idealizing process in the literature that Elaine reads constitutes an important aspect of the civilizing process for her: 'Nothing in these stories is anything like my life. There are no tents, no highways, no peeing in the bushes, no lakes, no motels. There is no war. The children are always clean' (30). Elaine's past has taught her to associate Eaton's catalogues with outhouses, but Grace Smeath floats the genre by teaching Elaine proper reverence for consumer goods (56), a civilized economy that Atwood satirizes.

Although we are dealing with fictional personal and social histories, neither the rejection of the country in scatological images nor its nostalgic recuperation should be surprising. Canadian social historians emphasize the shift in the North American population from rural to urban (Woodcock 299, Clement 160), the decline in primary sector employment, especially of agricultural workers (Clement 76–7), and a significant post-1960s growth in non-farming country-dwellers (Woodcock 314). The biographies of many of the novelists prominent in this chapter suggest personal involvement in this social history. Most – Hodgins (Merville, British Columbia), Buckler (Dalhousie West, Nova Scotia), Laurence (Neepawa, Manitoba), Munro (Wingham, Ontario), O'Hagan (Yellowhead Lake area), Ostenso (small towns in Norway, Minnesota, North Dakota, and Manitoba), Davies (Thamesville, Ontario), Ladoo (McBean, Trinidad) – grew up in the country or in small towns and moved (usually for education or employment) to larger centres. Even those such as Thomas (Binghamton, New York), Roy (St Boniface), and Atwood (Ottawa) who did not grow up in small towns nevertheless did move to larger centres such as Vancouver (Thomas), Montreal and Quebec City (Roy), or spent significant portions of their lives in country areas – Atwood in northern Ontario and Quebec, Roy near Altamont. Finally, a significant number returned, some temporarily, some permanently, to smaller communities like the ones that they left. Buckler returned to the Annapolis Valley; Munro to Clinton, Ontario; Ostenso to Gull Lake, Minnesota; O'Hagan to Jasper and to an island near Howe Sound, British Columbia; and Laurence went to Lakefield, Ontario. Atwood (in Alliston, Ontario, for seven years) and Thomas (on Galiano Island) took up 'country' living while some bought summer homes: Laurence on the Otonabee River, Richler at Lake Memphremagog, Roy in Petite-Rivière-St-François, and Wilson in Kamloops.

Characters such as Lind Archer in *Wild Geese*, Elaine in *Cat's Eye*, Rose in *Who Do You Think You Are?*, Del Jordan (by implication) in *Lives of Girls and Women*, Mlle Coté in *La petite poule d'eau*, Morag Gunn in *The Diviners*, and Dunstan Ramsay in the Deptford trilogy all re-enact some aspect of their maker's movement from country to town.[7]

3

Doubling Back: The Rhetorical Recovery of the Body

People don't get any better as their language gets more sophisticated.

– Rachel in *Latakia*

The sequence, anus-to-finger-to-mouth, has proved to be commoner than people like to believe.

– Theodor Rosebury, *Life on Man*

In a third move, the novelist returns the character to his or her origins or, comparable to Michael McKeon's 'epistemological double reversal,' the novelist negates even town civilization in a scatological critique that often parodies the civilizing process.¹ The extreme form of the autonomous, civilized self, nascent in Atwood's *Cat's Eye* and Buckler's *The Mountain and the Valley*, threatens to abstract itself entirely from its origins and, therefore, from the body. Atwood satirizes the clean and proper body when she has Ainsley in *The Edible Woman* mock the dental students who check their mouths for cavities every time they go to the bathroom (9–10). Later in the novel, Atwood parodies the belief that not washing indicates insanity (183); parody calls into question the tendency of the civilizing process to appear 'natural.'

More often, scatology is allowed to break in upon the rising individual, and the doublings back to origins that occur in the biographies of many of these novelists may explain why. In *The Mountain and the Valley* David Canaan's father accuses him, in scatological language, of getting too 'high': 'Don't you want killin' ... you goddam snot' (165). There is also a curious bodily reticence; David and his father cannot even urinate in one another's presence. On the other hand, David processes bodily intimacy, the greatest of his many taboos, and betrays Bess, joking about her 'piss' in front of others (187). Through David's role in the pig-killing scene, Buckler sets up a series of attempts to exit from the scene of the body. When someone comments about David's attempt to leave the barn, he returns with a vengeance to the site, and is the first one at the frightened pig's dung-covered hind legs. In David's self-conscious and processed civilization, there are no innocent lacerations of the body as there seem to be for the other men. His drive is to transcend the filthy pig, his own bleeding hand, the bodies and roles of the other men, even his own limitations, but during his parodic attempt at transcendence on a barn beam, he falls.[2] He falls back into the body, because after this he is never free from pain. David's town-driven sensibility, which only doubles back to origins with violence, is not identical with Buckler's. We see hints of this in the more pastoral, almost nostalgic versions of scatology when a more omniscient narrator than the one usual in David's consciousness reports, late in the narrative, on David and Toby urinating and laughing together: 'It was the way two boys laugh who have both been uncomfortable in someone's parlour, though neither's fidget is realized by the other until they are outside and one of them grimaces back at the house and exhales a prodigiously drawn-out fart' (255). Because the return to bodily origins is not *inevitably* tragic in *The Mountain and the Valley*, the transgression against David's individual sphere seems self-induced.

Other novelists too allow filth to transgress against the rising individual. The communal and the scatological combine in Thomas's *Mrs Blood* to attack Dr Biswas's 'ethical idealism': 'He began to resent his wife's pale skin and the baby's diarrhoea' (24). In Laurence's *The Stone Angel*, despite Bram's attack on her persona, Hagar doubles back by presenting the filth nostalgically. This is understandable given that Bram is also the unacknowledged object of her desire; what is more problematic is Laurence's nostalgia, which at times confirms Bram's rather naïve theory of representation: 'Never gave a damn for living horses ... But when you seen them put onto paper where they couldn't drop manure, then its dandy, eh?' (83). Laurence's project for the self in *The Stone Angel* involves breaking through the entrainments of an overcivilized body, but Bram's disingenuous realist privileging of thing over representation is limited by Laurence's naturalization of the biblical text, so that she calls down scepticism upon both origins and the civilizing process. In *The Diviners*, Laurence gradually splits Morag in half. On one side is Skinner Tonnerre, who reduces women via scatological obscenity (68) and who dismisses the family romance of Piper Gunn and the Red River Settlement as 'crap' (72), a demythologization that Morag repeats when she calls the Gunn crest, motto, and war cry 'a load of old manure' (162). On the other is Brooke Skeleton, whose small bathroom (197) suggests overcivilization. The attack comes simultaneously against the sphere of the individual and against the town, so that Morag cannot relax until she arrives at the fictional equivalent of Margaret Laurence's home in Lakefield, the new Neepawa. *The Diviners* gradually effaces Brooke as Morag acknowledges her unclean kin: Skinner, Prin, and, above all, Christie.

As the references to the Red River Settlement suggest, the doubling back in Morag's personal history opens out into social history. Laurence counters romantic versions of the past with scatological revisions. She includes an 'outdoor privy' (95) in Morag's imagination of pioneer life; as well, because of gender identifications, Laurence cannot completely discount Catharine Parr Traill's enactment of the hardy pioneer, so she searches for repressed voices which qualify the enacted myth.[3] Laurence finds the scatological and the morbid in Traill's symptoms of the Water Hemlock: 'vomitting, colic, staggering and unconsciousness and finally frightful convulsions which end in death' (*The Diviners* 404).

Munro, Davies, and Richler too double over the civilizing process, recalling characters to their origins. While the avoidance of the school outhouse seems to be necessary for Rose in *Who Do You Think You Are?* to avoid the aggressive boys who assault Franny McGill, Munro eventually broadens the repression of filth towards the Freudian dynamic of civilization and discontent; the school gets indoor plumbing, and Rose, somewhat hypocritically, laments that 'there never was another honey-dumper' (37).[4] Rose appropriates the scatological bluntness of Flo as a psychological defence (155), and indeed wishes for the old home. Davies's *What's Bred in the Bone* involves Francis Cornish in a less ambiguous and more insistent recuperation of what is excluded from the social system. As Munro does with Franny, Davies codes the excluded filth through the near-idiot child, Francis I (called

'The Looner'). The attempts to protect the 'second' Francis Cornish (from scatological details) are characteristically successful: 'He was not yet such a close reasoner as to suspect that if Bella-Mae were thus burdened with the common needs of life, his parents might also share them' (75). But his *Bildungsroman* includes an excremental education into the senses: 'He ... learned the stench that rises when a hot shoe is placed on the horse's [manure- and tobacco-covered] hoof' (108).[5] Mordecai Richler, whose biography in contrast to Buckler, Laurence, Munro, and Davies is much more urban, does not double back in the way that they do, but he does use Joshua Shapiro in *Joshua Then and Now* as a mediator between an undercivilized past (Joshua's father Reuben, whom Richler treats nostalgically) and overcivilized Outremont, where Bertha says 'I only go at home' (24) and where the toilet-seat covers are covered: 'shaggy white rugs everywhere ... Do they walk on toilets in Outremont?' (21).

The doubling back also occurs in the East/West coding of the scatological image. This less common coding is layered over country and town in novels such as Howard O'Hagan's *The School-Marm Tree*. There, a Dutch painter in the Yellowhead attains some Eastern success through his paintings of Western outhouses. In the reaction of the townspeople, O'Hagan parodies the desire to rise – 'the showing of outhouses, they felt, was unjust when most of the people in town had bathrooms with modern appurtenances' (38). Outhouse and bathroom here measure O'Hagan's reaction against the ideological hold that the East has over the Western town and over a woman like Selva.[6] The town, at its own insistence, becomes a poor version of the East while the trailhands, especially Clay Mulloy, dream West. The Eastern bathroom apparently hides the body, and the dynamics of hidden sexuality in Branchflower and Wrogg, cynic and naif, are connected to this affectation. Selva's initial desires for the East (she wants Branchflower or Wrogg) are given parodic form in Rosie, who says that 'it's all right if you're a man to pick your nose with your thumb, but it's not good manners to use your finger' (106, 123). Like the writers of manners books in wanting to rationalize custom, Rosie unintentionally reduces shifts in manners to arbitrariness, encoding O'Hagan's scepticism about the value of the civilizing process.[7]

4

Extreme Scepticism: Parodies of the Civilized Self

What does this wild pig want soap for? Visions began to form of the creature returning to his friends with Pears Transparent Soap and then all of them bathing and scrubbing their armpits in the rain in a foul parody of us.

– Michael Ondaatje, *Running in the Family*

Once the civilizing process and the sceptical doubling back on that structure become commonplace, they invite an extreme scepticism which can trust neither the civilizing process nor the recuperation of origins. Such a scepticism is implicit in the scatologizing of the modernist city-wasteland (*Joshua Then and Now* 51, 55),[1] and explicit in Noah Adler's twentieth-century parody of 'The Passionate Shepherd to His Love': 'Let it be said of us that we made no plans ... We'll fart when we have visitors and drop rocks on passing cars' (104). The literary parody here mocks both pastoral hopes and the civilizing repressions because the bodily relaxation in the lack of civility[2] shades into Noah's uncivilized cruelty to Miriam.

In *Yesterdays*, Harold Sonny Ladoo neither valorizes the excremental cultural past nor the rising self, while Leon Rooke attempts (during his doubling back) to approach extreme scepticism in *Shakespeare's Dog* by parodying the civilized self: Rooke 'originates' man in dog and represents Shakespeare's cultural ambitions alongside Shakespeare's dog's desire to rise from among the 'dung-eaters' (52). When the dog Hooker contrasts Queen Elizabeth's civilized toilet (courtesy of John Harrington) against her bear-baiting, Rooke doubles back on civilized pretensions. The monarch has not gotten better or less violent just because her conveniences have become more sophisticated. The shift from medieval rulers who, if necessary, gave audience in the W.C. (Pudney 99–100) to the private modern bathroom thus inaugurates a purely surface civilizing. The same style of satire occurs during Hooker's philosophizing on the tell-tale excrement after he has illicitly poached and consumed a deer: 'I covered the dump over with a frantic scrambling of dirt. It's not mine, I wanted to say.' The other dogs join his protestations of innocence, and Hooker wonders, 'was this, too, part of our nature and birthright or had we picked it up as one of many – fleas, mange, phobia – in the Two Foot's curse?' (57). Hooker is safer than he thinks because humans have been educated to repudiate excrement and not to inspect it (at least in public) too closely. A traditional function of the scatological image, according to Bakhtin and Kristeva, is to erase the division between man and beast (Bakhtin 1984, 226; Kristeva 1982, 12). The most common function of this erasure is to lower man and return him to his origins. The deformations of Shakespeare's name – 'Shakespizzle' (72) and Anne Hathaway's coinage 'Shakeshitter' (95) – deform the classicist approach to authorship, and ally Shakespeare to the intimate descriptions of Hooker at stoole; certainly the dog's life of sensation, smell, and defecation determines literary history in *Shakespeare's Dog* because Shakespeare's move to London occurs only when the Regarders threaten Hooker's life.

Through Hooker, a dog who narrates, Rooke intends the parody to destabilize humanist certainties. Not so much a play on Richard Hooker as a near-anagram for Rooke, Hooker attains a sympathetic and humane persona that might surprise Charlotte Ford; he philosophizes about excrement and he refuses to urinate on a grave. And he feels grand when he finds that he can walk on his hind legs: 'to the left, then to the right, then over a muckhill' (150) – but is unsure what to do with his tail. To this parodic scepticism, however, we must add that the increasing ability of people to identify with animals may be connected to the civilizing process (Mennell 315).[3] The beast fable always contains within it an inevitable tendency towards anthropomorphism (Ziolkowski 11), so that it confirms the human persona even despite the experimentation, the degradation of epic structure, and the identification with the slave that it allows (Ziolkowski 12–14). Hooker's written persona may confirm the civilizing process at the same time as Rooke parodies it.

Timothy Findley's parodic biography *Famous Last Words* and Harold Sonny Ladoo's parodic autobiography *Yesterdays* are less reassuring when they address the same problem: the crisis of where to place civilized values. Findley's Duke of Windsor desires to escape his civilized persona and, among other things, 'fart out loud' (245). At the same time, in order to discredit Rudolph Hess with insanity, his British captors must get around the civilized boundary-markers that show up in loathing and vomit; the captors teach him not to throw up at fishheads, to 'become' a cat. Findley satirizes the civilized, written persona through Hugh Selwyn Mauberley and yet presents the transgression against the civilizing process to be just as inhumane. George Bowering's parody of Canadian social history in *Burning Water* is much the same in this. Bowering cannot locate civilized values in the overdisciplined Vancouver who eventually '[goes] to war with his body' (207), nor do the scatological breaks in discipline – Vancouver vomits after his primitivist desire to eat Cook's body – signal anything better. In *Famous Last Words*, however, the need to resolve the crisis is more insistent. Mauberley's narration certainly cannot breach the problem: 'The tension in the rooms became so great that one of the dogs threw up, while the other lifted its leg against a Louis Quinze table (luckily an imitation)' (107). Scatology jars hilariously against Mauberley's bracketed overvaluation of the art-object, which, after all, is only a *sign* for the civilized preservation of tradition, and is not civility itself.

Findley identifies the 'present' narrator, Quinn, with Mauberley in his fastidiousness, but there is no simple lionization of Mauberley (who has adopted the simplistic Fascist equation in which clean equals good)[4] or of social realist terms (in which dirt equals human, and therefore equals good). Quinn and Mauberley are seen ambivalently: their horror of filth is clearly represented as an ordering function (which makes them capable of society, of writing), and yet that fastidiousness is also represented as a refusal to see Dachau (for Quinn) and the dark side of the attractive male (for Mauberley).

Choonilal, in Ladoo's *Yesterdays*, alternates between overvaluation – 'Me son so educated dat when he talk, I does only feel to shit man' (34) – and undervaluation of his son's ability to rise above village life: 'It look like English does flow from you ass. But all de book you read Poonwa, and all dat education you have in you ass is notten' (76). Although at times Ladoo seems to set up an attack on European rationalism in Poonwa's use of Descartes (29) (an attack that comes from the scatological position that England has defined for the Trinidadian), the insistent reduction of all worlds to filth and to animal eroticism destabilizes a potential anti-colonialist norm. Poonwa attempts a material philosophy, but it degenerates, almost immediately, into misogyny, cliché, and childish scatological verse:

> The philosophy of Poonwa.
> A treatise on God and other matters.
> Philosophy and the philosopher's stones (Women excluded).
> What goes in must come out (Related to pregnancy and such matters).
> Philosophy and the philosophers' stones (Women excluded).
> The philosophy of a philosopher's hole (Women included).
> Once there was a girl
> with two cracks in her hole
> she pissed in a bowl
> until she grew old. (42)

As I will argue in Chapter 8, this destabilization of perspective is connected to the technological aspects of the civilizing process in William Gibson's *Neuromancer* and Leonard Cohen's *Beautiful Losers*. In the latter, F. dies 'wiping his ass with a curtain' (40) and the narrator echoes the primitivist impulses of his mentor: 'I salute my monsterhood. I urinate everywhere on the linoleum' (67). The problem of extreme decivilization is overcorrected and 'solved' by the technological sensorium: the narrator goes into a total fast, so that he no longer fouls his shack with excrement (246), and finally turns into a movie of Ray Charles. Cohen's evasiveness is calculated to undermine any confidence in a solution to the binaries of scatological origins and the civilized self.

Apparent in these Canadian literary versions of the rising civilized self and of the doubling back process, but most clear in extreme scepticism is how self-consciously Canadian novelists approach the process. Peter Stallybrass and Allon White in *The Politics and Poetics of Transgression* assume that a central self or central authority is always undesirable. They, like Bakhtin whom they seek to revise, demonize the civilizing process, although they do not follow Bakhtin in his belief that carnival (a type of doubling back) automatically undermines internal and external authorities: 'Often it is a powerful ritual or symbolic practice whereby the dominant squanders its symbolic capital so as to get in touch with the fields of desire which it denied itself as the price paid for its political power' (201). For Stallybrass and White, the bourgeoisie are again and again ready to be surprised by information about bodily repressions and the social scatology that constitutes the self, but St Urbain's Jake Hersh is quite conscious of the ideological implications of his disgust:

There's a simple solution. Wrap the stool quickly in your underwear, lean back and heave it into the bushes. *Yes yes*, Jake agreed, *but how do I pick it up?* It's yours, isn't it? Your very own bodily waste. Disgust for it is bourgeois. Yes, yes, but how do I pick it up? Sunshine soldier! Social democrat! Middlebrow! Unable to face life fully. Everything is holy, Jake. Holy holy. *Yes, but how do I pick it up?* (171)

The self-identification of the 'social democrat' in this resistance to filth can hardly be a 'festival of the political unconscious' (Stallybrass 201). Richler does not double back over the history of manners, but he does indicate that scatology is connected to a social rhetoric. It is to this rhetoric that we now turn.

PART II

THE SOCIAL BODY: SCATOLOGY
AND IDEOLOGICAL HIERARCHY
IN THE ENGLISH-CANADIAN NOVEL

5

Immigrants, Foul Ghettos, and Social Climbers: Marking Fictional Class Structures

Nous imaginons bien plus sortablement un artisan sur sa garderobe ou sur sa femme qu'un grand President, venerable par son maintien et suffisance. (We imagine much more fitly an Artificer upon his close stoole or his wife, then a great judge, reverend for his carriage and regardfull for his sufficiencie.)

– Montaigne, '*Du repentir*' (Florio translation)

Ein starkes Vergnügen an analen Witzen und Schaustellungen, wie es sonst der natürlichen Derbheit mancher Gesellschaftsklassen entspricht, hatte sich bei ihm ... erhalten. (He found a great deal of enjoyment – such as would tally with the natural coarseness of many classes of society, though not of his – in anal jokes and exhibitions.)

– Sigmund Freud, *Aus der Geschichte einer infantilen Neurose*

I'm glad to be near [the garage mechanic] and enjoy the distance that separates us ... Remarkable how any comparison always favors me! Thank God for dirt.

– Christian Enzensberger, *Grosserer Versuch über den Schmutz*

Stallybrass and White, like Elias, show that the civilizing process creates a number of class markers through the definition of manners. Elias argues that particular manners were considered good in medieval times *because* they belonged to a certain social class, and not that a social class was considered honourable because it obeyed particular manners injunctions.[1] The feudal sense of difference is still instructive in a democratic society because while class difference loses some political valence, it certainly does not disappear from the symbolic realm. While Douglas notes how standards of purity and taboo function to organize societies which are without modern political and technological differentiation, and how caste systems function on the metaphor of the body (123), she also notes that even in secular societies marginalized people continue to function under the signs of the unclean.[2] Stallybrass and White map out a particularly convincing example of this when they reread Freud to show how maternal abjection is coded among his patients through the social order of the maid, how there is no simply 'personal' abject (Stallybrass 153).[3] Washoe, the chimpanzee, signed 'dirty' when she was forced back into a cage among other monkeys after having been allowed to roam about human dwellings – a 'downgrading of her status from human to animal' (Linden 9) and a rather poignant social echo of the expanding sphere of the bourgeois individual.

If we consider the represented society made up of characters from Canadian novels, it quickly becomes clear that scatology marks a dialectic between broadly imagined upper and lower classes. At the same time as signifying origins in a past or in the country, the scatological image also marks the lower class, while a concern for cleanliness marks many attempts, both among characters and among authors, to situate themselves in an upper class. As in the rhetoric of the civilizing process, we sometimes see a scatological doubling back, when an author or character tries to regain something that has been lost in the class shift.

Depending upon the researcher's standards, Canadian classes can be divided in terms of 'income, ownership of property, level of education, degree of occupational skill, or position of responsibility and power'; in terms of 'popular evaluation of occupations ... or the opinions and judgements of some members of a community about the class position or class reputation of other members of the community' (Porter 9); and in terms of the social relations of production (Clement 143).[4] Novelistic *discourse* about class, however, tends towards more simple dialectical maps, and this may be why Porter wrongly claims, in his seminal study *The Vertical Mosaic*, that class is not a theme in Canadian literature (Porter 6).

An early novel like Moodie's *Mark Hurdlestone* conveys the external markings of class in its consistent emphasis on the *forms* of speech, courtesy, and physiognomy (24, 301). In the twentieth-century novel, this confidence in and ensuing scepticism about surface markings is partially transferred to the scatological image, and the lower class is consistently represented in scatological terms. Morley Callaghan's Marxist priest, Father Stephen Dowling in *Such Is My Beloved*, is especially moved by 'the smell of bodies' in the confined space of the confessional (77) because the scatological sign of materiality confirms, he thinks, his lower-class ideology in the Catholic Church. The tramps in Davies's *Fifth Business* (46), the lower-class Baptists in Munro's *Lives of Girls and Women* (177), Lora's impoverished past (111, 114) in Atwood's *Bodily Harm*, the poorer part of town in *Cat's Eye* (332) and in *The Edible Woman* (281), the Newfoundland fisherman in Johnston's *The Story of Bobby O'Malley* (85), the gypsy-foot whores in Ondaatje's *Coming through Slaughter* (119), and Annie Oakley, the lowest-ranking soldier in Findley's *Famous Last Words* (41, 56), are all represented scatologically. Del Jordan, but not Alice Munro, approaches a limited nostalgia in *Lives of Girls and Women* – thinking that she is approaching nature and approaching her own body among Garnet French and the Baptists. Despite the association of filth and humanity in *Not Wanted on the Voyage*,[5] Annie Oakley in *Famous Last Words* is sinisterly uncivilized; the novel's postwar rule among Private Oakley, Sergeant Rudecki, Lieutenant Quinn, and Captain Freyberg is that 'the higher the rank, the more civilized.'

Both A.M. Klein's and Mordecai Richler's Jewish ghettos are marked scatologically. In *The Second Scroll* the Casablanca ghetto is 'thick with offal and slime' and with 'signs of a donkey's passage' (62). Although the novel constantly works to subvert the sense of sight (and its implied idolatry), narrator and author very readily accept the evidence and symbolization of smell (64). The Montreal ghetto in *Son of a Smaller Hero* is full of 'garbage and decaying fruit,' 'horse manure,' 'odours' (15),[6] and the Adler family business is scrap collecting. Rubbish collection was often entrusted to the poor as a form of 'social welfare,' and contributed to the excrementalizing of them (Corbin 117, 143–4). Richler explicitly sets the classes against one another when Noah Adler crosses class lines to enter, uncomfortably, Miriam Hall's Anglo-Saxon world: 'She must be very well-educated, he thought, rich. He wanted badly to say something that would fit.

Finally, he asked for the toilet' (45). Once in the bathroom, Noah recognizes its cleanliness as the material opposite to the ghetto: green enamel, many taps, green tiles, initialled towels, sunken bathtub, and half-concealed pink toilet paper. The young and credulous Noah is at first awed; this, apparently, is what a ghetto boy can aspire to.

Of course, by making Miriam's bathroom the main index for class difference, just as Libby Gursky's bathroom is in *Solomon Gursky Was Here* (23), Richler satirizes the terms set by the dominant class. This scatological reduction functions in Noah too, eventually allowing him to escape from the feigned coarseness of the Halls' social set (194) and to return to the 'real' scene of the body, the ghetto. Dominant classes and races can use the civilized self and these perceived differences in cleanliness as social controls. To destroy lice, Mengele gasses an entire block of Jewish women's cells (*St Urbain's Horseman* 163); in an unnerving echo of this, Joey's head is shaved to destroy lice when he enters a Canadian juvenile detention centre (112). When Duddy Kravitz tries to rise from the ghetto, he meets the power of the cleanliness discourse in Irwin Shubert; Irwin prevents Duddy from socializing with a higher class by pretending that Duddy filled a wine bottle with urine as a mean trick (*The Apprenticeship of Duddy Kravitz* 70). Irwin manipulates the *appearance* of filth to keep Duddy in his place. Herky in *St Urbain's Horseman* is typed by his association with excrement, although in his case Richler is the nemesis. Untouchable because his occupation has to do with toilets, he lives among the 'lower' class of literary characters designated as satiric butts.

What we see of Noah, Duddy, and Herky confirms Douglas's contention that pollution occurs very often at the boundaries of social or cosmic structures, and when people are placed in ill-defined positions (Douglas 113, 133). The class position of the immigrant in the Canadian novel also confirms this. In David Williams's *Eye of the Father*, Magnus Vangdal immigrates to America. He finds, however, against the grain of the democratic myth, that he 'can't be comfortable anywhere but the bottom' (35), and he remains in a self-initiated and societally confirmed anal role throughout the novel. The immigrant in Brian Moore's *The Luck of Ginger Coffey* is more forcibly scatologized. Before the Canadian employer hires Ginger, he says, 'What a PR man knows about the wurrkings of a newspaper could be written twice over on the back of a tomtit's arse ... So you'd best start at the bottom' (51). Ginger descends even lower and works for a diaper service, having to choose between actual excrement – thanking women for soiled diapers (129) – and something worse: playing 'personal bumboy to old Cleery' (198). This type of scatological image qualifies George Grant's claim that North American optimism has been long maintained by the immigrant who found opportunity and freedom here (G. Grant 193); on the other hand, the comic form of many of these immigrant novels suggests that rising to another class is possible, though mostly so in the second generation.

Since the lower class is marked by its scatology, once a character attempts to rise in class he must find a way of denying any scatological role. In a magazine article, 'Canadians Old and New,' Grove placed a great deal of importance on manners of bodily cleanliness in the process of assimilation: 'I have known any number of Ruthenians, Russians, Poles – as I have known some English people – who never dreamed that a head is not the proper recreation ground for minute inhabitants. I have never known any who did not at once try to rid themselves of them when they became aware that I, or anybody, objected to their sojourn there' (3, 55). Grove argues that immigrants are not less clean than Canadians, but then takes them as the image of disease, saying that Canadians are to blame if immigrant settlements remain as a 'foreign body within the tissue of the commonwealth' (55). When Philip Branden experiences status inconsistency, losing his inheritance and having to leave Europe in Grove's *A Search for America*, he pretends to jettison his aristocratic ideology with a comment on royal digestion – 'upon what meat does this our Caesar feed?' (57)– in favour of a democratic ideology that he thinks is more appropriate to his adopted place.

However, Philip's circumspection about the body and his ready classicism prefigures that he will merely transfer hereditary economic markers over to the intellectual sphere and to the moral sphere of clean and proper bodies (as Grove himself did).[7] Philip aspires 'to neatness and cleanliness' (139).[8] Via taboo, Philip separates the moral classes at the restaurant into those who laugh when Jim secretly spits into an obnoxious customer's soup and those who do not laugh (62). For a time Philip wants to remake himself as Frank, at ease in the New World: 'He did not recoil from the common drinking-cup or the general washing-room in public places' (74). This remaking is, however, immediately stalled by Philip's discovery of Frank's graft. The cross-purposes of a societal attack on the immigrant's ill-defined position and the immigrant's simultaneous scatologizing of the lower class in his own attempt to rise can be seen in the contest between Philip and the cooks. Philip carefully distinguishes between cookery and his so much superior job of waiting on tables; the cooks pretend to acknowledge the distinction, but acknowledge it only in parody: 'The kitchen-personnel ... called me "the baron" there, addressed me as "Sir Phil," and in high-sounding phrases spoke to me mostly of things and parts of the body that will not bear print' (64). The cooks speak obscenely against Philip and against his style of language, while Philip maintains his own 'clean' and well-mannered sphere by reporting the obscenity and attributing it to them, but not reporting it verbatim. To fit his special situation, Philip strangely coordinates the Old World 'romance of the younger son' with the more American 'progressive' narrative of the industrious apprentice: if he maintains his clean and proper sphere he will someday be recognized as the aristocrat he really is.[9]

Because of his wealth, Jake Hersh in *St Urbain's Horseman* emigrates the opposite way, eastward and upward, moving from Montreal's Jewish ghetto to the suburbs of London. This is what McKeon labels a 'progressive' narrative: 'Princes, the founts of honor, create knights; industrious apprentices internalize princely absolutism and create themselves' (McKeon 246). Since Jake is a social democrat, he enters the bourgeoisie without a mythology to tell him why he belongs there. The reason that his status insecurity manifests itself most obviously in the scene at Ormsby-Fletcher's house, when he cannot pick up his stool, is because his inhibitions are partially a function of his status as a colonial. Even though he is an intellectual superior, he is nevertheless Ormsby-Fletcher's social inferior according to the British scale.

As with the immigrant, the ill-defined position of the physically and mentally handicapped helps to relegate them to scatology: Gabriel in *The Story of Bobby O'Malley*, the Dukes' 'mongoloid' son in *A Jest of God,* Franny in *Who Do You Think You Are?,* Francis I in *What's Bred in the Bone,* and Buddy Bolden in *Coming through Slaughter.*

In Findley's *Not Wanted on the Voyage* Dr Noyes monitors the toilets and then scolds Emma for losing control of her sphincter: 'What can you expect from someone whose sister was an ape?' (205–6) The selective use of Darwin marks Noyes as a nineteenth-century anthropologist who still believes in hierarchies of cultures. Dr Noyes's sign of the precivilized is, of course, an element in Findley's polemic against Noyes, so that the transgression against the handicapped girl identifies the abuse of power in Noyes's maintenance of a social hierarchy. Richler uses the same moral rhetoric in *The Apprenticeship of Duddy Kravitz*. To make Duddy repentant about his role in Virgil's accident, Yvette informs him that quadriplegics 'can't control their bowels and they don't know when they're urinating' (246). Richler signifies Duddy's rejection of a moral conscience when Duddy loses his fear of the urinal attached to Virgil's bed (277). In *Not Wanted on the Voyage*, the scatological marginalizing of the handicapped is performed by an externally presented melodramatic villain.[10] By setting *The Apprenticeship of Duddy Kravitz* in Duddy's consciousness Richler complicates civility and class, because the same consciousness that is responsible for the novel's sphere of language is also responsible for the marginalizing of the epileptic become quadriplegic. As Yvette's comment implies, the 'real' (not just represented) lack of muscle control moves the quadriplegic's excretion and urination into a public sphere – thus bringing the residual classifying power of the civilizing process arbitrarily to bear upon the handicapped 'transgression.' Given such symbolizations, the empowerment offered to a paraplegic by a wheelchair-accessible washroom is more than simply utilitarian. Both the crippled Michael Riches and his wife Meg are signalled as victims very early in Findley's *The Telling of Lies* by the proximity of the flushing of a toilet to Meg's voice (33). The flushing surreptitiously indicates that Meg must intrude upon Michael's private sphere because of his infirmity.

Against the drift of such symbolizations, the will to maintain a clean private sphere coordinates with the will to attain or maintain class status. For First Samuels in *The New Ancestors*, the initial step towards revolution means refusing to assist his father in the collection of night soil (Godfrey 230). In *Such Is My Beloved* Mr Robison will not 'soil his hands by appearing in the police courts' (38), and he is also careful to avoid the dirty rooms of the prostitutes. Peter in *The Edible Woman* understands quite well the relationship between not only manners and class, but between scatology, manners, and the *representation* of class: 'Unintentional bad manners was something Peter couldn't stand to be accused of, and I knew it. It put him in the class of people in the deodorant ads' (87).

While Callaghan and Atwood in these instances satirize the simplistic class conceptions of their characters, the insistent attempts of their protagonists (Stephen Dowling and Marian McAlpin respectively) to escape the sphere of the body nevertheless give a certain importance to the clean and private sphere. Callaghan, whose social- and Christian-problem novels are haunted by the images of Christ in a stable and among prostitutes, senses this irony with particular acuteness: the ex-convict Kip Caley's interest in 'janitors taking out their garbage' (15) initially 'exalts' Senator MacLean, but such prodigal joys in *More Joy in Heaven* do not last long. In Richler's *Joshua Then and Now*, Jack Trimble tells the story of his father. Wounded in World War I, his father loses one lung while the other fills with green slime. Much later, he also loses his position as a barber because his coughing out slime makes the customers feel bad: 'My father, far too polite to upset a rich customer, finally drowns in his own snot' (366). Jack knows that to rise in class he must efface such a past and avoid filth. This he does, but as with Kip Caley's prison friends, the return of the repressed enervates Jack's social determination and indeed constitutes his reformed self: 'You are looking at the man who was going to get his dirty fingernails under Jane Mitchell's skirt' (367).

More often the desire to create a clean sphere occurs through language and authorship. Robertson Davies makes a claim for a compensatory understanding of obscenity by quoting what the old painter Northcote said to William Hazlitt: 'The common people sought for refinement as a *treat*; people in high life were fond of grossness and ribaldry as a relief to their overstrained affectation of gentility' ('In Pursuit of Pornography' 275). Whatever the theoretical value of such a statement, one need not ponder long to realize the problem with which it would confront the writer: to whom, then, should the writer's voice be directed? Davies's solution in *The Lyre of Orpheus* is to find voices which can exploit the relief involved in 'grossness and ribaldry' without leaving the propriety of the upper class:

'Libretto – well, Schnak has a word for it.'
'Shit?'
'Of the most rejectable and excrementitious order.'

The Latinate, academized cushion not only identifies that a professor (Penelope Raven) is speaking, but also indicates a strict linguistic hierarchy between professor and student (Schnak). Against Barbara Godard's conception of Davies's dialogism, this passage indicates how a many-voiced form and the bodily lower level can *support* authoritative languages, especially since the professor is allowed the last, rhetorically the strongest, position.[11]

Davies follows Stephen Leacock by stabilizing European academe against the challenges of American popular culture. In *My Discovery of England*, which Davies ranked among Leacock's best books (Davies 1957, 107), Leacock apparently sets out to satirize Britain, but then continually mocks the New World from the perspective of the Old. The North American persona is defined by his modern interest in London's system of 'sewerage' (32) rather than in the British Museum, in Oxford's lack of sanitation (77) rather than in the Humanities. The persona's lack of refinement in his interests gives his lower position away; this is modified in Davies, where the Anglicanized professoriate subsumes *all* of experience. Despite jokes which hint at the anal-retentive possession of knowledge, the professors (who are not just the objects but also the originators of those jokes)[12] consistently mediate between the languages of upper and lower classes. This is especially clear in the nightwatchman Wally Crottel's constant interruptions of his lawyer, Mervyn Gwilt. Although Crottel and Gwilt unite in an attempt to sue for the possession of the Parlabane novel, the scatological 'plain speech' of the masses in Wally repeatedly erodes the overdetermined authority of Gwilt's legal Latin: 'You said it was, like, Latin, *De Mortos* or something. "Don't crap on your folks" you said it meant' (159).[13] While Crottel and Gwilt separate low and high languages, the professors are allowed to combine both rhetorical levels, attacking the authority of Gwilt's Latin, but *not* from Crottel's position. They speak of Gwilt's 'admirable *argumentum ad excrementum taurorum*' (162), expanding the *upper* sphere to include scatology rather than contracting the circumference of their own authority as Leacock does when he rails against slang (*My Discovery of England* 184).

The complexity of Davies's simultaneous recuperation of and distancing himself from filth means that the privatization of the body may result, as Francis Barker claims in a brilliant but flawed argument, from the discursive practices of a particular social group.[14] Davies also uses an academic mediation to structure the representations of Maria and Mamusia in their respective upper and lower worlds – the daughter in the penthouse and the mother in the basement. The basement is filthy, with 'Yerko's pungent farting' (35). The metaphors, however, move from fart and 'midden' to 'foul rag and bone shop' (76). The Yeatsian allusion, not available to Mamusia or Yerko but a function of the narrating professorial voice, keeps a strict separation between the classes (no matter how central Mamusia is to the recovery of the past).[15] A parallel authorial stance qualifies

Duddy Kravitz's attack on the intelligentsia: 'What a pack of crap artists! Writing and reading books that make fun of people like me' (242). To the extent that reception theorists such as Wolfgang Iser and Georges Poulet are correct when they show how the reader identifies with the narrated consciousness, Richler's scatology is directed at the intelligentsia; but to the extent that the reader recognizes authorial and readerly self-reflexiveness, the scatological attack never disturbs the sphere of sophistication. Since Richler has written a novel making fun of people like Duddy, and since the reader is reading such a novel, reader and author conspire to laugh at Duddy.

One of the satisfactions of those apprentices whose apotheosis stalls is to see scatology turned against the clean and proper sphere of the more powerful classes. This doubling back, which Duddy cannot engineer for those who laugh at him, occurs in *Eye of the Father*, where Hilda, forcibly barred from polite circles in a Saskatchewan town, laughs to see her social superior and nemesis, Mrs Pederson, squatting and wiping her rear with brome grass (105). If the rich were for a long time unique in having bathrooms (Corbin 175), then one way of mocking status is to represent a return to older excretory habits among the rich.[16]

Because Del's mother in *Lives of Girls and Women*, Addie Morrison, finds only high-minded intellectual domination in Dr Comber and his wife, she temporarily shifts her own ideals: 'What good is it if you read Plato and never clean your toilet? asked my mother, reverting to the values of Jubilee' (62). According to Bakhtin, grotesque realism posits a body that is not private or egotistical, but whereby the people challenge the bourgeois ego (19). Thus the thirteenth-century 'Ass's Will' – a poem which bequeaths the ass's head to the Pope, the ears to the cardinals, the voice to the choir, and the feces to the peasants – seems to contain a social critique (Bakhtin 351).

However, while a social critique is intended by Del's mother against the Combers, it cannot attack the class structure in any immediate way since the association of the scatological image with *Addie* primarily confirms her *own* position in a lower class. Indeed, Addie's claims to a superior breadth of experience eventually end in her own unconscious subordination to a hardly exclusive upper class: 'No flush toilets in that town. "I have cleaned out chamber pots to get my education!" she would say, and not mind who was listening. But a nice class of people used them. Bank clerks. The CNR telegraph operator. The teacher, Miss Rush' (66).

This ensures that mimetically scatology always belongs to the lower class. Stallybrass and White attack Bakhtin on precisely this ground, claiming that carnival often 'demonizes the weaker, not the stronger social groups ... in a process of abjection' (19). Corbin similarly argues that 'the scatology of Shrovetide Carnival, the derision directed at hygienic consciousness, and the streams of abuse might be interpreted as acceptance of an allotted role in society' (Corbin 214–15). Yet this conception of how scatology can freeze a class hierarchy may overstate the case. A more balanced assessment would follow Natalie Zemon Davis's explanation of the effects of Misrule festivities: for many French urban magistrates, Misrule was a safety valve, 'deflecting attention from social reality,' but because festive life perpetuates certain community values, Davis adds that it also functioned rhetorically to 'decipher king and state' (Davis 97). Since Addie by rejecting the Combers' discussion group rejects an apprenticeship in a male-oriented and Eurocentric syllabus, her ideals at this point track those of Munro, giving Addie in moral power what she lacks in social or intellectual acuteness. If Addie is the object of satire, at least doctors and those measures of princeliness, bank clerks, are measured by *her* scatological standards.[17]

Not surprisingly, attempts to devalue an upper class far outnumber the attempts to double back to a lower class. In comparison with doubling back to the country or to a past, the taboos surrounding class positions are more powerful, even though both class and the civilizing process are coded through similar scatological images. For Davies's professors and for Munro's Addie, the doubling back is clearly only a tactical move, allowing a sceptical critique of class structure, but never reaching the point where the character renounces class gains. Similarly, Bernard Gursky uses 'a Jackson Pollock,' one of Bernard's daughter's *'fershtinkena* aquisitions,' to put job applicants in their places, asking them if they think the painting is good. Once they commit themselves, he pounces: '"It's hanging upside down. Now what can I get you?" Mr Harvard Tuchus-Face MBA' (116). Uneducated and from a lower class, Bernard's impulse is to turn the world upside down, but not so completely as to put away the artwork that signifies sophistication. Neither does Richler completely reverse the world. Moses Berger, the writer, is not taken in by Bernard's ruse, but like Davies's professors, mediates upper and lower.

'On reste toujours à l'intérieur de la sphère de ceux qui ont réussi, dont la vie a acquis une valeur sociale' (Lejeune 1980, 253; 'We always remain within the sphere of those who have succeeded, whose life has some social value' 199). Although Lejeune means that autobiographies 'sont le lieu où s'élabore, se reproduit et se transforme une identité collective, les *formes de vie* propres aux classes dominantes' (1980, 252; 'are the place where a collective identity is elaborated, reproduced, and transformed, *the patterns of life* appropriate to the ruling classes' 198), there is no reason to exclude fiction from this assessment. Laurence has Christie, a character at the bottom of Manawaka's social order, articulate a theory of unconscious community: 'Garbage belongs to all. Communal property, as you might say' (*The Diviners* 46). At this level, that which is jettisoned from the social order is actually what implies the denied unity of that order. But even though Christie has the intuitions of a Leveller, narratively he helps to support *Morag's* persona at the end of the novel. Morag will certainly not make her home in Manawaka (nor did Laurence in Neepawa) much less return to poverty, but in order to create an authorial persona able to mediate the range of culture from town garbageman to English professor, Morag needs, among other things, the authority of the lower class. A guarantor of many academic enterprises (de Certeau 3), the 'common man' also underwrites the narrative enterprises of Morag Gunn and Margaret Laurence, not to mention Richler and Davies.[18] To acknowledge this is not to deny class boundaries, but simply to make explicit the *rhetorical* uses to which marginality, and in particular scatological marginality, can be put. Munro's Rose, after all, uses scatology to 'queen it over' (23) people who would have liked to have been poor.

6

'This Is the British Fucking Empire': Race

The body ... will always exist in relation to some text: that is a given. The only question is, 'Which text?'

– Elaine Scarry, *Literature and the Body*

i

Societies create boundaries (and the concomitant dangers of 'pollution') also along racial lines. The citations in the previous chapter from Klein and Richler just as clearly mark racial difference, and often it is impossible to separate race from class in either history or literature. John Porter, in *The Vertical Mosaic*, notes congruencies between class and race divisions in Canada; more recently, Peter Pineo's and Porter's research indicates that the effects of ethnic status on job status have diminished, leading them to hypothesize that the 'vertical mosaic' is connected to periods of greatest immigration (390–1).[1]

It is therefore not surprising that novels such as Adele Wiseman's *The Sacrifice* and John Marlyn's *Under the Ribs of Death*, in which an Eastern European faces Anglo-Saxon notions of cleanliness, would come out of Winnipeg after a period of heavy Eastern European immigration to that city in the late 1940s and early 1950s. The latter novel begins during the other great period of Eastern European influx, just prior to World War I. After a visit to River Heights, Marlyn's protagonist Sandor Hunyadi for the first time 'sees' his own North End neighbourhood as filthy, scabrous, and rotten. More recently, when the novelist Margaret Sweatman returns to the 1919 Winnipeg General Strike in her award-winning novel *Fox*, she has one of her Anglo-Saxon characters undergo the matching experience to Sandor's and nearly become ill at the smell of cabbage cooking in a North End home (134). The initial 'soul' that Sandor creates for himself under the ribs of death is the soul of an Anglo-Saxon, 'Alex Hunter.' His hopes of rising in business are fed by what we might call 'entrepreneurial romances,' in which the hero keeps himself 'clean and presentable ... honest and neat and tidy' (108) until he can rise. But Sandor underestimates the *discourse* of the filthy immigrant, and each time that Sandor gives out his true name or his Selkirk Avenue address during a job interview, he loses whatever chance he has at success.

The scatological image in novels generally follows the lead set by the Canadian government's cultural policies, which until very recently encouraged emigration from Western and sometimes Central Europe while severely limiting emigration by non-Caucasian nationalities.[2] Particularly resonant cases of immigrant discrimination include the 1914 expulsion of the Sikhs on the *Komagata Maru* from Vancouver harbour, the head tax on Chinese immigrants, and the internment of Japanese citizens during World War II. Before 1953 the Immigration Act included a clause on 'climatic unsuitability,' a cover for the barring of immigration by people of colour (Hughes and Kallen 228). According to Howard Palmer and to Rohinton Mistry our immigration record is not as far removed from the American one despite the Canadian government's sponsorship of multiculturalism. Only in 1953 was the Fair Employment Practices Act passed, so that it became illegal to discriminate in hiring on the basis of race, national origin, colour, or religion. Bill S-5, the first bill against hate literature, was passed by the Senate in 1967, but died in the House of Commons. Bill C-3, a watered-down version of the same bill, was finally passed in 1969 (Rosenberg 196). Not until the 1960s, and perhaps only because of economic prosperity (Craig 12), did culturalism become fashionable (Woodcock 352) in some quarters with the Pearson government's introduction of bilingualism and biculturalism. Native culture was also suppressed and then sought along much the same timetable.

Thus while Brian Moore quite naturally focuses on the pollution attributed to his fellow Irishmen in *The Luck of Ginger Coffey*, he also represents the unclean among the Algonkians in *Black Robe*, at some distance from autobiography. For Williams the racial code is even more insistent because it initially seems to supersede autobiography: in Williams's first novel, *The Burning Wood*, the scatological images gather mainly around the Native; in his second novel, *The River Horsemen*, they are shared between the Native and the Ukrainian immigrant; and only in his third novel, *Eye of the Father*, do the images reach into Williams's personal Norwegian genealogy via Magnus Vangdal.

ii

Like the lower classes, marginalized immigrant and indigenous races become figures for the origins of the civilized self. Kristeva argues that the first constitution of the object is as 'abject.' This holds true not only in psychoanalysis (Kristeva), ethnography (Douglas), and sociology – Canadians tend to rank visible minorities in the lower echelons of the economic system, sometimes despite social reality with Asian groups (Ramcharan 90) – but also in imaginative literature, where the structures of the European civilizing process are brought to bear upon the writer's fictionalization of his or her own culture. Jake Hersh projects his son Sammy's loss of Jewish culture as an inability to say Kaddish during Jake's imagined funeral; instead, Sammy learns other idioms: 'I say, what shall we do with the old fart's ashes?' (285). The voice begins as a parody of British upper-class language and ends by disposing of Jake in scatological terms. However, in order to undermine the Germanic rhetoric of cleanliness which contributed to the Holocaust,[3] a milder version of which informed Canadian immigration policy,[4] Richler elsewhere gives scatology a more ambiguous valence. During World War II in *Solomon Gursky Was Here* Sir Hyman Kaplansky tricks his English Passover guests into eating *matzos* filled with ritual blood (509) to embody their complicity with the Nazis. The degrading conditions in the German concentration camp of *St Urbain's Horseman* – where drinking water was next to the latrine, where the same water was used for drinking and washing away excrement – signify the scatologizing and subsequent genocide of the Jew in German racial policy. The excremental nightmare becomes far preferable to the monstrous cleanliness of Mengele, who had all the women in a cell-block gassed in order to get rid of lice. Because of the Nazis' demonization of the Jew in images of uncleanliness, Richler must find some way of reversing the traditional association of excrement with degradation (an association that Jake, like other satirists, relies on) without smoothing over Nazi prison conditions. Richler mediates these competing values by splitting scatology between Harry Stein and Jake Hersh. Jake's persistent scatological concerns – 'Look out, Yankel, any minute now the shit hits the fan' (359) – carry a worry about his children in a racist society quite unlike the self-interested anal eroticism of Harry.

Similar concerns about race, the body, and illegal crossings over national boundaries appear throughout Richler's two later novels. In *Joshua Then and Now* a Jewish artist-protagonist again finds his way, by means of interracial marriage, into a United Empire Loyalist family, but the racial binaries are shifted from German/Jewish to English-Canadian/Jewish. Searching his ancestral past, Joshua discovers that his grandfather came from 'some shitty little village in Poland' and crusaded against Yiddish names like Bishinsky and Pfeffershnitt: 'You crazy Jews, this is the British fucking Empire and you can't call yourself by such horseshit names here. You there, you are now called "Bishop"' (289). The immigrant masters the discourse of 'Anglo-conformity' (Palmer 83), enunciating its unspoken prejudices.[5] The grandfather's intended conformity, however, is not quite enough to subdue his colloquial and scatological language; Richler thus degrades the empire because of its association with its newest subject.

By having Joshua join the satiric William Lyon Mackenzie King Society, Richler connects the horrifying but distant territory of the Holocaust to a less dangerous but more immediate Canadian territory. Mackenzie King pretended fairness to the Jews, but referred to them as junk collectors and advocated racial restrictions which would spur assimilation by preventing the formation of foreign ghettos (Mackenzie King, *Toronto Mail and Empire*, 25 Sept. 1897, quoted in Rosenberg 226). King's post–World War II immigration policies were geared towards nationalities that could be easily assimilated (Palmer 89).[6]

Richler's anti-Semitic White Anglo-Saxon Methodist customs official Bert Smith stands almost allegorically for the old empire in *Solomon Gursky Was Here*, but his scatological denigration of the Jew identifies a repression, satirically exaggerated, at the centre of Canadian culture. 'He had a strict upbringing. When he wet his bed, his father clipped a clothespin to his penis' (84).

Elsewhere Richler's allegories are less divided. He approaches the myth of cultural adoption in *Joshua Then and Now* through Joshua's marriage to Pauline, but parodies it through the relationship of the two fathers.[7] The senator, Joshua's father-in-law, is thrilled when his association with Joshua's father, Reuben, leads to outdoor urination:

'"I pissed outside," the senator told [Pauline], excited, "out in the field there"' (298). What the lower-class Jew provides for the Loyalist senator is a body. The satirist's revenge against the scatologizing of his culture is to entertain the logical conclusion: the Anglo-Saxon cannot dispel his bodily waste without the assistance of the degraded race. This conclusion is, of course, available to Anglo-Saxon writers as well. In Atwood's *Bodily Harm*, Jake, who bears a number of similarities to Jake Hersh in *St Urbain's Horseman*, responds to Rennie's comment that he has a poker in his anus: 'That's not a poker, it's a backbone ... I got it from pretending to be a goy' (73).

iii

Representations of Third World race – Atwood's *Bodily Harm*, David Godfrey's *The New Ancestors*, and Harold Sonny Ladoo's *Yesterdays* – put the Black, like the Jew, in a scatological position. Although intertribal repressions appear after the independence of Lost Coast (Gold Coast was the colonial name of Ghana) in *The New Ancestors*, the main lines of power in all three novels are North/South – White colonial oppression and Black suffering. Despite the White man Michael Burdener's sympathetic intentions in *The New Ancestors*, he must stand in as *pharmakos* for all colonial powers and put up with his mother-in-law's scatological abuse of him. In an ecstatic trance, 'she makes an obscene gesture, as though she is a man painfully pissing' (64); the gesture is not entirely symbolic (as Michael believes) since there are hints that White educators forced her to change her elimination patterns (73). Michael's effort at racial reconciliation becomes tragic, and that tragedy is signalled very early by scatology: 'The blacks do stink differently, don't let a liberal tell you other, for once the scientists and the Smethwicks agree' (17).[8] This 'material' differentiation between races proleptically dooms Ama Awotchwi's and Michael's interracial marriage – a personalized White man's burden – before the reader even knows much about the two characters.

Much later, Michael (under the pseudonym Burr) discovers a primitive sense of joint ancestry, imaginatively recovering 'Olduvai Gorge' (133). The mode of the recovered community is geographic and historical (in the proto-civilization along the Niger River), but also excremental, when Burdener wipes himself with pages from his notebook and no longer wants 'to let his body slip off after the diseased, mucoused shit' (347) which he left in the Niger. The use of the civilizing process in this late and excremental recourse to origins ultimately subordinates racial experience by implying a basic civilized parallelism between cultures, but it does not mitigate Michael's or Ama's personal tragedies.

For Ladoo, the colonial attack on non-White cultures is more insidious and the process less amenable to symbolic reconciliation. Like Richler, Ladoo inflates the racial self-critique by placing the people of *Yesterdays'* Carib Island entirely under the rubric of scatology: 'De only future in dis island, is drinkin rum and playing de ass' (26). Whichever way one takes Ladoo's semiosis of Trinidad, this attack on the racial self coheres with the self-image that the West Indian tends to receive in Toronto, Ladoo's adopted home: according to Raymond Breton's study of the perception of discrimination against minority groups in Toronto, West Indians consistently report far higher levels of discrimination than other ethnic groups. Ladoo's difficulty in getting a job consistent with his educational attainment – he worked as a short-order cook after graduating from university – graphically particularizes Breton's study. But balancing the scatological version of Trinidad is Tailor's information about the English who colonized Carib: Tailor appalls Choonilal by telling him that the English do not like to take baths and that they wipe their bums with paper. Choonilal has no confidence in Indian or Negro doctors, but it is the English doctor who apparently cannot be trusted,[9] who slips his fingers up Basdai's 'two holes' (65).

Ladoo's use of scatology maintains, in Choonilal's son Poonwa, an extreme scepticism about even his own marginal race. Because of the Canadian teacher's whip, Poonwa hides in the only safe place, the toilet. He begins to eat in the toilet, breaking his parents' Hindu dietary laws, and continues this practice later in the home of his employer. When his parents build a house, Poonwa ensures that a modern toilet will be part of the layout. As in Leonard Cohen's *Beautiful Losers* where F.'s vision of the 'Bhagavad-Santa' generates a response of 'you soil everything' (60), Ladoo intentionally soils Trinidadian Hindu culture. Mary Douglas cites studies which claim that in India a strong ritualization of defilement can co-exist with blindness to actual filth (Douglas 124). This is essential to Ladoo's satire in *Yesterdays*, where Choonilal's sacramental attempts to mollify the Aryan gods via his toilet manners include, unconsciously, the intrusion of the anal into all levels of his being and language.[10] The racial-colonial critique is corroded by the insistent association of excremental imagery with Hindu culture once it is put under the gaze of Western versions of the civilizing process. Poonwa's inability to make even ritual cleanliness distinctions makes his Hindu status even more parodic.

In Poonwa the scatological image does not mediate between cultures, since Ladoo has him simply reverse the signifiers of colonialism in his planned Hindu mission to Canada: 'How come dey make de Indians Christians? Well de same way Poonwa goin to beat dey ass and make dem learn Hindi' (67). The studied naïvety, especially in a character who has long been forced to compromise his culture, means that Ladoo concedes moral superiority neither to the colonist nor to the racial margin.[11]

Rohinton Mistry's parody of the Western gaze, 'Squatter,' is more sympathetic to the plight of the Torontonian immigrant – in this case a Parsi from Bombay. The protagonist, Sarosh, is a squatter in both senses of the word; he lives on a land not his own and cannot excrete his waste if he follows the Canadian practice of sitting, but must climb onto the toilet seat to 'simulate the squat of [his] Indian latrines' (733). In the new place, the old practice seems like a 'simulation,' highly artificial and eccentric: 'There had been a time when it had been perfectly natural to squat. Now it seemed a grotesquely aberrant thing to do' (739). Mistry links this eliminatory disorder to a series of social, not private, alimentary disorders, such as that of the immigrant who cannot eat 'pure white Wonder Bread' (736). Although the story is narrated in Bombay and the glimpses of Canadian characters from the dominant culture are very brief, Mistry's social semiosis creates what we might call an 'implied Canadian' to counterpoint Sarosh. Repressed on the level of narrative, this implied Canadian is nevertheless signified in both the bodily practices that give Sarosh's attempted conversion an urgency and in the unlocated gaze which, seeing no legs in front of the toilet, detects 'a foreign presence in the stall' (735). To this gaze, the immigrant exposes the arbitrary nature of cultural practices, and this exposure forms a prohibition where there was none, a taboo around the sitting that once had been simply habit. The immigrant, caught by this gaze between two cultural practices, begins to see two simulations where he had seen one nature. The implied Canadian, looking upon an alternative practice, can also no longer *really* see one nature. Yet emanating from the hypothetical movements behind the story Sarosh detects the malodor of 'xenophobia' (735); therefore the implied Canadian must still be defensively insisting that there is one nature, newly converted to *doxa*, set against one simulation, that now appears as foreign, unclean, taboo.

iv

The most pervasive representation of race by means of scatology in the Canadian novel occurs in the image of the Native. Terry Goldie has shown, in *Fear and Temptation: The Image of the Indigene in Canadian, Australian and New Zealand Literatures*, how the indigene functions in White semiosis at the poles of denial and embrace. This is most clear in the representation of sexuality, but it also holds for scatology: the Native functions to restore origins or the lost body to White culture, but that restoration generally takes place under the auspices of the white sign-maker (Goldie 24–5, 77, 119–20). Scatology that is peripheral to a novel's dominant concerns demonstrates how associating the Native with filth has become a 'second nature.' John Richardson in 1832 described what goes on outside the garrison: the Ottawa 'occupied themselves by the firelight in parting the long black matted hair and maintaining a destructive warfare against the pigmy inhabitants of that dark region' (243). This 'warfare' parodies the British/Indian wars in the larger narrative, but parodies it in such a way as to displace North American content onto African signs (the pigmy), and to interweave the markers of civilized cleanliness with colonial warfare, so that the Natives are *agents*, not subjects, of colonial enterprise. What the Natives do to maintain civilized cleanliness in their hair thus justifies what the British (making the analogical leap) do in their own 'dark regions.' In Roy's *La petite poule d'eau*, Luzina fears catching lice from the Indians (40) and is upset that the 'grimy' and 'dirty' Natives will not support her civilized desire to open a school (92), while in Atwood's *The Edible Woman* the disgusted Millie believes that menstruating Native women use moss instead of sanitary napkins. The representational traditions of 'reek' and 'vermin,' which appeared most famously in Pratt's *Brébeuf and His Brethren*, still signify preliterate cultures, even though both Roy and Atwood satirize the beliefs of their characters, attributing the beliefs to the false superiority created by 'common knowledge.' Farley Mowat, a less sophisticated writer than Pratt but one with at least a little firsthand knowledge, offers less culture-bound versions of common sense: in his autobiographical *People of the Deer* he has diarrhoea only as long as he refuses to eat the Native Ihalmuit diet.

The *type* of scatology associated with First Nations reveals the White literary use to which the Native is put. In Peter Such's *Riverrun* and Rudy Wiebe's *The Temptations of Big Bear*, blood signals not just gender, but also genre. The blood emphasis maps the cultural past through elegy. This departs from early works such as *Wacousta*, where the Natives taunt the inhabitants of the garrison at Detroit with blood (195, 199, 223) and then make them bleed. Blood in *Wacousta* is most important in the description of murdered British soldiers such as Harry Donellan – 'the scalpless crown completely saturated in its own clotted blood and oozing brains' (58); Such and Wiebe, though more sympathetic to the Native point of view, are not thereby more 'Native' in structuring their work. Despite archaeological precision, Such's account of the Beothuk is complicated by elegy, in which blood signals death and pathos. Thus the bloody representations of the dying stag (59) and caribou (75) function mainly as European tropes for the extinguished tribe, indeed almost in the romance convention of the wounded hart (which operated at a more conscious level in *Wacousta*),[12] and cannot function according to Native traditions of the hunt in which animal blood stands for power and plenty.[13]

Such does attempt to evoke alternative interpretations when he describes Waunathoake's birth – 'the cord still throbbed with life' (76) – but generally he sticks to elegy. Wothamisit's and Demasduit's cough and spit are eventually tinged with blood (43, 112, 114), Demasduit weeps (90),[14] Osnahanut vomits from hunger (65, 69), and his 'fearsweat' has a cultural meaning: 'If all the people die, there will be no one to remember our spirits' (128). During her captivity, Demasduit, 'remembering the forgotten uses of her body,' leaves the house to get near the gardener's 'sweatsmell' and 'the reek of the nearby outhouse' (108). Here, even without blood, vomit, or 'fearsweat,' excrement is elegiac, mediating loss and only allowing for pathetically limited forms of bodily return.

Still, near the end of the novel, Such does reach a moment when the Native body does not fit generic patterns. The last Beothuk, Shawnadithit, makes an image of the governor of Newfoundland with her teeth; the spittle that we see has no edge of blood (which would be superfluous by this time), and tells the reader nothing generic about how we should interpret Shawnadithit's absolute historical isolation in a boundless display-case. Does the last bearer of the culture carry the whole structure in her art, or since the culture has collapsed into a single lore, is there no longer any measure?

First Nations, again like Richler's Jews, often become alternatives to British Canadian repression of the body. This happens very violently and inconclusively in *The Temptations of Big Bear*. John Delaney's obscenities and blasphemy project onto the Native what Delaney dare not acknowledge within the frame of his Orange culture. He speaks to the uncomprehending Native woman of 'pawing through the wounds and private pricks of Jesus' (232) and of the 'most absolute pure frozen Christ shit' (233). In the Freudian model of the self, the movement outside of 'civilization' discloses the repressed phallus and anus, in this case of Aylmer, Ontario.[15] Inevitably, some of the projection is Wiebe's. Like Such, Wiebe attempts to get at how alien Native culture is to European understanding, despite the lack of homogeneity in European cultures and despite any difficulty in assessing what exactly is 'marginal.'[16] The use of scatology becomes a mimetic technique whereby cultural difference can be presented in an anthropologically correct and immediate way through taste and smell (which are seemingly outside of language): 'Has he ever tried to swallow buffalo liver steaming from the carcass, and sprinkled with gall for taste?' (36); 'slowly the smell gathered of horses and sweat and buffalo grease' (40). Moore's Algonkians (*Black Robe* 39–40) and Laurence's Métis (*The Diviners* 338, 423) also emit a strong odour.

Adding to these circumstantial signs, Wiebe attempts to portray modes of being that are prior to European standards of civilization by representing his Cree as unconscious of filth. Big Bear toes aside excrement (50), buffalo chips are used for fire (87), and Horsechild picks his nose to eat the mucous (94). Nevertheless, Wiebe's desire for anthropological accuracy balances uneasily against the Christian epigraph under which he sets his entire narrative, the Pauline attempt in Acts 17 to convince the Athenians that the unknown god they worship is actually Jahweh. By making Big Bear into a precursor of Christianity and in giving the most power to his *words*, particularly about the 'Great Spirit,' Wiebe lets the alien body go in favor of Paul's assimilative tendency.[17] Big Bear's fear – 'He had not thought The Only One would permit such *blackness* to be found in him; opening endlessly' (150, my italics) – seems curiously identical to an existential (disembodied and post-Christian) fear.

The difficulty of using scatology to represent another culture is perhaps most evident when Big Bear dreams of the pink liquid (blood and milk) flowing from a cow after the last buffalo hunt. Blood and the 'last' hunt combine to signal elegy, but the slicing off of the buffalo's teats to add milk to the flow creates a strange, generically indeterminate effect, an effect which one suspects cannot be translated across cultures. The bodily sign of death – the mingling of blood and milk in the cut teat – cannot be fully elegiac, either in the writer's context of twentieth-century Canadian society when such an act must seem barbaric, or in Big Bear's tribal culture where the sign must take a form of *nostalgia* for the hunt (and the pink liquid), *not* for the dead cow or anything that she represents. In this latter case the anthropological narrative's signs move tangentially to Big Bear's tragedy. Wiebe's failure to fully process this Plains custom as elegy is an important failure, since it sets anthropological accuracy against literary coherence, and highlights the difficulties attending the mimesis of race.

Wiebe recognizes these difficulties in the person of Kitty McLean. Kitty romanticizes Native life (272, 276–7), yet she also adopts Cree attitudes towards the body, saying that the only way to kill a louse is to crack it between the teeth (291). But in this presentation of Kitty, Wiebe seems to claim a mastery over Native attitudes, a mastery that he later disavows when Kitty becomes the figure for the author-translator of Native thought systems. In her despair at properly translating Big Bear's voice during his trial, she begins to think that she is menstruating: 'She thought in a revelation it was the monthly *blackness* seeping through her and momentarily she would feel dampness, she was certain she felt it, once, and when she could look at herself there would be the dark worm crawling between the blackish hair inside her leg out of that unstoppable entrance into herself, she could never squat now as she had as a child and not feel herself opened uncloseably' (384, my italics). Kitty's comparison is not metaphor so much as bodily *condition* or habit – as the conditional construction suggests. As the internal representative of the author-translator, it is appropriate that she uses Wiebe's Christianizing language – 'revelation,' 'worm' – even as she despairs of the ability of Christian figures to make typological sense of Big Bear's story: she can no longer read languages as parallel allegories of one another. This is one of the most evocative moments in Wiebe's writing because it transgresses against his Christian figural use of Big Bear. Kitty is one of those 'she-things' (*femelles*) who '*gâchent tout infini*' (Céline 531; 'wreck the infinite'). Unclean, if we invoke the terms of Old Testament law, she is one whose flow of blood (not just the parallelism of existential doubt) allies her with Big Bear. And, as a bronzed woman, bleeding, she is alien from the White male author even if she belongs to his elegiac conventions.

W.O. Mitchell's Natives in *The Vanishing Point* satirize and then modify the Protestant body: 'So that's the whole situation with civilization,' Archie Nicotine concludes, 'a lot of people – a lot of germs – a lot of shit' (39). Mitchell's semiosis has its romantic side – the Native children are public and unselfconscious about eliminative functions (114) – but it too contains a potential tragedy in the undifferentiated and self-injuring tricks of 'Weesackashack,' looking for 'scabs from his rear end – eating them because he mistook them for food' (13).[18] If, as Goldie argues, Mitchell uses Natives mainly to address White concerns, at least he does so by using the cultural mechanism provided by the Cree Trickster, Wisahkecahk: the Natives' subversion of Reverend Dingle's sentiment when they have him translate his 'thank-you' into the Cree for 'bullshit' is rooted in the traditional culture-mocking techniques of the Trickster.[19] According to Douglas, observational bias entails that filth seems to jump out from another culture under observation (97). In particular, she suggests that the Amerindian Trickster cycle is not as scatological as Norman O. Brown's reading of ethnography makes it seem.[20] Yet Douglas does not make allowance for Amerindian suppression of their own stories (in order to avoid being made into a scatological object by the dominant Caucasian culture), allowance for obscenity standards in publications prior to the 1960s, or for something as mundane as the history of reservation housing – by 1987 in Canada, for example, only 10 per cent of dwellings on reservations had running water and sewage disposal compared to 98 per cent of the occupied dwellings in the rest of the country (Clatworthy and Stevens). Archie Nicotine's mockery of urban washroom architecture thus has a social basis. Furthermore, Amerindian writers represent the Trickster as scatologically as Mitchell does.[21] Mitchell does not naturalize scatology as an inbred Native predilection, but presents it satirically as a function of White actions: 'That nurse she'll just stuff Fyfe Minimal Subsistence Biscuits up my red ass you see' (239).

Mitchell's Stoney Cree also use the Trickster's scatological scepticism against their own traditional culture: 'We don't buy that Bony Spectre bullshit any more' (29). This self-reflexivity recognizes Native traditions of satire. Rudy Wiebe too has Big Bear deconstruct his culture when instead of recounting a vision quest he gives a satiric and punning version of how he acquired his name: 'I was so eager to get out my mother had no time to spread the clean hide ... and I fell with my nose in something the bear had left behind. Since then I have always had something big with bears' (206). Wiebe represents a dialogism within Native culture so that the native does not just perform the nostalgic function of primitive 'belief' for a sophisticated white culture.

Leonard Cohen, George Bowering, and David Williams all use parodic scatology to carefully differentiate the *narrated* Native from the *historical* Native. In *Beautiful Losers* Cohen's unnamed tribe becomes a trope for death: 'A ——— is the word for corpse' (5). The Freudian equation of the corpse with feces – the entire body as waste material – prefigures Cohen's primitivist connection of the excremental with the pre-Conquest Iroquois (54–5). Cohen's purposes for such a connection appear to be double. On the one hand, F.'s project is a figural recovery of what he thinks is a pre-Enlightenment body; he, and Cohen too I would argue, thereby have the Natives agonize for a repressed White culture: 'The Company of Jesus had their way with them. Lots of semen in the forest, I'll bet' (16). This theory is enacted in Moore's *Black Robe* where Father Laforgue spills his semen in the forest while watching Annuka and Daniel in coitus (56). On the other hand, this repression simultaneously identifies the history of White masculine abuse of the Native. Edith's bum becomes the focus of the White town's desire in *Beautiful Losers* (28), and her victimhood is signalled just before her rape, when she urinates in fear: 'It was a sound so majestic and simple, a holy symbol of frailty' (64).

The difference between Cohen's sense of Native frailty and Such's or Wiebe's sense is that Cohen's Natives, though suggested by the Abénaquis, are purely hypothetical. The overemphasis on Native filth thus becomes self-conscious artifice and invites scepticism about narrative structure and ideology in a way that anthropological accuracy does not. This happens in *Burning Water* as well. Instead of just using the First and Second Indians to signal a pre-Enlightenment body, Bowering has them mimic *English* scatological language: the First Indian's 'first ceremonial English words,' learned from the *Discovery*'s crew, are 'Aeh shitt!' (128). Most important, these words, like the rest of the narrative, break out of historical voices and documented events. George Vancouver 'discovers' the Northwest Passage when his ships rise and fly over the Rockies. During this anachronistic passage,

Lieutenant Puget says, 'Those superstitious heathen would be fouling their breeches, if they had the decency to be wearing any' (134). The complex parodic structure – a parody of eighteenth-century language set inside a parody of a twentieth-century airplane ride – does not allow the attribution of uncivilized filth to the Indian to be a 'natural' mimesis of eighteenth-century attitudes. The Indians also speak in twentieth-century clichés, including scatological clichés:

> 'I suppose you get a lot of rain in these parts,' suggested Vancouver.
> 'Not so much in the summer,' said the chief. 'In the winter it rains all the time, but we always say that at least you don't have to shovel it.'
> 'I could think of a good use for a shovel right now,' whispered the first Indian. (141)

History recedes infinitely before the twentieth-century novelist, and the unclean Native becomes a doubly hypothetical proposition.

The first two novels of David Williams show a progression from the use of the Native as a figure for the lost White body towards the more sceptical position. For Joshua Cardiff in *The Burning Wood* the Native acts as a scatological counter to the bodily repressions of White fundamentalist religion. The associations are metonymic when Joshua uses the toilet as an excuse to leave the Bible camp and follow his Cree friend Thomas to the reservation; the type of transference in which Joshua engages is more evident in his metaphors:

> An Indian man stood at the foot of the driveway and, facing the house, urinated in the snow. He took his unrelieved time about it, sending up a great cloud of steam above his head, catching the last of the sunlight, so that he began to resemble the picture of an angel alighting in an old illustrated Bible. Joshua was relieved because his mother was in the kitchen at the time, peeling potatoes. He kept Janie forcibly away from the picture window. (41)

Despite the religious adoption in Joshua's language, his historical intent is to keep his blood family from his imagined kin. While Williams's rewriting of Rudy Wiebe's Old Testament Indians doubles Native filth onto Christian spiritualizing in an attempt to naturalize and pluralize Christianity, Joshua's 'relief' is only emotional at this point. The use of the Cree as a generalized trope for the body is perhaps inevitable, given the opening scene of the novel where Joshua imagines himself as 'David in the cave at Engedi, approaching now so carefully, carefully, to cut the skirt of the sleeping king's robe' (1). In the original text, Saul was not sleeping, but excreting. When culture and acculturized text (the *King James Bible*) veil the body, one response is to turn to a culture where bodily functions are more apparent.

In his next novel, *The River Horsemen*, Williams incorporates a whole range of Plains Cree culture in his characters Fine-day (the shaman in the novel who, historically, survived the Northwest Rebellion of 1885) and Many-birds (the Trickster Wisahkecahk, the key causative agent in Cree mythology according to Jennifer Brown, 120).[22] With revivalist preacher Jack Cann and a Ukrainian boy, Nick Sobchuk, the two Natives paddle a canoe up-river to Saskatoon during the Depression, parodying not only *Adventures of Huckleberry Finn* but also Wisahkecahk's mythic canoe-journey during which he helped to restore the world after a great flood (George Nelson in J. Brown 46). The ex-convict Many-birds forces Jack to readopt the lost body of Christianity, but this is strictly inadvertent. Many-birds is antinomian and somewhat sinister:

Never have got outa the pen alive if I worried. Keep your mind a blank. Every day drain it dry.
  Then I feel something else about to drain ...
  'Water to water,' I say, 'dust to dust.'
  It's what the priest said over Billy Left-hand after he got outa the hole. Throat cut the same day. In the dining hall.
  At the last minute I think to stick out my cup. My friends all sit, blinking like owls.
  'What's wrong with you birds? None of you ever laugh?'
  I put the cup to my lips, swallow fast. Hot ...
  At once I know a way to beat that fucker, bald Head Moon. Outshine him myself.
  The cool air licks at my crack. Between my legs I see the old man grin at last.
  'Hey, old man, I think you should kill yourself. That would be the funniest thing. Here, it's easy. So easy a guy like you could do it. Let me show you.'
  I flip over the rail, headfirst. I hear them all gasp just before I start to fall.
  Upsidedown I grin at a starry sky. Old Bone, I think, your light is put out. You won't dare to show your face again.
  Then I land, like a cat, in mud to my knees. (148)

Many-birds' scatological parody here mocks Fine-day, the shaman who has had an initiatory dream of dismemberment, death, and rebirth. Earlier, and therefore doubly the wrong end round in the shaman's narrative, Williams had Many-birds satirize the shaman's birth experience: '"You was born out d'wrong end, old man"' (70). Parody does not attempt to get the culture 'right,' even though it does still reserve a special status for the sign-maker. Williams thus, like Mitchell, imitates the self-injuring scatological jokes and cultural scepticism of Wisahkecahk.

v

One of the difficulties with the representation of marginality and race (especially of an oral culture) is that the scatological image is coded through the civilizing process and its proxy, writing. This means that with our alphabet it is impossible to be both anthropologically 'correct' and completely avoid racism. Williams partially avoids this through parody, but Brian Moore has greater difficulty. Although the Natives in *Black Robe* consistently turn the scatological image against the Normans, they are still *bearers* of the image, unclean and 'low.' On the other hand, when Moore has Annuka vomit after bludgeoning her captor to death, this represents a fairly recent decorum about the treatment of enemies that may be historically inaccurate, but Moore does so to make her sympathetic. The imaginative effect of the scatologizing of marginal races seems to be that while the author maintains a civilized persona (as writer), he also embraces the marginal position, so that the repressed culture and its trope (the filthy body) become another basis for a revised aesthetic. As with class, the effect is partly an increasing rhetorical identification with the 'low.'

As with class, the rhetoric of racial marginality creates status ambiguity for those at the margins who wield the alphabet. Michael Greenstein notes how Jewish writers maintain the marginality of the Diaspora against Zionist institutions (Greenstein 12). Greenstein's deconstructive reading, however, does not address the writer's class position. If, as has often been argued, 'literature is elite-oriented' (Craig 19), we may be witnessing the broadly based production of new elites along ideological and intellectual, not racial or class, lines. As mediator between 'lower' and 'upper' levels of language, the writer retains the rhetorical advantage offered by the position of the marginal by identifying his persona (Jake, Joshua) in some way with a lower class (by means of genealogy or by having him mock authority). To call A.M.

Klein 'marginal' (Greenstein 5) is inaccurate, unless "marginal" refers to the way in which most verbally inventive authors need time to acquire a fit audience. Jewish class positions in Canada have generally been higher than other non-Anglo racial groups (Marchak 31; Porter 80, 85).[23]

The class solution, in which the writer mediates between 'upper' and 'lower,' cannot always work in the topos of race. Greenstein notes how Richler uses 'the coprophile' to debase Jews who have conveniently forgotten their origins (Greenstein 157), but we must add that Richler also has other criteria when he divides his Jews into those who do not deserve to be defiled, such as Jake Hersh, and those who do, such as Harry Stein. Both Jake and Harry acknowledge their racial past, but Harry, a cruel man, is punished legally and symbolically (when Jake shuns him). In this Richler expresses, as all writers do, a more specified version of the power that shares out society. As well, Richler's alternation between Yiddish and English can solve the writer's status ambiguity linguistically by combining a marginal and a dominant language (just as Tomson Highway does with Cree, Ojibway, and English); politically, the birth of Israel in 1948 has complicated the question of marginality for Richler and Klein.[24] The paradox already existed for Klein in the 1950s as Terrence Craig has argued (126), even when Israel was still a marginal proposition, and presents itself in *The Second Scroll* through the narrator's attempts to find a Jewish epic poet. The political incarnation of racial power in Klein and Richler is met with uneasiness: neither actually scatologizes the Jewish state since they identify with its racial basis, but both mistrust the position of power from which all states operate (having suffered a version of that power at French- and English-Canadian hands).[25]

Klein's distrust for the material representation of culture ensures that the literary form which the celebration of culture and race once took, the epic, will not answer to the search even though Klein personally allied himself with the Zionist cause.[26] The circumspect 'Poet of Tiberias' displaces the epic poet or novelist, and writes only aphorisms.

Two of the seven reported poems rely upon scatology:

Pity emetic and the enema, Terror (83)

and

On the clearing of the swamps at Esdraelon
The little arrows pierced; we fevered; we pissed black.
Anopheles, his hosts! (83)

In the first poem the chiastic play on Aristotle's metaphor creates a neoclassical but scatological and abbreviated aesthetic. Although the collected works of the Tiberias poet have been read as a burlesque of Imagist doctrine (Spiro 222), they only sound satirical if we determine ahead of time that scatology is inevitably satiric. Spiro notes that part of Klein's purpose in the first poem is mimetic – 'to produce an elementary image of terror, some of the physical effects of which are vomiting and diarrhoea' (222) – and admits that in the latter poem the satire is less apparent (224). In the latter, the scene is the epic reconstruction of Palestine, but by means of scatology and aphorism Klein retains the position of marginality vis-à-vis epic literature and, by means of renal malaria, vis-à-vis nature and the Anopheles mosquito. Although Klein elsewhere certainly mocks Imagist prescriptions,[27] in *The Second Scroll* (seventy-seven pages of text and forty-seven pages of glosses) he arrives at Imagist tendencies because of a distrust for the grand traditions of epic which synthesize disparate strands into one culture. It is therefore easier to feel sympathy for Klein's Zionism than for the cultural visions of Pound or Eliot, particularly after one of the Ministers of Immigration in the Mulroney government, Bernard Valcourt, tabled (and later withdrew) a bill which included the fingerprinting of refugees and would have forced some specialists (such as doctors) to locate in designated rural areas for at least two years.

Richler also distrusts the solidification of race into nationhood, even though that distrust is expressed mostly thematically. Duddy's acquiring of land is too literal, not quite what his *Zeyda*, raised on the yearning poetry of the Diaspora, had in mind. Although the relation between Canadian land and Zionist hopes is not altogether clear in the novel, by the time Duddy possesses the land in stylized primate manner – pissing his name into the snow – he has clearly compromised himself with power. Richler, Klein, and even those writers who attempt to synthesize cultures hesitate at what Theodor Adorno calls 'the premature reconciliation in art and criticism of unreconciled social conflicts' (Fekete 56). This hesitation, born of the experience of racism and not evident to the same degree in the representation of class, occurs especially when writers recognize the beginnings of new empires.

7

Allegories and Sites of Power: Politics and Economics

We have a saying which is, 'The mind, Emperor of the body,' though we now, like you, have driven out all emperors and imperialists.

– Ling Huo in *The New Ancestors*

i

Klein, caught between the desire to affirm a political structure and the reluctance to do so, is certainly not alone in using scatology to address the tensions in a political structure. For many writers resistance is less complex, but in any case, national or party or economic abstractions are embodied allegorically by means of scatology. Barbara Foley convincingly argues that even the most resistant texts are to some degree mimetic.[1] While we might hesitate to attribute ontological priority to either world or text (Shell 1), the technology of writing is of course symbolic – 'other-speak' in the broadest sense – needing things against which to send sonic or post-sonic echoes. This ensures, according to Fredric Jameson, that any attempt to distinguish between socio-political texts and those that are not is 'a symptom and a reinforcement of the reification and privatization of contemporary life' (Jameson 1981, 20). Even if the movement towards the civilized self (which we have seen is not always negative) takes part in that privatization, Jameson is nevertheless right in his claim, especially since he, like Foucault, theoretically links the body to what can never be outside of the collective – the text; the body is that which gives us a particular *concern* in histories and texts (Jameson 1981, 31). Allegory connects the privatized meaning of any narrative with the polity. We have seen in Part I that the impulse towards privatization is paradoxically but inevitably enacted in the public sphere through personal and social histories.[2]

There are two opposing versions of how power can be registered on the site of the body. The semiosis of World War I repeatedly involves scatology (*The New Ancestors* 84; *The Diviners* 90; *Two Solitudes* 309; *Fifth Business* 70) as a mimetic marker, a way of substantiating the narrative's 'reality.' On the other hand, Atwood *parodies* the analogy of politics and the body in *The Edible Woman*. Ainsley connects Quebec laxative surveys to a collective Québécois guilt-complex and to the Quebec language-problem (21–3).

Jameson could no doubt show how these two extremes of realist detail and parodic negation convey political meanings, but for the moment I am more interested in a conscious allegory whereby Canadian novelists register political concerns in the body. Despite the negation of political allegory in *The Edible Woman*, in *The Handmaid's Tale* the lockless bathroom doors (58) of Gilead are Foucauldian symptoms of totalitarian control. Because the bathroom retains its signification of privacy, it also becomes the site of minor insurrections against the collective. The handmaids purposely clog the toilet with wads of paper (122), write anti-authoritarian graffiti in the cubicles, and one handmaid begins her escape in the bathroom: 'Moira was our fantasy ... [the Aunts'] power had a flaw to it. They could be shanghaied in toilets' (125). Offred extrapolates from the toilet into politics: 'There is something reassuring about the toilets. Bodily functions at least remain democratic' (235). The Natives in Moore's *Black Robe* follow a similar line of reasoning against European ascendancy: 'Normans shit and eat and bleed and die just like other men' (109). The body, which abjectly registers Offred's sympathy with other victims of Gilead when she retches during the Salvaging (259), is that by which Atwood means to register the past politics of Puritan New England, contemporary politics in Iran, and her fears about the future; but the body is also that through which she imagines the democratization of power.

As in *The Handmaid's Tale*, there are in Godfrey's *The New Ancestors* no simply personal bodies – all register power. Pobee-Biney describes his prison term: 'They only let us empty our chamber-pots once a day, if we infracted nothing' (192).[3] Michael Burdener speaks about his wife, Ama Awotchwi, who was a 'dirty woman' for President

Kruman: 'There was no other word for it really than the white word, the urinal word, fucking ... "What is my body," you said when that latrine-cleaner Samuels offered a chance of your father's freedom' (141–2). Michael interprets Kruman's erotic domination scatologically, degrading Kruman, but although Michael means also to degrade Samuels by mentioning Samuels's former job, that job registers an earlier victimhood: avoidance of latrine-cleaning was Samuels's personal stake in political change. A prerevolutionary incident in which he refused to clean the outhouse pail of Hastings Awotchwi (Ama's father) allegorizes Lost Coast's socialist revolution, which in turn is an allegory for the bloodless rebellion against British rule that took place in Ghana ('Gold Coast') during the late 1940s. Hastings, from a managerial class,[4] could not at that time quite put himself into Samuels's shoes, and he said to the boy, 'You must not be sullen so' (232).

Later Samuels, working as an enforcer for Kruman's regime, cannot quite put himself into the shoes of the students who challenge the new government (and the *new* managerial class) with 'END TRIBALISM NOW' (180), a slogan which echoes the slogan that former president Kwame Nkrumah used just after the 1949 founding of his Convention Peoples' Party and long before he attained power in 1957: 'Self-government Now.'[5] Samuels unconsciously echoes Hastings's imperative by playing with deterministic mutations of the banner's words, until political power is mystified in eternal verities: 'End Rain Now! ... End Rain & Sea. Now. Double Quick-Quick' (180). In sentence mood, play, and deterministic cynicism, these words parallel Samuels' reworked memory of 'being God and watching Hastings Awotchwi, in his Senior Service Whites, address that nightsoil pail, "Do not be sullen so, pail. Do not be sullen, soil sullen, sullied soil, shit sullen, sullied, sullen soiled, shit"' (233). By means of this language and structure Godfrey allegorizes his earlier, more general comments on Ghana: 'What is happening here, in a word as Marx would say, is the transition of a Western-type parliamentary system into a single-party communistic state. As far as *Realpolitik* goes ... the shift is essentially theoretical' (*Man Deserves Man* 187). Through bodily impingements, especially on and by Samuels and Kruman, Godfrey allegorizes both the sources and betrayals of Nkrumah's slowly adopted pan-African 'socialism.'[6] The incredible optimism, even utopianism, that Godfrey found among Ghanaians in *Man Deserves Man* (189) is ventriloquized in the novel as an *outside* voice, coming from the Chinese diplomat Ling Huo: 'We have a saying which is, "The mind, Emperor of the body," though we now, like you, have driven out all emperors and imperialists' (42). The saying holds true neither in the novel's personal sphere nor, as the Maoist Huo's inability to manage the metaphor shows, in the political sphere from which Huo gets his language.

Despite appearances and despite historicist critics' near-equation of modernism and imperialism, Godfrey's bodily determinism is not intended to paralyse with pessimism the West African drive towards independence. Gamaliel Harding fears that his son, whom he has long repressed, has joined the Kulungugu killer boys: 'They would shit in a church, such children' (281). The implied post-colonial fantasy is parallel to the sodomy in the Anglican church during *Yesterdays*; despite his initial 'moderate' position, 'El Amaliel' (Gamaliel's 'altered' ego in Mali) conspires in the torture of Rusk, the American spy. During the hallucinatory interrogation, El Amaliel transfers Rusk's neocolonial dynamic from the erotic to the scatologic, just as Burdener did Kruman's: 'Your very balls are constipated with inklings of conquest ... a woman is nothing to you, how can you fire your thirteen mile guns into her' (358).

Godfrey's refusal to fully identify the narrative with either the post-colonial government or with neocolonialism is ultimately in keeping with his vision of himself as one who, having worked for CUSO, can mediate between Canadians and the abstractions of statistics about the Third World (Godfrey, 'Doomsday Idealism' 416).

Other novelists too register neocolonialism in the body. In Atwood's *Bodily Harm*, the West Indian characters believe that there is 'nothing like a Revolution to make the States piss money' (277), and vandalism against the public washrooms used by tourists is the meagre (though unnerving) response to North–South economic inequities. In Lowry's *Under the Volcano* that monarchial representative, the Consul, goes to a toilet which he describes as 'this final grey Consulate, this Franklin Island of the soul' (336). There he reads a travel brochure containing unintentional puns – 'SEAT OF THE HISTORY OF THE CONQUEST: VISIT TLAXCALA!' (336) – setting up an uncalculable homology between the British post-colonial diplomat and the Spanish conquest of Mexico. For the Consul, who has lost his public status, the symbols of imperial office are only displayed ironically in the toilet. A Mexican paramilitary group of neofascists overestimates his importance, eventually murdering him as a political threat, but in the same manner as they previously murdered an indigenous Indian peasant, the *pelado*, and throwing the Consul into the *barranca* which doubles as a garbage dump and 'gigantic jakes' (174). In Lowry's ironic representation of both colonial and post-colonial Mexican authority, then, it is repeatedly the *pelado* who is degraded and destroyed under occupation. The history of the conquest has frightening consequences in that public place, the private body, self-government again notwithstanding. The Consul sees himself as King Maximilian, the well-meaning and eventually broken proxy of French imperialism in nineteenth-century Mexico. If the puppet monarch ineffectually challenged the French who propped him on the throne, was he an imperialist or did he become one of the conquered?

For White Canadians, post-colonial experience is vastly different from Third World urgency because White settler groups very quickly outnumbered marginalized groups, permitting early independence and yet nominal European control of the Canadian government through the British North America Act. The difference between toilets in Klein's Moroccan ghetto and Richler's Canada is perhaps instructive: 'There is no water in the mellah. The mellah's alleys are its cloaca' (*The Second Scroll* 65). Water is first used for drinking, then for washing hands, then for dishes, then for clothes, and only then for flushing; meanwhile Richler's Herky speaks of four gallons of fresh water per Canadian toilet flush.

Despite the two different levels of bodily comfort, the racial scatology that we have seen in Chapter 6 occasionally addresses Canadian politics overtly. Bakhtin recognizes scatology as a dethroning gesture (Bakhtin 1984, 372–3),[7] and even if British monarchial power in Canada is now largely ceremonial, in Williams's *The River Horsemen* we see the dethroning (coded through Western populism) when Nick Jr exposes his penis during the British anthem. Nick Sr ingeniously defends his son as an imitator of Edward VIII: 'The former king give up his throne that way didn't he?' (111). Similarly, when Moore's immigrant, Ginger Coffey, unsure where he is in the darkness, urinates in the Royal Family Hotel, the act has an uncrowning effect no matter how 'accidental' Ginger claims that it was. In both novels the characters pay a price for undressing even a figurehead emperor, but these latter-day confusions of the king's 'two bodies' underwrite a democratic mythology, and are particularly effective in attacking nostalgic throwbacks to aristocratic ideology which mask a moral or racial philosophy under the guise of a political philosophy.[8] Following the tradition of seventeenth-century progressive narrative, Williams and Moore use scatology to undermine the belief that 'honour' in the external social system corresponds to a moral order.[9]

Dethroning applies to prime ministers as well. In Hugh MacLennan's *Two Solitudes* Tallard says, 'The French are Frencher than France and the English are more British than England ever dared to be. And then you go to Ottawa and you see the P.M. with his ear on the ground and his backside hoisted in the air' (48). Despite Robert Borden's 'democratic' hope to be the populist leader of two divided camps, Tallard's scatological cartooning expresses Bakhtin's populist response to political authority.

ii

What Bakhtin downplayed, unfortunately, was money. 'The site of popular uncrownings, the fair, is also the marketplace ... Where Bakhtin emphasized the dirt of the fair and the bodily lower stratum, the pedlar displays soap, mirrors and items of dental care, commodities of beautification (particularly for women) of a cosmetic nature ... If the fair displayed the grotesque body, it also displayed the "fair"' (Stallybrass 30, 39). This revision of Bakhtin is crucial in order to see that in novels such as *The Edible Woman* the disappearance of the national domination of the body does not mean the disappearance of power. The power of the nation over the body's fortunes has now often been superseded by the economic power of the multinational corporation.[10] Atwood exposes what Stuart Ewen (after an analysis of the self-critique implied in Listerine ads) calls a 'commodity self' (Ewen 47).[11] Marian's identification with and refusal to eat animals coordinates her role as female victim with her culturally *approved* anorexia.

As Bryan Turner argues, diet, which was originally intended as a brake on desire, has presently come to signal the enhancement of desire: 'The internal management of desire by diet was transferred to an external presentation of the body through scientific gymnastics and cosmetics' (Turner 3). In *The Edible Woman* the commodity self, created in part by diet, becomes more and more parodic as Marian gradually narrows the list of foods that she can stomach. As well, fashion and consumer packaging can be seen as interchangeable forms of hygiene (Enzensberger 90, 94), and when Ainsley overdoes Marian's make-up, everyone again approves. Marian, however, feels 'distaste,' noticing that 'her mouth had left a greasy print on the rim of the glass'

(255). In this way Atwood forces the 'commodity self' or consumer body, which *seems* clean in the media simulacrum, to appear filthy as well, as if it involves a new kind of unclean secretion. Atwood thus uses the civilizing process – Marian noticing a form of pollution and feeling revulsion – to attack the 'commodity self,' which was created, in part, by similar civilized disgust.[12] This doubleness has consequences for the interpretation of the novel. Whereas early on Clara looks very like a parody (of the back-to-the-farm element in the 1960s counter-culture, unable to keep her house clean and her children from excreting in untoward places), she slowly becomes an alternative to the overly cosmetic culture of Marian and Peter.[13] But at the end of the novel Atwood cannot stabilize her satire against the economic system of getting and spending. Marian finally eats again. At the very moment that she rejects the commodity self she again becomes a consumer.

Once the body is no longer 'with the king,' the sources of power's impingements on the body become more abstract and difficult to identify (Barker 12). As Foucault argues, the last three hundred years have seen a large-scale dispersal of power into bodily details. A telling case occurs at the end of *Beautiful Losers*. Cohen seems aware that his repressive hypothesis in regard to the Jesuits is already out of date in the age of subliminal seduction, but he nevertheless rents the ending to the Jesuits as if they were still the narrative's antagonists. Whatever historical repression the Jesuits stood for has long been written over by the incitement to speak about the erotic and the anal.[14] The leasing out of our biology to the corporations (Kroker, *Technology* 79) is the *real* present imitated in *Beautiful Losers*, a present which gets effaced when Cohen (too late) attacks the old corporation, the Jesuits. The field of play for F. and then for the narrator is the technological sensorium; the field of coercion is that of the Jesuits. Even though Cohen teases out the effects of present technology just as often as he teases out the clichés of print, he only hints at the way in which F.'s anal climax is produced by the dictates of the pornography industry.

William Gibson is explicit about how corporations design their messages on the body; in his futuristic dystopias, corporations (mostly Japanese) control the biotech trade in body parts.[15] A character such as Turner, who retains archaic (that is, twentieth-century) individualist attitudes, vomits to see how the human body is co-opted when a Sense-Net executive recovers company property – the eyes of the dead star Jane Hamilton (*Count Zero* 94). Business, at best, creates new virtual environments for the disencumbered mind; at worst it repeats (on a different level) the early twentieth-century assembly line in front of a computer terminal. Much like Williams and Moore, Gibson gives the new king, the self-regulating market, a body. In *Neuromancer* Henry Dorsett Case, who had always believed that the real powers were more or less than people, invades the computer cores of the Tessier-Ashpool Corporation and is surprised at 'the soiled humanity' of Ashpool's room (203), much as Marly is in *Count Zero* when she arrives, years later, in the same place and senses the same thing – 'a darkness that smelled old and sadly human, a smell like a long-abandoned locker room' (195).

Atwood works more subliminally in *The Edible Woman*, where a man who claims to be doing an underwear survey makes obscene suggestions to women. Technically he appears to be a parasite on an otherwise 'legitimate' function of consumer culture, but Atwood purposely confuses consumer culture surveys with 'private' transgressions against women. As Bakhtin claims, stupidity and misprision often point out the flaws in a discourse; Atwood pretends to be unable to negotiate between social tensions (a traditional function of the novel) – and she therefore indicts not just a particular perversity, but an entire economic system's victimization of women. David Ricardo's vision of a battle to create and control wealth is thus localized in the body.

Both Gibson and Atwood reposition 'things' at the centre of what more and more threatens to become an abstract economic sign. Again we are in the realm of allegory, but now, dealing with economics, we can easily see that it is not only the novelist who allegorizes. Reading *Duddy Kravitz*, we might (rightly) conclude that through Hugh Thomas Calder's 'shameful little experiments with money' in the urinal (194) Richler means to allegorize *avaritia* in medieval fashion.[16] But money, Freud insists, is an allegory with feces as its referent, feces being the original form of exchange. The child has no money of its own, except what is given, and during toilet training feces becomes the first material thing which it is in the child's power to give or to hold (*Über Triebumsetzungen, insbesondere der Analerotik* 131).[17] Money's *significance,* psychoanalysts claim, depends upon the value with which the child regards its feces (N. Brown 293).[18] Because the 'self-made' Calder puts $100 bills in the urinal and then guesses who has pulled them out, he reveals a deep ambivalence about what might more properly be called the 'money-made' man.[19]

Freud's identification has serious difficulties, of course: psychoanalysis fails to engage its own reliance on paid therapy with its 'discovery' of the money-filth complex (Shell 196f), Freud unambiguously uses the economic metaphor elsewhere in an honorific way (Heinzelman 9), and other forms of material exchange (toy-sharing and food-sharing, for example) may predate toilet training.[20] Nevertheless, Freud isolates an important image-pattern in Western literature; like language, currency and credit exchange systems are undoubtedly allegories, at least allegories for labour, production, or land.[21]

In Moodie's *Mark Hurdlestone* patrimonies (entirely divorced from labour) are necessary and honoured, and money appears not as a sublimation of feces but of eternal life into social status.[22] Even so, Hurdlestone handles his gold as a material thing, to be occasionally fondled. Grove's Hannan, in order to get in with Philip Branden (and steal his money), calls Howard's bankroll 'filthy trash' (*A Search for America* 115). If early Canadian novels hint at the money-complex, post–World War II novelists make conscious use of it specifically to embody and devalue money or commodities. Hagar Shipley compares her constipation to being 'locked like a bank vault with no key' (Laurence, *The Stone Angel* 191). In Moore's *Black Robe* the Natives define the French so that French mercantilism is equivalent with excrement in identifying the self: 'They are the shits who love furs' (66). Ozias Froats and Mamusia in Davies's *The Rebel Angels* both pay money for feces, Froats to his test group (109) and Mamusia in order to supply her *bomari* (155). The humour of Davies's satire against the town-hall crusader Murray Brown depends upon Freud's logic. Brown wants to stop the university from spending money on Froats's experiments (in which feces is analysed in order to somatotype individuals); despite the scatological associations of his name and namesake (N.O. Brown), Brown is unconscious of the Freudian meaning of sublimated money. Ladoo reverses the terms, but not the equation in *Yesterdays*. When Choonilal and Tailor argue about the latrine, the real issue is whether or not Choonilal will mortgage the house for Poonwa's Hindu mission to Canada (5). When Poonwa demands the money, Choonilal feels the need to defecate (32). In Johnston's *The Story of Bobby O'Malley* Agnes's purchase of a white marble headstone for her husband, Ted (184), effaces the real man in an expensive revision of his character. Ted himself had called the toilet his headstone (184), but the commodified burial practices which deny the body of his death also deny his unclean individuality.

More than other Canadian novelists, Richler develops this reverse allegory, in which exchange value is purposefully reduced to excrement. In *Duddy Kravitz* Jerry Dingleman corners the market on Mr MacPherson's classroom merit cards. The system of exchange that MacPherson hopes to create – an accumulation of time off from school in exchange for good behaviour – is subverted in the bathroom (8). There the boys gamble for the merit cards and the cards lose their symbolic function as indulgences, becoming only manipulatable capital, which attaches itself arbitrarily to the winner of 'nearest-to-the-wall'; the *site* of this transformation ensures that 'good,' 'high,' and 'neat' (MacPherson's moral code) is degraded and revealed, by means of the boys' instincts, as a materialist system. However, although Richler's economy approaches the symbolism of Freud, the boys evidently have no difficulty leap-frogging over Freud's intermediary (and literalistic) step of precious metals (coins) to the more abstracted representation of paper money.

Historically the shifts from specie to fiduciary systems did not occur easily since the newer systems always provoked questions about the relationship between the monetary sign and its substantial referent,[23] but the boys immediately recognize the power of authority to provisionally abstract itself from its delegated symbols. The boys – Dingleman, then Duddy – who subvert MacPherson, finding new markets outside of MacPherson's feudal arrangements, graduate to larger economic systems where they authorize credit and expenditure. Duddy learns from his father's material and circumstantial worship of Dingleman, the 'Boy Wonder': 'He's got a whang that could choke a horse. I know, we had a leak together once' (60). The sidelong glance that mythicizes, coordinates capitalist successes with virility. By the end of the novel Duddy has entered his father's entrepreneurial romance, and Max gives his blessing by in turn mythologizing Duddy (315), the newer boy wonder.

iii

But the ascription of bodies to political, corporate, and monetary authorities or, conversely, to the people who suffer under these powers can be very ambiguous. While the racism associated with nationalism may explain Richler's resistance to economic nationalism, the satire against Duddy co-exists uneasily with Richler's public support of Canada–U.S. free trade. Materialist criticism freezes capital, but capital's injunction is to keep moving (Baudrillard 1980, 106). Baudrillard describes a circuit in which desire and the unconscious are 'the trash heap of the political economy and the psychic metaphor of capital' (1980, 94). The 'repressed' portion of the self (money, anal eroticism, or a conflation of the two) enters a novel and is dismissed (or not) by the novelist as immoral; that 'repressed' portion can loop back to confirm not its dismissal, but its own continued presence. For example, Duddy and the boys initially appear as desires (to manipulate capital, not to pledge allegiance to entrenched authority) and a system (capitalism) that Mr MacPherson has repressed. But what Dingleman/Duddy signifies is that MacPherson's system of feudal responsibility *always was* driven by capital and not by moral right: MacPherson could command the price of a day off because he controlled the boys' time in school. The effect is something like the doubts arising about the Renaissance aristocracy after the sale of honours (McKeon 151). Although Richler satirizes the capitalist, Duddy with capital keeps moving: Richler's picaresque novels *allegorically* insist upon a free market. In Richler's later novels (where the image of the rich artist unconsciously represents the businessman), the self-made character constantly reappears and repeatedly provides a human face and body for capitalism. In Gibson's *Count Zero* and *Neuromancer*, although the corporations are reduced to individual bodies by means of scatology, the 'cyber-space cowboys' (as they are known) confirm the individualist myths that inform American capitalism.[24]

The perhaps insoluble problem may be that the body is consistently imagined by novelists to contain an integrity above political and economic considerations. In what Octavio Paz calls the shift from the old 'economy of things' to the new 'economy of signs' (not so new if we keep in mind Plato's *Gorgias*) bodily reference is never secure – not for the novelist, not for the critic. In *Two Solitudes* Marius identifies the working men as those who sweat and stink. The man with the most positive reaction to Marius's anti-conscription speech is the one who also stinks the most. This too-ready identification of labour with a scatological sign appears to be MacLennan's, not just Marius's, since it appears again in a different context (115). MacLennan is certainly not alone in providing such identifications.

More unconsciously, *The Collected Works of Billy the Kid* conveys a specific and recent historical allegory. Ondaatje means to address the problem of beginning orders, for which the American frontier is the mimetic surrogate, and he creates an initial differentiation between Billy and the animal: 'The windows looked out onto fields and plants grew at the door, me killing them gradually with my urine ... I saw no human and heard no human voice, learned to squat the best way when shitting, used leaves for wiping, never ate flesh or touched another animal's flesh, never entered his boundary' (17). This disingenuous version of Billy almost implies that he can be read as a Paleolithic artist antedating American frontier politics. Ondaatje sets Billy's systematically destructive human nature against other natures in the Freudian terms of repression and civilization, but more specifically, since the book was written during the time when the American frontier was displaced onto Southeast Asia, Billy's minimal defoliant unintentionally echoes the billions of tons of defoliant (Agents Orange, Blue, and White) that American planes dropped on Vietnam while ensuring a free market. I do not mean to argue biographically that Ondaatje took the 'wrong' side in the Vietnam war – an Ondaatje poem such as 'Pictures from Vietnam' would invalidate this; rather, I mean to suggest that an Americanist semiosis of the frontier can perhaps not avoid some inertia of the usual symbolic codes of the Western – which often link a free market in weapons with the rugged individual. Even a theriomorphic moment in *Coming through Slaughter* is not exempt from political gestures. Buddy Bolden seems to pause his destructive 'rage to order' when he mimics the way a dog urinates and scuffs dirt over the spot. But this is more than a 'little sensa humour' (90). In imitating the dog's 'system' (90), Buddy does not change order for pre-order; he exchanges one kind of order for another, beginning again with a very simple sign-system – the primate excretory marking code which is territorial and proto-political, indeed is 'hound civilization' (90) as Buddy, intending to be ironic, remarks.

Ondaatje wants to display individual artistic activity as subversive of political structure. In *Running in the Family* the schoolboys must write lines in Sinhalese: 'We must not urinate again on Father Barnabus' tires' (83). Freedom, on the other hand, consists in writing rude expressions; this links the boys to the graffiti poets of the fifth century BC who wrote on the despot king's rock fortress, and to the campus graffiti during Sri Lanka's 1971 Marxist insurgency (84). Scatology thereby signals a folk voice of political protest, one of the terms whereby Ondaatje, like his fellow Ceylonese poet Lakdasa Wikkramasinha in 'Don't talk to me about Matisse' (85), posts himself far from modernist complicity in imperialism. Given the graffiti politics in

Running in the Family, it is not astonishing that when Ondaatje deals with the artist's lust for destruction in *The Collected Works of Billy the Kid* he should want to prevent the reader from taking the driven artist as a political symptom. Indeed, the picaresque hero (Duddy, Billy), ordinarily represented as an individualized 'will' in contest with the force of authority (McKeon 97), becomes highly ambiguous once we recognize that he can embody the *collective* will (and, I would add, *body*) of a powerful society.

This obliquely provides an interesting gloss on Haliburton's Tory humour. The competition between the traditional Nova Scotia fishing/shipbuilding economy against the new capitalist economy of steam and steel (Naylor 297–302) is ignored in Sam Slick's 'ciphering,' as Slick brings the railroad down to practical matter by filling out the allegory of debt: 'The Nova Scotians ... have been running back so fast lately, that they have tumbled over a bank or two ... A bear always goes down a tree starn foremost. He is a cunning critter; he know 'taint safe to carry a heavy load over his head ... I wish the Bluenosers would find as good an excuse in their rumps for running backwards as he has. But the bear "ciphers"; he knows how many pounds his hams weigh, and he "calculates" if he carried them up in the air, they might be top heavy for him' (*The Clockmaker* 25). Slick at this point moves to actual calculations in favour of the railroad, but the initial naturalizing tendency in the analogy deflects assessments of who loses and who gains by railroad construction. More broadly, the naturalizing of bank interest calculations ('all natur' ciphers' 26) contains just enough of the bear's 'starn' to make the banks and their economic policies seem homely, but not enough scatology to degrade the economic system. If, as has been suggested, Haliburton is the Victorian heir to Swift,[25] Haliburton is much more circumspect and stable in his satire than Swift, with a greater sense of propriety when it comes to business and capital. Swift's excessive scatology challenges the polity in a way that Haliburton purposely does not.[26]

Natalie Davis argues for a comprehensive circulatory process in which transgression confirms authority in its role, blows off steam from the political system, and yet momentarily licenses (thereby prefiguring) alternatives to the system.[27] Depending then upon how we read the emphasis, Duddy, Billy, and Sam Slick can seem like transgressors or the ventriloquized voices of the free market newly naturalized. Quite reasonable expectations about mimesis make scatological rhetoric powerful. Not unique to free-market discourse, this tactic also appears in the positivism of a socialist text such as *Not Wanted on the Voyage* where Findley writes as if the body were an entirely unproblematic signifier of political resistance.

Findley's earlier work, *Famous Last Words*, did not rest in such simple techniques, but attacked the powerful Imagist doctrine wherein the 'thing' is emperor, and did so by undermining Ezra Pound's materialist rhetoric. Findley's Pound says that he wants to drown like Li Po chasing after the image of the moon (or a young lady's behind) in a pond, and originates his mockery of Mauberley in the body: 'At least I am not impeccable: stiff from spats to collar. And I don't wear gloves when I undo my flies. And I am not a flit' (81). The Imagist poet acts as if his visual signs of an anti-aesthetic and of insistence upon bodily functions were enough to excuse his political actions, and later, as if his willingness to suffer in his own body because of his words could excuse the suffering caused by his propaganda campaign on behalf of Mussolini's fascist government.[28] On a 'tour of Ezra's mind' Mauberley encounters 'mounted heads and horns and hooves without bodies' (80), a hint that Findley's Pound, despite his scatological language, has not fully judged the physical implications of his radio speeches. For once, though not throughout the novel, the overmannered aesthete comes off rather well in the allegory of body and power.

By the time of *The English Patient* (1994), Ondaatje too is less sure that the body is the greatest good. Katherine Clifton tastes the blood from a cut on the 'English' patient's hand just as he has 'tasted and swallowed her menstrual blood' (170), but these intimacies do not make the lovers innocent of history. When Kip accuses the patient and his 'fragile white island' of standing for 'customs and manners and books and prefects and ... precise behavior' (283), Kip is wrong on several counts – the 'English' patient (Almásy) is not English after all and his behaviour is not especially precise. But despite all this, Kip's imputation of Almásy's guilt in World War II and as a representative of the West is correct, unmitigated by any bodily intimacies.

8

Hygiene Guidelines for Virtual Bodies: Science and Technology

With regard to the meanness, or even the filthiness of particulars, for which (as Pliny observes) an apology is requisite, such subjects are no less worthy of admission into natural history than the most magnificent and costly; nor do they at all pollute natural history, for the sun enters alike the palace and the privy, and is not thereby polluted ... For what is deserving of existence is deserving of knowledge ... Nay, as the finest odors are sometimes produced from putrid matter (such as musk and civet), so does valuable light emanate from mean and sordid instances. But we have already said too much ...

– Francis Bacon, *Novum Organum*

Under the microscope ... we look at earwax, or snot, or dirt from our toes, checking first to see that there's no one around ... Our curiosity is supposed to have limits, though these have never been defined exactly.

– Elaine Risley in *Cat's Eye*

My repeated recourse to social allegories and the unspoken limits of ideological structures could make scientific reasoning about filth an extended footnote to rhetoric. Stallybrass and White turn science into simple ideology, discounting, for example, nineteenth-century miasmic theories of disease as purely social signifiers; such is not my intention even though works such as John Bourke's *Scatological Rites of All Nations* in its encyclopedia of primitive scatomancy confirmed racial and colonial hierarchies, even though I have already emphasized that disgust for bodily ejecta long antedates Pasteur,[1] and even though washing has been used in Canada to lacerate offenders against the code: a shower bath, perhaps for its 'educative' possibilities, was in fact used as a punishment in Kingston Penitentiary between 1855 and 1859, but was discontinued after Samuel Moore in Auburn State Prison died of it in December 1858. Nevertheless, we cannot discount the way that many novels – however 'ideological' and inseparable from a preceding social discourse they be – refer in some way to the world. One of the weaknesses of political, especially utopian, readings of 'the material bodily lower stratum' is that an author's scientific understanding may be sacrificed to rhetorical clarity.

In Atwood's *Cat's Eye* Elaine mocks both the women who fear dirty toilet seats (253) and the discourse which once encircled polio with a broad range of possible contaminants, making it 'something you breathed in or ate, or picked up from dirty money other people had touched' (8). She, like Stallybrass and White, lives under the confidence that bacteriology begets. When Susanna Moodie, writing 130 years earlier, had Juliet Whitmore go bravely among the infectious poor (*Mark Hurdlestone* 153–4), the episode may not have been as condescending as it now appears. One does not, for example, normally question the motivations of those who work with AIDS patients. In *Roughing It in the Bush*, where the format of travel narrative obviates the need to flourish a heroine's selflessness, Moodie reported that the sewers in Montreal were opened in order to purify the place and to stop the cholera. Ernst Platner, a late-eighteenth-century authority, claimed that dirt could obstruct the pores and hold back excremental humours (Corbin 71). Analogies between body and world (relying on such biochemistry) likely led to the opening of the sewers, but Moodie did not trust the 'repression' theory and instead connected sewage with the cholera, claiming that the opening 'loaded the air with intolerable effluvia' (51). Although the miasmic theory that Moodie (like Melville and De Mille) got from early nineteenth-century science proved just as wrong,[2] the stakes – a 60 per cent death rate among the infected, 4,000 cholera deaths in Montreal and 3,800 in Quebec City between June and September of 1832 – make it difficult to dismiss her association of poverty, odour, and disease as the social distinctions of one who imagined herself a gentlewoman. Moreover, the popular intuition that cholera was connected with odour and effluvia was confirmed (though not in the way expected) in 1849 when John Snow mapped the disease in London. He noted the contamination of the water supply with raw sewage, had the Broad Street pump changed, and saw the epidemic wane. The reinterpretation of cholera as a water-borne disease (Marks 191–207) did not gain widespread acceptance until after Moodie's death.[3]

Stallybrass and White are correct to argue that 'the mapping of [London] in terms of dirt and cleanliness tended to repeat the discourse of colonial anthropology' (130),[4] but they assume that the ideology of sanitation can be separated from the referent of cholera. Referring to cholera from the distance of twentieth-century antisepsis, they speak as if the disease were not just *interpreted* discursively, but *constructed* by discourse, and as if the ego structured in language bore no relation to any body. The actual situation was quite complex. Cholera was both the effect of class difference, since poorer quarters were less sanitary, and a contributing cause of class antagonism, since cholera confirmed the upper classes in their avoidance of the 'dirty' poor, while many of the poor blamed an upper-class conspiracy for the high incidence of lower-class infection (McGrew 62; Heine 64–75). Moodie's body was under more danger from the collective than ours are, and seen from that perspective her attempt in *Mark Hurdlestone* to mediate between upper and lower classes at the point of disease does not seem quite as high-handed.

Even if Moodie had known of Snow's findings, miasmic theory arguably has a physiological basis. Stallybrass and White treat the sanitary reformer E. Chadwick's claim – 'all smell is, if it be intense, immediate disease' (quoted in Stallybrass and White 139) – on the level of class differentiation, but smell is a cue that often allows vertebrates to recognize spoiled food. The tendency to generalize and group smells may be better approached as something that must be painstakingly unlearned in a social context – as a construction of the primate ego, not just of a 'bourgeois' ego.[5]

This is not, by any means, to reassert a version of medical materialism by assuming that there are hidden hygienic reasons which explain social or religious purification rites.[6] Ama Awotchwi, in Godfrey's *The New Ancestors*, rejects her earlier Westernized self, that 'total-foolishness girl ... seeking scientific remedies at Kingsway or U.T.C. for her bowel disorders, her menstrual disorders' (156). In Richler's *Joshua Then and Now*, Joshua notices a certain Hebrew anxiety in his father's explanation of sex: 'There seems to be an awful lot of washing up involved, Daddy' (68). But if Godfrey implicates science in imperialism, and if Richler qualifies Maimonides, the twelfth-century Spanish rabbi who argued that every aspect of Pentateuchal law had a hidden medical reason,[7] Godfrey is also an apologist for Western technology and Richler also ridicules discourses which forget the medical referent: Aunt Ida, newly literate in psychology, explains that Uncle Benjy's cancer is psychosomatic (*The Apprenticeship of Duddy Kravitz* 236). Once we analyse the different ways in which novelists on the edge of science undermine or confirm the categories of hygiene, it is important to remember that hygiene, when it orders fictions, makes a double reference to what is known about a real, permeable body (which can easily be put in danger), and to a rhetoric which maintains vested social or religious interests.

Scientific hygiene can organize present and past hierarchically. One form of this is in the use of the filth-cure to signify the prescientific. Western education about what is clean and what is not lets the *bomari* in Davies's *The Rebel Angels* signify the 'primitive' for the reader as well as for the novel's academics. Likewise, during a trip to the fictional Caribbean island of St Antoine, the narrator of *Bodily Harm* is given a surprising remedy for sea-urchin swelling – urination on the infected foot (192). Ladoo, representing a very different Caribbean society from Atwood's, nevertheless reports a filth-cure for Balraj's and Rama's scorpion bites. Nanna feeds the two boys roasted scorpion, they urinate in his hands, and he rubs the urine onto their hands and even into their mouths while reciting mantras from the Hindu scriptures (*No Pain Like This Body* 50–1). Ladoo's reference to the filth-cure is most instructive because it signifies the past in a complex of ways. Since Ladoo writes about his native Trinidad (the fictional 'Carib Island') from the distance of Canada and a Canadian university education, the past is partly biographical. Ladoo's representation of homeopathic magic (a scorpion as an antidote to a scorpion bite) and sympathetic magic (the destruction of a scorpion to gain power over the scorpion venom in the boys' bodies) sets Trinidad beneath an implied Western rationality. The biographical allegory is thus also cultural, since the two forms of magic are the most prominent ones displayed as signs of the primitive in the cultural genealogy of Sir James Frazer's *The Golden Bough*. Ladoo does not connect his description to any science of homeopathic inoculation, but gestures back to a naïve medical tradition which maintains that 'the main principle of any "physick"' is 'its nasty taste or smell' – the use of filth to drive out filth – a tradition which extends back into the Middle

Ages (Rawcliffe 212) and which occasionally reappears in advertisements, such as those for Buckley's cough mixture and for Listerine.[8] Ladoo's interplay of magic, Hinduism, and filth-cure suggest a composite past controlled by a sceptical authorial voice. In the case of *Bodily Harm*, the semiosis has some referential basis, because urine has been and still can be used as an antiseptic while it is fresh (Rosebury 178; Anthony Smith 448), but the readers of *Bodily Harm*, *The Rebel Angels*, and *No Pain Like This Body* are made to feel as if a disappearing past is being recovered for the post-scientific self. In each of the three novels the filth-cure makes the past radically other vis-à-vis the 'scientific' present, whether that other is treated ironically (in Ladoo), as folk wisdom (in Atwood), or as desirable arcana (in Davies).

In order to challenge 'scientific' hygiene, Wayne Johnston creates a marvellous satire preceding Bobby O'Malley's stage kiss with Mary Hart. The director, Sister Haymond, wants to counterpoint St Joseph's (Bobby's) kiss on the Virgin Mary's (Mary's) cheek with 'the somewhat less chaste kiss' that two other children imitating 'the restrained, respectful passion of the modern Catholic family' (110) will perform – but Bobby's mother, Agnes, is still uneasy:

My mother ... was the only person in Kellies who opposed even the chaste kiss. 'My concerns, I assure you, are purely hygienic,' she said. She had long believed that people were contagious, 'not just when they're sick, but all the time.' She said the body was a breeding-ground; it was a little-known fact that each of us carries around inside us at least one of every kind of disease-causing germ known to man. 'Our germs can't hurt us,' she said. 'Disease occurs when people start exchanging germs.' She said we had to keep a proper distance between ourselves and others. We must imagine ourselves encased in a sterile bubble, and let no-one come inside it. 'Remember the bubble, remember the bubble,' my mother liked to say. 'If someone comes too close, step back.' What about married couples and families, I wondered. My mother said that, by the grace of God, a man and a woman became 'immune' to one another at marriage. 'I'm immune to your father, and he's immune to me.' It worked with children, too. 'We're immune to you, and you're immune to us. Isn't that wonderful?'

The problem with Mary Hart, my father said, was that her germs were bigger than mine. Her germs were 'bully germs' that had been lifting weights and jumping rope since birth. My mother denied this, saying that Mary's germs were not bigger, 'just more numerous.' (112–13)

While Agnes is Catholic, in the nosological recuperation of the doctrine of original sin her discourse parallels Cotton Mather's description of microscopic life, except that Johnston (non-Mosaically) suppresses the diseases of the father:

> The egges of these Insects (and why not the *living Insects* too!) may insinuate themselves by the *Air*, and with our *Ailments*, yea thro' the Pores of our skin; and soon gett into the Juices of our Bodies. They may be convey'd into our Fluids, with the Nourishment which we received, even before we were born; and may ly dormant until the Vessels are grown more capable of bringing them into their Figure and Vigour for Operations. Thus may Diseases be convey'd from the Parents unto their Children, before they are born into the world ... And Vast numbers of these Animals keeping together, may at once make such Invasions, as to render Diseases *Epidemical*; which those particularly are, that are called, *Pestilential*. (Mather, *The Angel of Bethesda* quoted in Limon 78)

Johnston uses hyperbole ('contagious ... all the time,' 'one of every kind of disease-causing germ,' 'let no-one come inside') as a solvent to weaken the scientific referent of such discourse, and he has Agnes's husband use anthropomorphic language to reveal the bias with which she inflects the microbiological level.[9]

But Johnston's most devastating image is that of 'the bubble.' In both its precise reference – the sterile environments manufactured for immunodeficient children[10] – and its broader hint at an existential quarantine, the image sets hygiene and isolation (under the sign of religion) against filth and community (under the sign of secularism). The existential horror in *The Story of Bobby O'Malley* is that the family members *do* become effectively 'immune' to one another. Johnston's angst is precisely opposite to Moodie's fear of the cholera. Whereas Moodie represented the fear of disease through contact, Johnston fears the social and religious appropriation of a scientific discourse which would use scatology to naturalize 'proper distance.'

Although environmentalist discourse usually relies upon metaphors of scientific hygiene – of 'cleaning up' pollution – the attack on scientific hygiene is nevertheless often associated with an ecological impulse.[11] Mitchell's Stoney Cree in *The Vanishing Point* are depicted as excremental and thus 'natural,' while White civilization keeps mum about excretion even while following Enzensberger's market pattern, turning the world into a waste (Enzensberger 98). Mitchell's civilization defecates grandly at one remove via industrial waste, but inhibits defecation on a personal level in the Native and the child – the Fyfe Minimal Subsistence Cookie, an oatmeal cookie made to prevent starvation among the Cree, constipates them (91); Carlyle Sinclair's Aunt Pearl is overly zealous in toilet training him.

Mitchell's rhetoric discourages large-scale industry, but encourages the relaxation of personal hygiene. The logic of this split signification depends heavily on Freud. Industry is understood as displaced bodily function, and yet at the same time Mitchell substitutes cathexis for a lament about the objectification of nature in the American 'will to technique' (G. Grant 183–4). Mitchell emphasizes the oil field's 'stink of hydrogen sulfide' (28) and Dr Sanders offers a psychoanalysis: 'Your anal erotic Aunt Pearl – responsible for the whole mechanistic mess we're in ... sent us all to play in the technological toy room – she's still burning her string you know – in that great bathroom in the sky ... if only she'd toilet-train the hydro and pulp and gas and oil and the little automobile boys – before they do it all over the whole wild green broadloom' (243–4). What would the cathexis of an entire industry look like? On the personal level, Mitchell confirms Dr Sanders's interpretation of Aunt Pearl's white stool as a sign of the overcivilized anal erotic. Aunt Pearl is a fictionalization of the hypothetical character in Freud's *Charakter und Analerotik* (1908), and Mitchell seems directly indebted to Freud's *Ein Traum als Beweismittel* (1913), in which the analysand defies an aunt who wants her to be a nun. Aunt Pearl is the exact image of this Aunt-Superior – orderly, possessive, repressed – and both belong to the folklore of the maiden aunt. Granted, Mitchell is not working in a narrowly realist mode, but his use of scatological symbolism is deceptive, particularly in the matters of constipating oatmeal cookies and white stool. Oatmeal is fibrous and thus would aid, not prevent, excretion. As well, psychosomatic conditions cannot turn stools white; a blockage in the outlet of bile (which contains the pigment stercobilin) into the small intestine or an excess of fat is required.[12] In Mitchell's case, 'what is known' is unconsciously (not ironically) sacrificed to the symbolic and humorous effects of white constipation. Although Mitchell uses language adeptly, his elisions from a real body limit his ecological assessment.

Those novelists – Gibson, Cohen, perhaps Bowering – who engage the technological sensorium generally share Johnston's and Mitchell's fear of disembodiment. They do not focus primarily on hygiene, but use scatology as a counterweight against technological advances which threaten more than hygiene to turn the body into a virtual body, and older versions of the real into simulacra. Gibson's Henry Case spends most of his time beside (but for all real purposes *inside*) a 'cyber-space' computer deck. This deck projects 'his disembodied consciousness into the consensual hallucination that [is] the matrix' (5) and, in creating a computer simulation of the world, invites new responses to biology: 'Sometimes he resented having to leave the deck to use the chemical toilet' (59). In order to stay in the matrix and in his 'virtual' body for more than eight hours, Case hooks up a 'Texas Catheter' (168). 'Il est difficile de ne pas établir au moins un parallèle entre [la] version technocratique "dure" de la société et l'effort aescétique qui est demandé ... au sociétés industrielles les plus développées pour se rendre compétitives' (Lyotard 26; 'It is difficult to deny at least a parallel between [a] "hard" technocratic version of society and the ascetic effort that was demanded ... of the most highly developed industrial societies in order to make them competitive' 12).

Although Gibson does not equate humanity with eliminatory functions – the Artificial Intelligence Wintermute creates a 'man,' Corto, who eats, sleeps, and masturbates, but who stares into space during his spare time – scatology nevertheless becomes a basic constituent which still allies Gibson's characters with past times. Human affect is signalled by the unclean: a sympathetic bartender's tooth decay (*Neuromancer* 3), Turner's nausea upon receiving raw computer data (*Count Zero* 23), Jones's grime under his fingernails (216). Against Virek's transcendental and disembodied search for the fountain of youth, Bobby Newmark's experience of simulation engenders an abject but more human version of the self. Virek comes very near to the condition which McLuhan calls 'angelism.' 'At the speed of light ... everybody is discarnate, a nervous system without a body' (*Letters* 515). 'Electronic media literally translated us into angels. On the phone "we are there" and "they are here," and so with radio and T.V.' (*Letters* 422). Virek's here-and-thereness is convincing but false because he appears in holographic images. On the other hand, Bobby's mother's wholesale entry into her simstim soap operas – she even drools a little during good shows (33) – sets up new social relations and self-perceptions for Bobby: 'He still harbored creepy feelings that some of the characters she talked about were relatives of his, rich and beautiful aunts and uncles who might turn up one day if only he weren't such a little shit' (34). The illusory corporeality of the elevated actors in the new media are directly linked to the abject version of the self. This historicizes Kristeva's 'abject mother': since Bobby's mother had 'jacked that shit straight through the pregnancy' (34), she is not only the biological and psychological inscription that Kristeva theorizes, but also a *technological* inscription of the abject.[13]

Scott Bukatman has suggested that Gibson is complicit with technological advance, that by making the virtual world of the computer phenomenal Gibson gives these microscopic sites a deceptive coporeality and that science fiction deceptively compensates for the loss of human agency in a technological society. David Porush conversely argues that science fiction's techno-inoculation serves as a way for the writer to preserve a core of humanity within new simulacra (171). Certainly Gibson addresses a world in which 'all that is the case' may be technologically simulated. Marly comes to such a conclusion in *Count Zero*: 'The sinister thing about a simstim construct, really, was that it carried the suggestion that *any* environment might be unreal' (139). Towards the end of *Neuromancer*, Case lands on a beach where the dead live again and considers his state: 'Hot urine soaked his jeans, dribbled on the sand ... You needed this world built for you, this beach. To die' (234). Although Case on the beach becomes a figure for the civilized man deprived of his technological productions, we discover that even the beach has been simulated by the artificial intelligence, Neuromancer. In Gibson's sufficiently advanced technology, urine too is condemned to the virtual and the problem of 'angelism' is heightened at the end of *Neuromancer*, where Case splits into two selves.

Gibson does not exempt literature from his definition of simulation: 'I think that a number of reviewers have mistaken my sense of realism, of the *commercial surfaces* of characters' lives, for some deep and genuine attempt to understand technology' (quoted in Gunn 117). The question of simulation is thus transposed from bodily realism to the level of the artwork. The characters in *Count Zero* discover in the end that the Cornell boxes sold anonymously to art dealers throughout the narrative are the productions of an artificial intelligence which puts together human waste in an evocative art of garbage: 'They send me new things, but I prefer the old things' (226). In a marvelous ventriloquism of agency, the computer itself wants to support Porush's humanist thesis.

It is much less clear whether Leonard Cohen prefers the old things, because although *Beautiful Losers* evokes a prescientific cosmos and scatologizes the disembodied aspects of modern popular culture, his ethnographic collection masks a profound scepticism about recuperation. 'Are the stars tiny after all? Who will put us to sleep? Should I save my fingernails? Is matter holy? I want the barber to bury my hair' (6) – the accumulation of questions and desires does not mean that the narrator is serious about saving his bodily ejecta from the malignity of sympathetic magic, but that all times and beliefs have become a playground for the present.[14] Of course, the present too is a playground for the present. Of going to a movie, the narrator says, 'I have to take my eyes out for a pee ... I've leaked all over the kitchen from all my holes, movie will stuff pores with white splinters and stop my invasion of the world, missed movies will kill me tonight' (68). Cohen predicts what Arthur Kroker calls 'the phase of designer bodies' when F. and the other boys ritually remove the narrator's wart in the school bathroom and in the name of science (110), and when F. includes 'the sphincter kit' as part of the Charles Axis program for F.'s human creations. In each of these instances, the excretory supplement to the implied technology (or 'technification' of the body in the latter two examples) seems to subvert F.'s will 'to stop bravely at the surface' (4). Nevertheless, with the present as with the past, the overdetermined satire means that the will to play supersedes most embodiments and most orientations of past 'magic' to present 'science.'[15]

All Cohen's characters in *Beautiful Losers* are relentlessly unclean. However, in the fear of the technological appropriation of biology[16] (which is not really evident in Cohen) the image of the disembodied scientist becomes important. This figure appears everywhere in Gibson's work, from the artificial intelligence which recreates Corto and which manifests itself in the holographic image of another scientist, Finn, to the cyber-space cowboy who does the practical work of science while avoiding the bathroom. The figure also shows up in *Cat's Eye*, although Atwood's realist conventions refer more to present society. Elaine's brother, Stephen, gets a chemistry set which makes 'horrible smells' (109), but even though he also gets carsick (his only weakness) and urinates words into the ground that are 'like his real writing' (72), he progressively rejects filth. His Baconian project to measure and extend the limits of what is known comes to refer to astronomy, not to his youthful magnification of earwax. Elaine, but not Stephen, understands his scatological nicknames for teachers as a reversion to his true self (233). During the plane hijacking which eventually kills him, Stephen hopes that there will be no pants-wetting among the passengers.

This rationalist persona is not, of course, merely a construction of Stephen's, but belongs to the cultural fund of clichés as Cordelia's joke on Elaine indicates: if the person who catches fishes for a living is called a fisher, what should a collector of bugs (Elaine's father) be called? When Elaine answers as expected, Cordelia says, 'He's an *entomologist*, stupid. You should be ashamed. You should have your mouth washed out with soap' (144). Atwood satirizes the dignity that the Greek suffix confers upon scientific and other selected academic occupations.

The novel's epigraph makes Stephen a parody of British theoretical physicist Stephen Hawking, who in the popular press appears as the disembodied and overcerebral scientist, naturalizing the topos of body/mind conflict in the image of the quadriplegic, and invigorating the topos with the moral force of the marginalized person.[17] Stephen Risley's – actually Stephen Hawking's – astronomy pushes Elaine into the virtual; when he describes the stars as echoes, she feels as if her body is dissolving (110). But Atwood intends the image of Stephen writing 'the whole solar system, three times over, in pee' (72) to have another effect: framing the impulse to name and investigate the supramundane is a biological situation which belies the disembodied conclusions. Against the trend towards cybernetic models of the human, which 'subsume the messiness of the human observer's role into a system of positive math' (Porush 375), Atwood reduces the scientific impulse until it is not so different from Elaine's hard education in the laws of hygiene, especially as they apply to gender.

Not entirely separate from the figure of the scientist is that of the doctor. Lennie Kravitz, Richler's budding doctor, does not become 'another Pasteur' (*The Apprenticeship of Duddy Kravitz* 173), but a backdoor abortionist. Lowry's Dr Vigil makes vast claims on his office front for the extent of his knowledge. '[The Consul] passed Dr Vigil's windows on the far side: *Dr Arturo Diaz Vigil, Médico Cirujano y Partero, Facultad de México, de la Escuela Médico Militar, Enfermedades de Niños, Indisposiciones nerviosas* – and how politely all this differed from the notices one encountered in the *mingitorios!* – *Consultas de 12 a 2 y 4 a 7*. A slight overstatement, he thought' (69). While Lowry contrasts the doctor with the urinal, the Consul's sensitivity towards exaggeration undermines the public printed discourse of the doctor, if only in regards to hours. Bowering's Dr Menzies in *Burning Water* is both scientist and physician. George Vancouver wants to urinate on Menzies's precious ferns (46) even though the cartographer (Vancouver) and the scientist have both done fundamentally the same thing in North America. In this implied power struggle between European political and European scientific ends, the scientist comes out less tainted, but the effect is merely local as elsewhere Bowering's Amerindians collapse romantic poetry and scatological implications into technological activity. Reasoning from the absence of women on the ship, the 'second Indian' arrives, deductively, at an explanation of European scientific and explorative advance as a male activity: 'Maybe when men fuck men all the time they learn the lore that takes them great distances on wingèd homes filled with useful objects made of iron' (148). While not meant to be taken seriously, this bit of social logic does tie the bearers of technology in with anal sexuality. Gibson's and Atwood's scientists and the doctors of Richler, Lowry, and Bowering are created unable to escape the unclean significations of the body.

If via the image of the scientist we loop back to *The Rebel Angels* and to Davies's desire to gain access to primitive arcana via the filth-cure, we notice that this desire is articulated through Ozias Froats, a biologist who analyses people's feces and who therefore belongs to both the modern (and respectable) typology of the scientist as measurer, and to the older (satirical) typology of the doctor or alchemist as scatophagus holding up a bottle of urine (Agrippa 184; Bakhtin 1984, 179). Medical science followed the contributors to the Hippocratic anthology in the belief that urine and feces could symptomize struggles within the body (Bakhtin 1984, 357; McGrew 104). The analysis of urine began to be applied to specific diseases in the second half of the eighteenth century with, for example, Matthew Dobson's important discovery in 1776 that the residue of diabetic urine smelled and (in what we might call a curious learned intersection of measurement and scatophagy) *tasted* like sugar (McGrew 74). While Davies satirizes Froats's personality, he does not satirize Froats's alchemical science. In devising the 'lost' letter that connects Paracelsus and Rabelais, Davies ignores Rabelais's attacks on alchemy: Rabelais's alchemists claim to cure seventy-eight kinds of illnesses with turds (*Pantagruel* 4.7.464) and 'la dame Quinte Essance ... ne fiantoit sinon par procuration' (5.23.813; 'Queen Quintessence never excretes except by proxy').

For Rabelais as for Swift, excrement functioned to demythologize science. During Gulliver's voyage to Laputa he visits the grand Academy of Lagado, a parody of the Royal Society, and sees one particular researcher who is a parody of Baconian investigation into mean particulars: 'His Employment from his first coming into the Academy, was an operation to reduce human Excrement to its original Food, by separating the several Parts, removing the Tincture which it receives from the Gall, making the Odour exhale, and scumming off the saliva. He had a weekly Allowance from the Society, of a Vessel filled with human Ordure, about the Bigness of a *Bristol* Barrel' (Swift 1965, 173). Davies may well have had in mind another Swiftian version of this tradition from 'A Discourse Concerning the Mechanical Operation of the Spirit, Etc.' in mind: 'Certain Fortune-tellers in *Northern America*, who have a Way of reading a Man's Destiny, by peeping in his *Breech*' (Swift 1939, 186). But Davies never gets too precise or too satirical about the nature of Froats's excremental operations. For Davies, filth's evocation of past time moves it outside of science or the critique of science into a perception in which dung is lyrical.[18]

Similar authorial impulses suspend Froats uncomfortably between science and popular images of science. As a measurer of excrement, Froats succeeds the sixteenth-century scientist S. Santorius, who measured ingestion and excretion and whose emphasis on quantitative measurements are part of the tradition that led to William Harvey's discovery of the circulation of blood.[19] As a student of somatotyping, however, Froats follows the popular but discredited work of W.H. Sheldon, whose constitutional psychology has proved so far to be a dead end. Davies does not appear conscious that Sheldon's ambitious correlations between body type and personality were not found by subsequent researchers, and Davies's 'science' has fooled even the ablest of critics. Elizabeth Harvey, for example, treats somatotyping as an established technique, and repeats Davies's uncorroborated assertion that penicillin began as filth therapy (Harvey 93). Other authorities give far different accounts: 'Body type and personality type correlate about 0.80 in Sheldon's work; however, such high correlations were not found by others' (Peyser 1037). 'Both ancient medical texts and folk traditions recommend the use of molds, especially in wound dressings, but there is no known connection between these folk practices and the modern discovery of penicillin, which is strictly a twentieth-century achievement' (McGrew 247). Like Hugh MacLennan in *Voices in Time*, Davies takes somatotyping more seriously than it deserves. Patricia Monk, who more carefully acknowledges the weaknesses of constitutional psychology (97), defends Davies's uses of and departures from Sheldonian orthodoxy. Although the referent in somatotyping fails, Monk shows how Davies uses it to address the relations between the body and the soul.

Montaigne said, 'Il n'est pas dangereux, comme en une drogue medicinale, en un compte ancien, qu'il soit ainsin ou ainsi' (134; 'It is not dangerous, as in a medicinable drug, whether in an old tale or report, be it thus or thus, so or so' 73). Yet while literary references to the body convey psychic and social structures, the referents outside the text cannot be discounted. The artist must submit to the rigour of what is known, argues Émile Zola (D. Grant 40), and if it seems anachronistic (especially where fantasy and post-modernism come under discussion) to cite realist jealousy of the scientific method (D. Grant 31), the reader, if not always the artist, is constantly involved in measuring the text against this hazy 'what is known.' Even a ludic departure from the history of science such as *Burning Water* depends for its rhetorical effect on its status as departure. Even an unconscious departure such as *The Rebel Angels* cannot be understood except as departure.

9

Polluted Women

The Lord said to Moses, 'Say to the people of Israel, If a woman conceives, and bears a male child, then she shall be unclean seven days; as at the time of her menstruation, she shall be unclean. And on the eighth day the flesh of his foreskin shall be circumcised. Then she shall continue for thirty-three days in the blood of her purifying; she shall not touch any hallowed thing, nor come into the sanctuary, until the days of her purifying are completed. But if she bears a female child, then she shall be unclean two weeks, as in her menstruation; and she shall continue in the blood of her purifying for sixty-six days.'

– Lev. 12:1–5

'When a woman has a discharge of blood which is her regular discharge from her body, she shall be in her impurity for seven days, and whoever touches her shall be unclean until the evening. And everything upon which she sits shall be unclean. And whoever touches her bed shall wash his clothes, and bathe himself in water, and be unclean until the evening. And whoever touches anything upon which she sits shall wash his clothes, and bathe himself in water, and be unclean until the evening; whether it is the bed or anything upon which she sits, when he touches it he shall be unclean until the evening. And if any man lies with her, and her impurity is on him, he shall be unclean seven days; and every bed on which he lies shall be unclean.'

– Lev. 15:19–24

i

If hygiene and the disgust for dirt have scientific referents at least partially independent of social rhetoric, hygiene has nevertheless repeatedly been used as a social control, particularly on women, complementing physiological rhetoric from Thomas Aquinas's reading of Aristotelean humours ('when a female is produced it is because of a weakness of active power or some material indisposition or some external change such as a moist south wind,' *Summa Theologiae* I.I Qu 92) to recent controversies about brain capacity and abstract thinking. More subliminally, and perhaps more immediately, 'hygiene' seems (as the work of Atwood indicates) to demand of women a clean and proper body. During a gender analysis of reader-oriented literary theories, Patrocinio Schweickart wonders, 'Where does the text get its power to draw us into its designs?' (27) Schweickart's answer is that the individuating impulse of a male protagonist arouses, even in the female reader, an authentic desire for 'autonomous selfhood' (28). The limits of this explanation become clear when applied to consistently ironic texts, but Schweickart provides a crucial link between gender theories and scatology. Schweickart's 'autonomous' self becomes not simply a figure of the enfranchised woman, but bears the trace of all civilized values, and she refuses to jettison those symbolic and real values even while criticizing the patriarchal symbolic order under which they were constituted.[1] One of those values – language – is, according to Elaine Showalter, 'the site of a covert struggle for gender meanings,' and the aquisition of language constitutes gender under what Jacques Lacan calls 'le Nom/Non du Père' (Showalter 3; 'the Name/No of the Father').

By 'the Name of the Father' Lacan means those structures in language which implicitly prohibit and permit certain actions; these prohibitions not only maintain a patriarchal legal system, however, but make possible the civilized self, as feminist analysts have suggested: the Name of the Father 'confirms in the child its attempts to situate itself in reality' (Gallop and Burke 110). The problem, therefore, is not simply that the traditional representation of the civilized self has been formed under the sign of the male. The general constitution of the civilized self against the scatological symbolism of origins also holds true for the female self – as the novels of Thomas, Laurence, Roy, and Atwood have already shown in Part I. The problem is that many novelists (both male and female) have tended to represent women at the discursive extremes – as either overcivilized or polluted by filth.

Where does this split discourse come from? One of the ruses of power is that those who are privileged demand a greater cleanliness from social subordinates (Elias 137) even while, or perhaps because, those subordinates are imagined to be dirtier. It is thus impossible to understand gender as 'difference' without some recourse to the institutionalization of male/female hierarchies (Showalter, 'Rise' 4). Second, the traditional use of women as exchange commodity has made virginity and other forms of cleanliness an important part of market value, even while the bodily and abject images generated by childbirth add a psychological pressure that increases the woman's association with 'precivilized' pollution (Kristeva 1982, 52–4).[2] In the nineteenth century the production of a female civilized self through education in courtesy included a strong anti-scatological component. Retention of urine and feces was considered by many educators at girls' schools as the trait of a gentlewoman, since it symbolized *not giving in* to bodily urges (Corbin 174). During the contemporaneous growth of bathrooms, women were enjoined not to let anyone, including their husbands, into a bathroom while they were inside (Vigarello 215–16).

In Moodie's *Mark Hurdlestone*, Mary Matthews's unfortunate maleness (noted by the narrator and later by Juliet and Anthony 139, 148) is expressed in 'coarse jokes' and 'profane songs.' O'Hagan, Richardson, and Haliburton are even more straightforward. Selva, in a bar, hears a man say, 'The world's a piss pot. And I've been all around it looking for the handle' (*The School-Marm Tree* 101). Her shock at the mild colloquialism marks off male and female worlds, just as Clara de Haldimar's shock at the sight of blood in *Wacousta* marks her sphere off from that of the British soldiers. Clara reproduces the Indian wars when she and Ellen Halloway (who has gone native) fight for possession of a knife, but when Ellen grasps the naked blade Clara faints at the sight of the blood that she has been the means of shedding, and this marks her off from even her feminized brother Charles de Haldimar. Haliburton has Sam Slick beat a man's wife to make her tractable, and Slick raises welts where no one can see. With a certain degree of cynicism, Slick transgresses civilized boundaries and then invokes those very limits, counting on the woman's greater civility: 'I calculate you won't be over forrard to show 'em [the welts] where they be' (122).

Grove follows a similar, if more sublimated, pattern. For him female civility either defines the woman or is a very thin veneer, because his idealist demands on women are great. Grove's *Settlers of the Marsh* represents bodily bases of motivation in both Niels Lindstedt and Clara Vogel, but Clara is also (in the tradition of St Jerome) the cosmetic mask of passion which Niels must see through in order to recognize the death's-head underneath. Lorraine McMullen's accurate social assessment that in Grove's work sex-centred relationships and physical satiety lead to disillusionment and payment (74) leaves out the tendency of Grove's women to have to pay more than men. Ellen Amundsen, who escapes social gender stereotyping, is nevertheless not allowed to display bodily passion. Of the two characters who do display bodily passion, Clara gets the novelist's death sentence, Niels thirteen years in jail and then rehabilitation.[3] Clara is only momentarily humanized when she imagines her degradation: 'You want to fling me on this ... this manure pile here' (153). Only when the ideal sphere of womanhood (which Grove both asks for and distrusts) is threatened can Clara become sympathetic. By comparison, Ostenso's *Wild Geese* (like *Settlers of the Marsh* published in 1925) does not demand the same ideal sphere of Judith Gare, and Judith is therefore not polluted by her associations with manure.

More surprising is the appearance of this naïve pattern of the overcivilized woman in quite recent novels where the writer is not attempting to represent early Canadian society. In Johnston's *The Story of Bobby O'Malley* Agnes O'Malley can 'never admit to using the bathroom' (13). She believes that men are erotic and filthy, while all women are potential nuns. In this way Johnston makes her enunciate what was and is really a male discourse: for example, medieval Catholic commentators suggested that because virgins were more continent than others, their urine was also clearer (O'Faolain and Martines 142).[4] Against such overcivilization of women, a state which must always seem like naïve sublimation in post-Freudian epistemologies, Johnston's men repeatedly insist upon the body. Schoolboys colour Kleenex red to mock Flo's menarche; encouraged by her dismay, they colour more and more Kleenex until Flo is confronted by 'a whirling vortex of sanitary napkins' (50–2). Even though one girl, Philly, farts in public without suffering socially, Johnston's narrative generally implies that the woman herself, not any social discourse, is responsible for the failed attempt to manufacture a clean and proper sphere. Indeed, Johnston's Agnes is doubly bound. Because Ted stands

Polluted Women 103

in for the filthy body, she can either let her civilized persona be degraded or set herself apart; however, because setting herself apart is not intellectually reputable in Johnston's epistemology, the option that he has her choose also degrades her sphere of rationality.

In Robertson Davies's system, art comes from an unclean underworld; this immediately sets art in dialectic with the sphere of sophisticated culture that Davies's novels always aspire to, and the dialectic is especially evident in the figure of the *female* artist. Since Hulda Schnakenburg, the graduate student composer in *The Lyre of Orpheus*, wears pants with a 'yellow stain around the crotch,' her dirt is 'the real thing' (25) lending substance to her music. But toward the end of the narrative she is washed, dressed up, and, in Davies's unconscious echo of Elias (court, *courtois*, courtesy), taught to curtsy. For Davies's male protagonists the civilizing process is not coded through hygiene. Hulda is first placed among civilized *women* and only then welcomed as a civilized artist.

ii

At the other extreme are the women who remain constituted by their bodily ejecta: Audrey Thomas's Rachel in *Latakia*, and Elizabeth Smart's personae in *By Grand Central Station I Sat Down and Wept* and in *The Assumption of Rogues and Rascals*. Traditionally this would make Thomas's and Smart's protagonists 'polluted women,' but given the materialist epistemologies that we have noted, pollution becomes a positive rhetorical value.[5] The two writers in *Latakia*, Rachel and Michael, fight over whose turn it is to clean the bathroom (41); Rachel at first interprets this in primarily social terms: 'Prince Charming probably chose Cinderella because she was the only one who could do housework' (87). In *The Double Ghetto: Canadian Women and Their Segregated Work* (1978), published one year before *Latakia*, Pat and Hugh Armstrong connect female subordination to the low prestige of household tasks (66). Despite new developments such as vacuum cleaners, automatic washers, and dryers, cleaning work had not really diminished because standards of cleanliness were rising (71), and the partial integration of Canadian women into the workforce did not generally result in a lessened demand upon them to do housework. Six years later, the Armstrongs' assessment was much the same. For example, they cite a Flin Flon study in which working women still averaged 31.4 hours of housework per week, in addition to an average of 42.5 hours at work. The men's labour at home increased slightly to 19.1 hours per week. A 1994 study in the United States shows working women doing 61 to 78 per cent of the housework, depending upon class and race (Perry-Jenkins and Folk 170). Thomas goes a step past social analysis, connecting the cleaning and not cleaning of toilets directly to Michael's aesthetics. He types and recites his novel out loud so that Rachel can hear him making progress while she is in the bathroom (30, 70). But he cannot urinate in a dirty public bathroom (113), old bodies disgust him (117), and Rachel implies that precisely because Michael ignores household chores his repression of the material world is much greater than her own: 'How are you going to write if you can't get outside yourself?' (118) Rachel asks, and insists that she has a 'greater faith in the material' (124).

Although she discounts Michael's claim that men and women write differently (133), she has reached exactly that conclusion. And, although Thomas sometimes treats Rachel with irony – for example, Rachel wants Michael to recognize that people cleaned him up as a baby (119), while she herself has temporarily abandoned her children – Thomas nevertheless emphasizes the social and literary importance of Rachel's experience. One of the first things that Michael learns to say in Greek is *kakń yvvń* which Thomas translates as 'bad woman' (50), but which has etymological connections with dirt and scatology. One of the most notable things about Thomas's writing is her rejection of the well-made plot, for which she sustitutes the minutiae of emotional and bodily states.

Men write with a larger historical framework, says Michael (133); his condescending theory seems to explain why the narrator of *By Grand Central Station I Sat Down and Wept* writes in a near-diary voice and gives only passing mention to World War II even though the novel was completed in 1941 and published in 1945: 'Why should even ten centuries of the world's woe lessen the fact that I love? Cradle the seed, cradle the seed, even in the volcano's mouth' (90). Elizabeth Smart's work departs from the traditional novel precisely insofar as she emphasizes emotional and bodily states, only acknowledging societal agencies such as the legal system when they impinge upon her narrator's love.[6] Smart may hint at less personalized referents through the idiot child born at the end of the novel, yet the female body supersedes historical symbolizations: 'I can only wait, like an egg for the twenty-first day' (100); 'Nature is using me. I am a seedbag' (113). These metaphors of deterministic biology imply the primacy of nature over the historical construction of gender.

The same primacy recurs in *The Assumption of Rogues and Rascals* (1978) where the body is much changed, but again determined biologically rather than historically. Replacing the tragic 'seedbag,' is a constipated old woman: 'The breakthrough is a bit bogged down. But on, on ... It will pour. The worry will there be paper enough. Look after the paper. Nappies too; though you can never really believe that a baby will come out' (107). Biological metaphors claim a symmetry between filth and birth, between female bodily processes and the process of writing, giving the female writer an authority to compensate for the lack of formal schooling (and Smart an authority to compensate for her innocence of literary theory): 'What about ... the wiped-out pioneers and lonely women agonizing at their too-far-off water holes? The long meaningless care of their outdoor lavatories? ... So girls, I recommend a study of manure, and the great rising and falling and fertilizing principles, which are not sad' (109-10). Although Smart's narrator initially seems to be about to address social history and the historical constraints upon female writing – thus invoking a larger historical framework – she eventually makes the pioneer women disappear under the larger scatological metaphor. This is far from dismissive: Smart agonizes for the extratextual and unclean body, while she sees the alienating histories (of pioneer women, of single mothers like herself) as axiomatic. Smart raises bodily states and functions to the level of theory, a room of one's own in theory where the single mother is not at a disadvantage for having raised children. The refusal of sadness is particularly poignant since Smart had to write throw-away articles for women's magazines to support her four children, no doubt while John Barth's Max Spielman of *Giles Goat Boy* studied post-modern proctocology on a grant at Johns Hopkins.

Whatever personal exigencies led to Smart's comic closure, one need look no further than the scatological metaphors to notice how a feminist approach to history makes the association of woman and body problematic. Male rhetoric from Aristotle to Freud has emphasized that women, often through excremental metaphors, stand in for the body. Aristotle believed that women contribute the *matter* to the foetus, while men give the *form*. Women's disorderliness was thus founded on physiology. Until the revolutions in chemistry, women were believed to be composed of cold and wet humours. Hebrew scepticism about the surrounding high cultures and their mythologies was often coded through a rejection of fertility practices and, therefore, through a rejection of women in favour of paternity (Schneidau 90f). Jerome, Tertullian, and Augustine associated women with filth because women represented an immediate danger to celibate and ascetic callings. Roger Caen in 1095 said that women are dung covered by white skin, and the bodily association of women was an important term during the centuries of witch hunts.[7]

To explain the psychology of this discourse, Mary Douglas says that pollution clusters around sex because sex is potentially explosive. But this does not explain why women historically have seemed to be more susceptible to sexual pollution than men. In Freudian psychoanalysis the association of women and excrement occurs because of childbirth; the bowel contents are given the meaning of baby by the young child. Because of the young child's ignorance of the vagina, Freud claims, the child believes that babies must be evacuated via the only route possible – the anus – a route which indeed is used among amphibians. The difficulty is that when these references appear among patients, Freud always detects a homosexual current, so that whatever is female becomes a filiation of male sexuality. Therefore, in Freud's attempt to explain, he also extends the old discourse in which the female body is a trope for suppressed aspects (homosexuality, excremental functions) of the male body. More important, Freud ignores the social code through which the anal birth is articulated,[8] an omission which Canadian novels correct. The 'abject foetus' appears in Laurence's *A Jest of God* where Rachel confuses a uterine tumour with Nick Kazlik's child, and in William's *The River Horsemen* where, according to Nick Sobchuk Sr, a Ukrainian woman gives birth: 'When I come up to her, she had a baby dropped in the back of her skirt, like a bloody shit' (73). In context, Williams's older Nick uses this anecdote to undervalue the labour (childbirth *and* housework) of his own wife; Nick Jr unlearns the patriarchal discourse only with great difficulty. Both novels examine the difficulties in female reproduction, especially following male abdications of responsibility; and while both in different ways make use of the more general Freudian typology of feces and death, neither suggests Freud's sublimated homosexual referent. Laurence addresses the painful connection between sexuality and childbirth through Rachel's reactions against her own mother's sexuality and her own abject 'child.'

Because the metaphysical epistemologies at the heart of the Judeo-Christian patrimony have to some extent been reversed (as we shall see in Chapter 10), it is not surprising that theorists such as Gilbert and Gubar, Cixous, and Kristeva, in an attempt to also reverse power structures, have retained the figural association of woman and body. Gilbert and Gubar emphasize how privatized bodily experience has often operated at the boundaries of and deformed the public alphabet (22). Natalie Davis has shown that in medieval times sexual inversion could give 'positive license to the unruly woman' (147). Male speech, argues Hélène Cixous, 'prive, le sait-il, de son propre territoire corporel' ('Méduse' 40; 'deprives him, he knows, of his own bodily territory' 247). Via 'mots-de-corps' (48; 'body-words') Cixous projects a new woman who engages in 'une expérimentation systématique des fonctionnements du corps' (39; 'a systematic experimentation with the bodily functions' 247). 'En s'écrivant, la femme fera retour à ce corps qu'on lui a plus que confisqué, dont on a fait l'inquiétant étranger dans la place, le malade ou le mort, et qui souvent est le mauvais compagnon, cause et lieu des inhibitions. A censurer le corps on censure du même coup le souffle, la parole' (43; 'By writing her self, woman will return to the body which has been more than confiscated from her, which has been turned into the uncanny stranger on display – the ailing or dead figure, which so often turns out to be the nasty companion, the cause and location of inhibitions. Censor the body and you censor breath and speech' 250). Kristeva follows Freud by asserting that the child 'crosses' the maternal bowels and thereupon takes the mother for the abject.[9] The body becomes a guiltless authority (the order of the mother), split off from the other universe of 'prestations sociales signifiantes' (1980, 89; 'socially signifying performances' 1982, 74), the order of the phallus. While Kristeva has felt uneasy under the sign of feminism and does not reify these differences into biological orders (despite her metaphors), she privileges the writer who allows the mother – abject and filthy – play in the text.[10]

This extension of what the 'polluted woman' means has come under the critique that for the new French feminists the body is too exclusively pleasurable (Eagleton 205). In fact, a social imperative may be operating in this 'pleasurable' body: according to the *International Encyclopedia of the Social Sciences*, research via projective techniques (onto inkblots and pictures) suggests that among females there is a moderate increase in body references beyond age fifteen, compared to a decline among males. D.J. van Lennep interprets: 'In Western culture men are supposed to transcend their bodies and turn their energies toward the world. Women, on the other hand, are given approval for continuing and even increasing their investments in their bodies' (Fisher 115–16).

The undercurrent of social oppression in Thomas and Smart suggests that they are aware of the limits to their bodily texts, even though the work of Thomas and Smart approaches Kristeva's notion of the 'feminine-gendered' text. Thomas's Mrs Blood knows that Jason, her husband, has bought her nightgowns in a bargain basement, which she associates with Lysol and dog excrement. More crucial than his economic devaluation of her is Jason's role in her split into Mrs Blood and Mrs Thing. Although as Mrs Blood she subverts patriarchal structures, it was Jason's demand for an abortion that named her, forever after, as one-who-bleeds. The patriarchal context of this bleeding does not associate it with radical female measures of reproductive control (like abortion or the diuretics which were believed to induce menstruation and prevent conception; O'Faolain and Martines 126); neither does the context fully confirm Kristeva's assertion that excrement represents danger from without while menstrual blood stands for danger from within (1982, 71). Mrs Blood is lacerated both from within *and* from without.

The association of women with the body is important because it posits a female narrative, originating in a female body, against the usual male narrative form of tumescence and detumescence (Winnett 509). However, Thomas's focus on violence and power qualifies the rhetorical utility of 'polluted' women. Kristeva recognizes as much when she says that defilement rites are evidence of the attempt by two powers (not necessarily men and women) to share out society without a central authority (1982, 70). In the Canadian novel, scatology often becomes a much more literal register of male oppression. In Ladoo's *No Pain Like This Body* female suffering, both from within – 'I bleed blood to make dat chile' (20) – and without – 'You shut you kiss me ass mout and cook!' (66) – is registered scatologically. Sexuality is the site of male violence in Williams's *Eye of the Father*, where Magnus sodomizes his unfaithful girlfriend. In Godfrey's *The New Ancestors* Ama Awotchwi Burdener inherits the soiled underwear of her estranged husband, Michael, in a dream (119). Michael eventually recognizes that social violence is mostly male when he sees that in Mali Islamic law puts a severe taboo on menstruation while ignoring venereal disease (314).[11]

Maria Theotoky, whom Davies constructs as a physical model of idealized femininity in *The Rebel Angels*, is harassed by Urquhart

McVarish, who paraphrases Rabelais's question – 'Pourquoy est-ce que les cuisses d'une damoizelle sont toujours fraisches?' (*Gargantua* 1.39.124; 'Is it true ... that the thighs of a gentlewoman are always cool?' *Rebel Angels* 50) – to validate his desire to degrade her. Friar John's answer in *Gargantua* – the coolness comes from shade, from a certain wind, and from something like rain – was at least partially a class attack and was evidently meant to subvert the courtly love tradition. Bakhtin defends Rabelais on precisely this ground: against idealization Rabelais gives women a material body which simultaneously degrades and regenerates (Bakhtin 1984, 239–43).

Davies, however, much more than Rabelais, deals consciously with the social roles in which gender and filth meet. McVarish's *instrumental* use of Rabelais qualifies the exorbitant pleasure-giving language by tying the fun to a specific context in the power relations between men and women.[12] Of course, Davies neutralizes the potential criticism of Rabelais by having Maria study him, defend him, and occasionally play Rabelaisian roles herself. Much less insidious than McVarish's harassment are the attempts by Penelope Raven and Maria to deconstruct perceived gender roles. Professor Raven says, 'You've no idea what the whole concept of womankind owes to sphincters!' (185). Although the emphasis is biological, 'womankind' is nevertheless understood as a social construction; Maria, less circumspect, shouts obscene verse in a restaurant (74). The linguistic play upon the name 'Maria' extends from the mother of Jesus to the alchemist Maria Prophetissa to the *bain-marie*, the rejuvenating dung-bath which, we are told, derives its name from the second-greatest Mary – Miriam, Moses' sister. These symbolic accumulations are compounded because of the way that the violin in the *bomari* is described: 'The great lady is undressed for her sleep' (155). The Swiftian echoes in this objectification of women do not reduce Maria despite what one might expect after reading about the disillusioned men in Swift's 'Strephon and Chloe' or 'Cassinus and Peter.' The danger runs the other way: 'woman' is both contained and excremental container, both the work of art and the excremental process without which the violin will lose its timbre. It is possible to see, in such a characterization, simply another version of the split between overcivilization and extreme abjection; however, by giving Maria such a wide range of signification and then allowing her, unlike Hulda Schnakenburg, to *refuse* the extremes, Davies avoids nailing her to an archetype.

iii

More compelling rejections of the split discourse appear in the work of Sylvia Fraser, Munro, and Atwood, where the poles of the overcivilized woman and the woman who stands in for the body are both clearly social productions and collapse into singlular protagonists. In her name, Fraser's Pandora Gothic reproduces discourses about the disorder and victimhood of women, and she is certainly well versed in the discourse of the overclean woman – 'I don't have a thing,' says Pandora, 'I have "insides," which are neater' (*Pandora* 56). Since the novel's schoolchildren ruthlessly imitate adult society, ostracizing Dirty Danny and Magda, Pandora adopts a clean persona and hides her intense bodily life. For her this duplicity almost has an autobiographical inevitability: her father sets the law in the house and speaks for the social order – 'everything *decent* you got from me' (134) – but also abuses her physically and sexually. Attempting to situate herself in the arbitary moods of the father, Pandora articulates her own punishments through the social images provided by school hazings:

'I'm not filthy!' wails Pandora. 'It isn't ME, it's Dirty Danny.'
The door is bolted, and sealed. Black Hands push Pandora's head towards the toilet bowl. It is full of ... No! it is full of flowers – red, gold, blue – floating in sweet milk. Pandora sticks out her tongue. She dips it into the milk. It scalds. It shrivels. It falls off. (135)

Attempting to situate herself ontologically in the Catechism, Pandora discards the Good Father of Christianity. She insists that it was her own father, who stinks, that made the world (136).

For Violet in Munro's novella 'A Queer Streak' the biographical documents from the past are similarly 'full of filth. Horse manure. Set out in rows. On purpose. Inside my trunk in my own house' (249). The duplicitous sign 'horse' gestures at both her dead horse, King Billy, and her dead father, also named King Billy – to whom Violet's sister, Dawn Rose, once anonymously wrote, 'You ought to be thrown down the toilet hole head first. You bowlegged stupid rotten pig. You ought to have your things cut off' (220). The wording of Dawn Rose's anger hints that Violet's later propriety and desire to forget the excremental past may really be a desire to forget some form of sexual abuse.

Male coercion also appears in *Lives of Girls and Women* and *Who Do You Think You Are?* In the former, although Del Jordan hates the well-bred girls who would not use the town toilets (131), she occasionally seems no different: ordinarily she will not say that she has to go to the bathroom in front of men (159). But the contextual reference to courtship rituals suggests that Del's overcivilized persona is not self-created, but follows what men seem to want. In the latter, Rose's urine retention is entirely circumstantial: she avoids the school outhouse only because it has been the site of rape. As a potential victim (like Franny McGill), Rose cannot be overly dismayed by a panoptic civilizing process which produces new washrooms inside the school, allowing the children to be supervised more easily. Neither scatological nostalgia nor bodily renunciation are essential values in Munro's text. When Rose needs to protect herself against male violence, she avoids the washroom; when, much later, she feels intimidated by a perfect housewife, she shares (with Jocelyn) the role of the scatologist who satirizes cleanliness:

'Do you use that special stove-knob polish?'
'I certainly do. And I use the special stove-knob cloths that come in that special package.'
'That's good. Some people don't.'
'Some people will use anything.'
'Old dishrags.'
'Old snotrags.'
'Old snot.' (101)

Munro's complex gendering shows itself particularly when Rose, to protect herself against the culture's demand for the type of female beauty that Cora epitomizes, reminds herself that Cora's grandfather cleaned out latrines. Rose only *seems* to be the satirist – since she really does worship Cora's image – and she critiques the 'clean and proper' body from the position of one who pretends (who *must* pretend) to be cleaner and more proper than she really is. Although the structures of gender have implications for the body, in Fraser and Munro recourse to the body as an essential value clearly cannot 'solve' the power structure.

Atwood at times uses the discourse which equates the feminine with the body. In *The Handmaid's Tale* the future is, for most purposes (including gender), the past. Because of the cultural premium placed on reproduction in post-nuclear Gilead, menstruation is understood as failure, so that the female body's normal discharge comes to seem (as it historically often has seemed) like a pollutant (69). Gileadean women are not allowed a refuge even in difference. 'Think of yourselves as seeds' (18), they are told, an intended self-identification which makes use of the biblical metaphor for semen – *male* sexual discharge. Against these conscious repressions, an unconscious discourse forms, a sensuous focus on eggs and ovaries (104, 131). The only moment of community in the novel centres around Janine's abject birthing. In *Cat's Eye* the female body too centres around blood discharges, from Mrs Risley's miscarriage which creates an enlarged egg-like image – 'a huge oval splotch of blood' on the mattress (178) – to Elaine's hyperbolic satisfaction at finally getting her period (244). Although Elaine for a long time believes that she is above gender and blames Susie's big rear for Josef's indifference, the gynaecological insistence of Susie's blood after her attempted abortion destroys Elaine's complacency (339). Marian in *The Edible Woman* recoils from the women at her bridal shower: 'What peculiar creatures they were; and the continual flux between the outside and the inside, taking things in, giving them out chewing, words, potato-chips, burps, grease, hair, babies, milk, excrement, cookies, vomit, coffee, tomato-juice, blood, tea, sweat, liquor, tears, and garbage ... She felt suffocated by this thick sargasso-sea of femininity ... She wanted something solid, clear: a man' (*The Edible Woman* 185). Whereas Atwood represents consumer culture as pure surface and surface rhetoric, a discourse which does not really acknowledge *bodily* consumption at all, the female is associated with that which goes on underneath in a real, not a media, body. Atwood therefore gains a rhetorical advantage against the patriarchy much as Thomas does, through exactly that subsphere to which the feminine has traditionally been relegated.[13] Once Marian breaks her engagement to Peter, the shift in power shows itself in muted insurrection against a clean and proper sphere: 'In a spirit of gay rebellion Marian neglected to erase her bathtub ring' (296).

But there is a flaw in Marian's vision of the female body: the details of consumption and excretion that she lists (except 'babies' and 'milk') apply just as easily to the male body. The real problem, Atwood implies, is the split discourse. In *The Edible Woman* sanitary napkins are much less surely the signifiers of femininity than in *The Story of Bobby O'Malley*. The survey supervisors appeal to female solidarity in an attempt to get interviewers to do the sanitary napkin survey (120); Atwood, however, hints that the suppliers are compromising feminism commercially. Elaine learns, in *Cat's Eye*, that female education into a clean and proper body is broader than any specific injunction. At first she thinks that Cordelia is her tormenter, but Cordelia is merely a personal face for the demands of consumer culture, which appear in women's magazines, the demands to get rid of toilet germs, unwanted odours, and pimples: 'I see that there is no end to imperfection, or to doing things the wrong way' (148).[14] Grace Smeath succumbs to the discourse; overconstituted as a civilized woman, she will not climb because others might see her underwear (66), but Elaine's cutting out of the paper women and her whole artistic enterprise is an attempt to gain control over these female images. She also recognizes that even the most euphemistic scatological language is a subversion, 'of Grace and Mrs Smeath, of tidy paper ladies pasted into scrapbooks' (134).

For a time Elaine is convinced that access to scatological language will break male power. She knows that it is not simply obscenity, but the back-and-forth play between 'higher' and 'lower' languages that gives a particular male discourse its power, and she imitates this play:[15] '"I wonder what Mary did for diapers? ... How come there are no pictures of Christ on the potty? I know there's a piece of the Holy Foreskin around, but what about the Holy Shit?" ... I enjoy pestering girls in this minor, trivial way: it shows I am not like them' (303). Despite the subject, Elaine's language is concerned with gender and not with religion at all. By means of the last phrase Atwood problematizes the ability of individual discourses to reform gender roles. Women in themselves apparently 'are' filthy, but men have control over discourse about filth; women 'ought' to be clean – a demand that is perpetually being renovated – so that when Elaine plays with religious scatology she thinks that she will not be identified with other women.

An earlier incident in *Cat's Eye* raises precisely the problem that we began the chapter with – Schweickart's problem of identification – except that Elaine must deal with an ironic text. The children make fun of their monarchist teacher, Miss Lumley, by inventing bloomers for her, so that the imagined bloomers stand for her paraphernalia of the British Empire. What begins as a Rabelaisian attack on colonial authority is suspended once Elaine recognizes the role of gender in the satire. Despite drawing the postcolonial Canadian reader into an identification with the children, Atwood has Elaine recognize that male underwear for some reason does not spark the same response, and Elaine starts to identify with Miss Lumley via the bloomers: 'Whatever is wrong with them may be wrong with me also' (85). Using linguistics to describe a lack of sensory enjoyment in Atwood, Robert Cluett (152–3) is insufficiently attentive to moments like this: moments during which the protagonist recognizes the gender biases in sensory languages. If Elaine identifies too closely with Miss Lumley, she could herself become the victim of social codes that attribute pollution. If Elaine joins in the mockery of Miss Lumley's underwear, Elaine would not only falsely distance herself from underwear, women, and thus herself, but she would also set in motion precisely the image that lacerated herself, the image of the overcivilized woman – without which the image of the polluted woman would have no context.

10

'The Hind Parts of God': Materialist Epistemologies and the Mimesis of Religion

That which cometh out of the man, that defileth the man.

– Mark 7:20

L'âme, prison du corps. (The soul, prison of the body.)

– Michel Foucault, *Surveiller et punir*

À chaque moi son objet, à chaque surmoi son abject. (To each ego its object, to each super ego its abject.)

– Julia Kristeva, *Pouvoirs de l'horreur*

i

It is impossible to understand the image of the overcivilized woman or the representation of the civilizing process, particularly its ambivalent nature (the reference to and then withdrawal from the body that keeps reoccurring), without acknowledging the central role which religious conceptions of holy separation, k-d-sh in the Hebrew tradition (Douglas 8), have played. Bodily discharges were seen as impure (especially during worship or war) by the Israelites (Douglas 51), and the scatological image has subsequently been understood in Western religions to be in dialectic with spirit. Since Calvinist practice has vastly enlarged the sphere of the individual (Weber 98–127),[1] an attack on the Protestant persona has come to mean an attack on a conviction in salvation that (according to Weber) the Protestant projects onto the physical and economic spheres. Because excrement is a nonproductive aspect of the physical sphere, the 'upward mobility of spirit' (McKeon 194) can be attacked at exactly that point at which the Protestant discovers his or her salvation enacted in the world. Such a dialectic is implied when George Grant claims that in Canada 'public religion has become an unimportant litany of objectified self-righteousness necessary for the more anal of our managers' (G. Grant 186). Even without analysing Grant's drastic reduction of social and religious complexity to sublimation and its discontents, it is evident that the Freudian metaphor off-handedly relays a tacit epistemology. At the centre of Freudian psychoanalysis, Marxist theory, indeed at the centre of most twentieth-century filiations of scientific ideology including, *mutatis mutandis*, the novel, is the belief that reality must always in the first instant be understood materially, an understanding with which the scatological image naturally sympathizes.[2] Thus, although a writer of immense sophistication such as Umberto Eco has his detective of semiology, William of Baskerville, read with irony the belief that jewelled crucifixes are 'theophanic matter' (*Il nome della rosa* 145), Eco also has William fix on, without irony, the Thomist argument that 'divine things should be expounded more properly in figures of vile bodies than of noble bodies' (*Il nome della rosa* 81).[3] A subliminal effect created by Grant in the image of anal retention only becomes clear once we analyse the statement according to Bakhtin's dialogic principle. According to Bakhtin's schema, Grant (like Freud in *Charakter und Analerotik*) is not engaging in psychological analysis (and the generality of Grant's essay confirms this), but is attempting to satirize 'high' religious authority by means of the low scatological image.

The dialectic of scatological matter and religious 'spirit' is carried out as a much more conscious fiction by a number of Canadian novelists. Some – Atwood, Findley, Ladoo, Scott, and Johnston – for varying reasons intend the material polemic to undercut the spiritual hubris involved in particular forms of religious faith; others – Davies, Laurence, Williams, Moore, and Richler – appropriate the culture's dominant material epistemology in order to naturalize faith in a bodily context. Excepting perhaps the romance *Shoeless Joe*, where W.P. Kinsella both tongue-in-cheek and very seriously treats baseball as a religion, Canadian novelists tend to double back over the religious persona just as they do over the civilized self. The novelist, using the Freudian model of personality, undercuts the religious persona with the persona's unconscious anality, with evidence of how the centre of his or her faith depends upon the (denied and often obscene) pollution at the margins.

The writer thus becomes the revealer and handler of unclean matter, while the religious persona (Mitchell's evangelist Heally Richards, for example) attempts, against the evidence of his body, to maintain an untenable metaphysical epistemology. Since social images tend to refer to a past reality, there is, however, an attendant irony when the writer overvalues the social power of the religious persona and undervalues (through euphemism) the persona's capability of direct expression.

The more experimental novels of Cohen, Rooke, and Klein are important in this context. They complicate the dialectic between excrement and spirit because these novelists recognize the parallels between the spiritualizing tendency in religion and the idealizing tendency in mimesis, as well as the epistemological irony inherent in all *representations* of even a filthy body: representations using the Freudian model insist that the body is the beginning of the real, but nevertheless rely on an abstracted textuality to convey that real.

Atwood maintains a fairly straightforward polemic against an imagined Puritan culture in *The Handmaid's Tale*. Although she intends to mitigate the strict parallel between the Gilead regime and religious fundamentalism by portraying Baptist resistance at the borders of her text, bodily and linguistic practices in the novel clearly mimic stereotypes of Puritan cleanliness. Offred has 'pumice for sanding off dead skin. Such Puritan aids are supplied' (60). She scrubs herself with the pumice after the horrifying Particicution, in what is clearly meant to indicate the regime's cynical acquiescence in the Freudian dynamic of (always Puritan) displacement.[4] The Aunts punish Dolores for urinating on the floor, and the regime's euphemistic bid to control language pits Aunt Lydia's word, 'unhygienic,' against Moira's words, 'crotch rot' (58).

Cat's Eye, which on the surface seems to be far less polemical, contains similar patterns. Grace Smeath's mother only allows Elaine Risley and Grace four squares of toilet paper per bowel movement; as with Aunt Pearl in *The Vanishing Point*, Freud's parsimonious and petty anal erotic is translated without alteration into the novel. Just as Offred does, Elaine internalizes the culture, feeling that just by looking she has helped the washing machine to clean things. After Mr Smeath cites the schoolboy rhyme 'Pork and beans the musical fruit,' Elaine is horrified to discover that 'toot' means fart, fearing that she has been enlisted in a scatological discourse. Again, Atwood does not complicate 'Puritan' society by means of Mr Smeath's transgression. His comment seems eccentric to what Elaine calls 'the Smeath dinner table, stronghold of righteousness' (133). That Atwood intends the Smeath household to ramify throughout the macrocosm of Canadian culture is evident in the adult Elaine's description of the art gallery: 'It's as if somebody's been around spraying the paintings with air freshener, to kill the smell. The smell of blood on the wall' (90). To counter this Puritan inheritance, Elaine paints works such as *White Gift*, four panels that progressively unwrap tissue paper surrounding the image of Mrs Smeath. In the final panel she is 'in her saggy-legged cotton underpants, her one large breast sectioned to show her heart. Her heart is the heart of a dying turtle: reptilian, dark-red, diseased. Across the bottom of this panel is stenciled: THE*KINGDOM*OF*GOD*IS*WITHIN*YOU' (372). After this painting is vandalized by a woman whom Elaine at first mistakes for Grace Smeath, Elaine recognizes that her painted distortions of Mrs Smeath are not modernist *Kunstwerke*, but 'washroom graffiti raised to a higher order' (373). Despite the superficial humility of such a statement, Atwood's surrogate artist has, in effect, cleverly traded any ties to Smeathean bourgeois spirituality for a more respectable material epistemology, and quietly associated herself with the master Jan Van Eyck, whose 'Johannes de Eyck fuit hic' looks 'disconcertingly like a washroom scribble' (347). In one of Elaine's last paintings, Mrs Smeath is 'bigger than life ... Blotting out God' (426).[5]

Findley's polemic in *Not Wanted on the Voyage* is as definite as Atwood's, though at times more playful. Mottyl the cat suspects because of Yaweh's smell that he is human, and Yaweh takes a long time to 'materialize' (66) from a carriage spattered 'with the remnants of excrement, eggs and rotten vegetables' (64). The marginal demos, *mise en abîme* in the mythical Genesis narrative, attacks Yaweh with filth just as the democratic twentieth-century writer, *mise en abîme* in a cat, does.[6] Allusion (to the medieval *festa stultorum*)[7] and generalized historical allegory (higher criticism has, since Julius Wellhausen, materialized the Bible) combine to send up Dr Noyes's denial of the body of his creator. Yaweh is, of course, in collusion with Dr Noyes: reporting the affront to his dignity, Yaweh euphemizes excrement as 'ordure' (70). The sign of excrement conveys the idea that Dr Noyes cannot entertain – but that the post-Nietzschean writer can – the death of God. During one of the few moments when νοῦς moves beyond the caricature of a villainous, authoritarian mind, the smell of animal and human manure on the sea suggest the disappearance which Mottyl has long expected: 'a silent God who refused to materialize' (241). In order to kill both patriarch and the father-narrative, the fooling author makes his own account the original, giving the belated reader the 'authentic' story against which the Jahwist's account in Genesis can be measured: 'During the summer solstice, the sun had stood still for two whole days and a storm of meteors had pelted the dung heap and killed all the Middenites' (22). Patriarchal political ends evidently distort what was originally a natural referent: midden first; 'Midian' only later. Although Findley purposely confuses Greek (Noyes) and Hebrew (Noah), and collapses forms of worship into one another (Catholic into the proto-Hebrew, 48), he still, however ironically, claims a type of fabular history.

Findley's theory of marginalia is more explicit in his earlier novel, *Famous Last Words*. Little Nell enunciates an almost Derridean conception of the 'parergon': 'His theory was that you could sum up the age you lived in by reading its walls. The truth, which loves to hide, had found the perfect hiding place ... the partitions of a comfort station' (275). The toilet walls parody the walls of the Grand Elysium Hotel on which Mauberley writes; the demotic scrawl replaces the stylus of the aesthete's classical paradise, although the toilet graffiti does not actually get reported. What appears to be *outside* the text is a tabooed scatological truth: 'La soillure est ce qui choit du "système symbolique." Elle est ce qui échappe à cette nationalité sociale, a cet ordre logique sur lequel repose un ensemble social' (Kristeva 1980, 80; 'Defilement is what is jettisoned from the "symbolic system." It is what escapes that social rationality, that logical order on which the social aggregate is based' 65). What is excluded – according to Kristeva the mother's body and all irrational (ego-threatening, parturition-threatening) analogues such as excrement and menstrual blood (71) – is what constitutes the symbolic order.

To make Little Nell bear post-structuralist theory may be too much to ask of a figure who is a caricature, a lesser aesthete. Yet most of Findley's novels, especially in their moral outrage, are constituted around notions of inner and social defilement. The genres that Findley tends towards (fable, murder mystery, espionage thriller) maintain a

Judaic code in their thrust towards moral separation. Although the author apparently forgets it in *Not Wanted on the Voyage*, Jahweh did show up in *Famous Last Words*. Holiness and boundary terror appear when an actual bomber drops actual bombs onto a Bahamian audience watching a film of the Battle of Britain. This transgression of the simulated by the real becomes explicitly Hebraic in the plane's sky-writing: 'mene mene tekel upharsin; the final scrawl, the ultimate graffiti' (287). At this point the Hebraic deity, who will not allow the moral code to be blasphemed, and the twentieth-century scato-humanist, who privileges the voice from the toilet, coalesce in the figure of an author-judge who (as a former journalist) wants to write his graffiti not on a toilet wall, but within reported history, so as to tell us what is right and what is wrong. The author-judge in *Not Wanted on the Voyage* may be more hidden, but is no less present. The difference between 'Yaweh' and Findley is that, for Findley, post-scientific and post-realist, scatology (as the type of all matter) marks what is human instead of the boundary where the categories of creation are mixed (Douglas 53) and where the human consorts with the beast.[8]

ii

Scatological attacks on religion are clearly responses to anti-bodily traditions in Judeo-Christian thinking, only a few instances of which can be cited here. In Deuteronomy the Israelites are enjoined to bury their excrements outside of the camp: 'The Lord thy God walketh in the midst of thy camp ... therefore shall thy camp be holy: that he see no unclean thing in thee, and turn away from thee' (23:13–14). Using these cultural boundaries, the Old Testament writers and, following them, Paul rely on the image of excrement to portray degradation.[9] Stressing taboo over sacrifice, the law forms an inner constraint (Kristeva 95), while Christ complicates the self by interiorizing abjection (107): 'Si l'abomination est la doublure de mon être symbolique, "je" suis donc hétérogène, pur et impur, et comme tel toujours potentiellement condamnable' (1980, 131; 'If abomination is the lining of my symbolic being, "I" am therefore heterogeneous, pure and impure, and as such always potentially condemnable' 112).

Despite this interiorization, the Christian West has often relied upon an external, almost Manichaean dualism between body and spirit. Among Gnostic-Christian epistemologies this dualism is especially developed, as can be seen in Valentinus's contention that Christ did not excrete his solids.[10] The motive force behind the monastic ideal was the belief that the body had been extensively corrupted by the Fall (Brooke 19). Augustine, under the spell of St Anthony's ideal and despite his attacks on the Manichees, identified the 'hind parts' of God that Moses saw (Exod. 33: 17–23) with Christ's flesh in *De Trinitate* (2.15–17). In Book Three of the *Confessiones* Augustine tried to balance his crucial personal (and figural) discovery – that God is spirit – by emphasizing the humiliation of the flesh in the person of Christ, but Augustine's terms are still heavily binary. The Arian controversies of the fourth century (including the temporary *rapprochements* such as ὁμοούσιον in the Nicene Creed), the Monophysite tensions of the fifth to sixth Centuries, and the iconoclast controversies leading up to Lent 843 AD centred not only on politics, but on the bodily identity of Christ. According to Thomist anthropology, the soul which apprehends God in Christ cannot be material, but is an incorruptible absolute form (*Summa Theologiae* Qu 12, Qu 75); eating, digestion, and all that they entail will disappear after the resurrection: 'The use of food serves the corruptible life, for we take in food to avoid the corruption which can follow on the consumption of natural moisture' (Aquinas, *Summa Contra Gentiles* 4.83).[11]

As a result of this separation of form and accident (soul and body), and since 'the localization of hell in the heart of the earth naturally followed upon the method of interment in the ground,' the devil has traditionally been represented in Western literature as belonging to the earthly realm (Rudwin 55), as an animal (Rudwin 36), and even as the inventor of lavatories (Rudwin 251). The phenomenon of the second face on the demon's buttocks in an illustration such as 'St Wolfgang and the devil' (1483) has been interpreted as 'a mark of the devil's lordship of matter and dirt' (Cavendish 58–9).[12] Supplementing eroticism and blasphemy, scatological obscenity has traditionally been attributed to the persona of the witch or warlock; among the charges brought forward at the sensational pan-European trials of the Knights Templars between 1307 and 1316 were spitting or urinating on crucifixes, kissing the devil's hindquarters in the form of an animal, and ritual homosexuality (Cavendish 72).

Although Nietzsche reads Luther as a dionysiac in *Die Geburt der Tragödie*, given medieval associations and given Elias's history of the civilizing process, Luther's farting at the devil or his experience of

122 Scatology and Ideological Hierarchy

grace on the privy (his '*Turmerlebnis*') is hardly surprising.[13] John Harrington, the English inventor of the water closet, was following a long monastic tradition when he wrote about praying at stool:

> Pure prayer ascends to Him that high doth sit,
> Down falls the filth for fiends of hell more fit.
> (quoted in Wright 74)

Protestant attacks on relics often had strong scatological elements. One assault on credulous pilgrims mocks 'Thomas a Becket's snotty handkerchief' in an attempt to shore faith in a spiritual, not an earthly, pilgrimage (McKeon 107). A parody of an indulgence might take transgressive form –

> Mossehor, qu'es eissi présen,
> Vos dona xx banastas dé mal dé dens,
> Et a tôs vôs aoutrés aoûssi,
> Donna una cóa de Roussi.
>
> (My lord who is here present
> Gives you 20 baskets of toothaches
> And to all you others also
> Gives a red bum.) (Burke 192)

– as did actual desecration of relics, such as the depositing of human excrement in holy water basins (N. Davis 179–80). In one 1545 German Reformation print, the Pope, with streaming excrement in hand, rides on a pig (Stallybrass and White 51).[14] On the other side, Rabelais's Catholic-humanist attack on the Pope – via the Popefigs who must pull a fig out of an anus with their mouths (*Pantagruel* 4.45.544) – and Catholic attacks on the Reformation used similar imagery, as noted in the Introduction with Thomas More.

In Freud's system, these spiritual self-fashionings and projective attacks are symptomatic of bodily repression, since 'der Teufel ist doch gewiss nichts anderes als die Personifikation des verdrängten unbewussten Trieblebens' ('the devil is certainly nothing else than the personification of the repressed unconscious instinctual life'), while 'die Sauberkeit, Ordentlichkeit, Verlässlichkeit macht ganz den Eindruck einer Reaktionsbildung gegen das Interesse am Unsauberen, Störenden, nicht zum Körper gehörigen' (*Charakter und Analerotik*

Religion   123

208, 206; 'cleanliness, orderliness and trustworthiness give exactly the impression of a reaction-formation against an interest in what is unclean and disturbing and should not be part of the body' 174, 172). Even Foucault's discursive analysis of the soul owes a lot to Freudian corporeality. For Foucault, the surplus power possessed by the king creates both the corporeal inverse – the body of the condemned man – and a non-corporeal *duplicate* – the 'soul' (1984, 176). By politicizing the soul, Foucault jettisons the universalist, strictly biological aspects of Freud's theory, but nevertheless retains ontological primacy for matter, with 'spirit' still a reaction-formation.

Puritan versions of the self give some support to these theoretical outlines of the unconscious. Like the monks who prayed at stool, Cotton Mather represented his religious persona in immediate reaction to the filthy body:

I was once emptying the cistern of nature, and making water at the wall. At the same time, there came a dog, who did so too, before me. Thought I: 'What mean and vile things are the children of men ... How much do our natural necessities abase us, and place us ... on the same level with the very dogs!

My thought proceeded. 'Yet I will be a more noble creature; and at the very time when my natural necessities debase me into the condition of the beast, my spirit shall (I say *at that very time*) rise and soar.'

Accordingly, I resolved that it should be my ordinary practice, whenever I stop to answer the one or other necessity of nature to make it an opportunity of shaping in my mind some holy, noble, divine thought.' (*The Diary of Cotton Mather* quoted in K. Thomas 38)

Atwood, by dedicating *The Handmaid's Tale* to Mary Webster (who was among those hanged as witches in Mather's New England), connects the Gileadean rejection of the body to religious persecution in a Freudian dynamic of transference. The same short polemic wherein Atwood claims Webster as an ancestor attacks Mather: '[Witch-hunting and torture] did not end with racks, stakes, and Grand Inquisitors, or with Cotton Mather' ('Witches' 332).[15]

Biblical translations in this century too are instructive. Where the Authorized (King James) Version identifies the free man as 'him that pisseth against the wall' (1 Kings 14:10), the Revised Standard Version contains only 'free.' The recent tendency has been to dignify references to the inner organs (for example, $\sigma\pi\lambda\acute{a}\gamma\chi\nu o\iota\varsigma$ or $\sigma\pi\lambda\acute{a}\gamma\chi\nu\alpha$, which indiscriminately refers to heart, lungs, liver, kidneys, and even

124 Scatology and Ideological Hierarchy

womb) by rendering them as 'heart,' instead of 'bowels.' Where the King James and sometimes Geneva versions render the Greek or Hebrew as 'bowels,' the Revised Standard Version and the American Standard Version substitute 'heart,' 'affection' (Job 30:27, Gen. 43:30, Phil. 1:8; Col. 3:12 and, 1 John 3:17 in the ASV only), 'stomach' (Job 20:14), 'womb' (Ps. 71:6), 'anguish' (Jer. 4:19), or leave the word out entirely (2 Chron. 32:21, Col. 3:12, and 1 John 3:17 in the RSV only). This is not always straightforward bowdlerism because in some places (for example, Deut. 23:13) the new translations have become more explicit; nevertheless, the changes confuse ancient boundaries of the body with modern boundaries by attributing modern scientific differentiation of organ functions and modern emotional 'seats' to the ancient Hebrews.[16]

iii

No matter what we make of the accuracy of the repressive hypothesis, it is certainly central not just to Atwood and Findley, but to religious discourse throughout the Canadian novel. The differentiation between 'body' and 'soul' may be seen in naïve form in Brooke's *The History of Emily Montague* and in Moodie's *Mark Hurdlestone*. In the former, the attack on monks 'who make it a point of religion to abjure linen, and wear their habits till they drop off' (33) is made from the simple viewpoint of Protestant 'cleanliness.' In the latter, Clary's post-mortem letter to Anthony sharply divides between 'the dust and rubbish of the gay world' (350) and the solitary heart (even though money and inheritance laws are what keep Moodie's narrative in motion at every turn), while profanities sound terrible to newly converted Mary Matthews's cleansed ear.

After Freud traded Christian literalism about the demonic for a psychoanalytic literalism about the body, the equation of religious respectability with a superficially clean and proper body became difficult to maintain. Stephen Dowling's difficulty mediating between matter and spirit in Callaghan's *Such Is My Beloved* owes much to the clash between Freud and external orientations in Christianity. Sinclair Ross raises the problem in *As For Me and My House*, where prairie realism demands that the privy be acknowledged, but prairie Protestantism demands euphemism. While Mrs Bentley defends the limited colloquiality of 'belly' (70) and 'sweat' (91) in Paul's classroom, and mocks a pool-hall sign demanding 'THE LANGUAGE THAT

YOUR MOTHER USED' (96), her sense of restraint is hardly less than Mrs Wenderby's censorship. The etymology of 'perspiration,' Mrs Wenderby's replacement for 'sweat,' has a built-in history of euphemizing: *per-spirare* (Latin, 'to breathe through') anthropomorphizes the pores and spiritualizes the outflow. Mrs Bentley, whose modernism so determinedly materializes religion, nevertheless has something of the Wenderby conscience. When Steve calls their outhouse the Leaning Tower of Pisa, she adds, 'a rather good name too by virtue of a bad pronunciation' (63). She implies, but does not say, the 'obscene' word. Ross not only breaks the 'luminous whole' of modernist theory in Philip's 'earthbound' art (Williams, 'Void' 38), but also by means of the Bentleys' privy:[17]

The privy leans badly, fifteen or twenty degrees anyway from the perpendicular. Last Hallowe'en it was carried off by the hoodlums of the town and left on the steps of the church with a big sign nailed to it *Come Unto Me All Ye That Labour And Are Heavy Laden*. They haven't been able since to get it straight again, but Mrs Finley says that we can use it with assurance. My neighbor, Mrs Ellingson, came over this morning to tell me how she and her husband laughed when they saw me go in the first time: 'Sven say she look so scared I maybe tink she vaste her time.' (13–14)

Scatology can become credit in a post-Freudian economy of confession. Mrs Bentley must be fallible enough to gain the reader's sympathy: when she acts as the Puritan and repeats the anal retentive joke against herself, she gains a materialist epistemology to subvert the older, no longer convincing respectability.[18] The symbolic realm is not separate, but a function of the self-interested artist. The woman who does not want to be a Puritan of course reports the hoodlums' dialogical reduction of the biblical text; more interesting is the word 'assurance,' which puns from grace and salvation across to the bodily context, perhaps parodying Luther's *Turmerlebnis*.

The objects and sources of Canadian scatological attacks on religious language are various. In Audrey Thomas's *Mrs Blood* a feminist problematic revises the old texts: 'I stink therefore I am. This is the bloody and bawd of Christ which was riven for thee' (21). The punning female recorporealizing of communion (less and less a bodily exercise with the historical shrinkage of the wafer) follows a materialization of the Cartesian credo, thereby attacking the two poles of Western male hegemony.[19] The narrator's blood is set in juxtaposition with Pentateuchal laws which name the menstruating woman as unclean, but Thomas's 'female' stands for the body in all its forms – not just in blood, but also in foulness.

In Ladoo's *No Pain Like This Body* and *Yesterdays* the attack comes from a less stable scepticism and is directed both at Trinidadian Hinduism and Christianity. In *Yesterdays* Sook and Choonilal sodomize each other in the Anglican church. The characters in *No Pain Like This Body* constantly speak of God in connection with the scatological image, as one exchange between Ma and Pa shows:

> 'But it have a God and he watchin from dat sky.'
> 'God coud kiss me ass!'
> 'Well wen a man could cuss God he deserve to dead!'

The scatological blasphemy is not simply a function of Pa's aggressive character, but Ladoo requires it to be enunciated by the innocent: Rama asks, 'Why God not kill dat lightnin ass?' (23) and Panday asks, 'You mean God does see wen Rama pee on me in de night?' (20).

Ladoo specifies the blasphemy by setting the terror of the novel's weather against the discourse of omniscience:

> 'Wot God doin now?' Panday asked.
> 'He watchin from de sky.'
> 'But de sky black like coals.'
> 'God still watchin.'
> 'Well God playin de ass now!'

By means of the rainstorms, Ladoo intentionally confuses Jahweh and the Hindu storm-god, Indra. 'God' is also signified in the unclean typology of father and priest, uncleanness signalled by the contravention of Hindu dietary laws when flies enter Pa's mouth (66) and try to enter Bismath Saddhu's mouth (101).[20] Although it seems superfluous given the broad typological attack on God, the technically inauthentic form of Hinduism transported to Trinidad by the indentured labourers in the nineteenth century also comes under attack when the one-legged villager mocks the priest: 'He is a modderass chamar and he playin Brahmin. Bisnath Saddhu is not a priest. He fadder used to mind pigs in Jangli Tola. He modderass chamar come to Tola playin holy' (98). Since Ladoo notes in his glossary that most of the Indians who came to Trinidad were lower-caste chamars (*panchamas*), the disruption of the social system because of the migration may be the reason that the religious system slips into parody.

In his unfinished and posthumously published novel *Yesterdays*, Ladoo takes more careful account of the mechanism of projection, abandoning the simple typology of Pa and God. Choonilal wants Tailor to repair the latrine because during Tailor's party women defecated by the Jandee pole, made messes on the outhouse floor, and knocked out the eastern wall.[21] Since Choonilal dreams that the stench will keep the Aryan gods from coming near, he projects his own concerns about cleanliness and reincarnation onto Tailor: 'Wen you dead you go born back a blasted worm in a latrine. Oright!' (3). According to Choonilal's form of religious nostalgia, the man of God is defined by external cleanliness rites, but in Choonilal's caricatured speech – 'I is a religious man, a kiss me ass religious man' (3) – and throughout the novel, religion becomes a mystification of bodily action. The attempted rape of Basdai after she visits the outhouse is explained as the work of an evil spirit (11). Tailor and Ragbir think that if someone will 'bull' Poonwa, he will forget about his Hindu mission to Canada (73). Religion is also understood as purely instrumental. The main reason that Choonilal wants the toilet cleaned is that he does not want his neighbour Ragbir to get a blessing for allowing Choonilal to use his toilet. Choonilal feels morally superior to modern Hindus with toilets in their houses, while the other characters feel superior to Choonilal after the climactic scene in which he falls asleep next to his own waste. Pandit Puru knows the materialist bias of Choonilal's religiosity, and he uses this knowledge to force Choonilal into remortgaging his house so as to finance Poonwa's Hindu mission – 'De Hindu gods go make you see trobble till you shit' (58) – while Puru himself can get away with scato-erotic advice because he is designated as a holy man (102). Ladoo's texts seem to admit no epistemological basis outside of the scatological, although the reappearance of the flies in *Yesterdays*, circling from the sleeping Choonilal's mouth to his waste and back again, suggests some fundamental outward distinction between the pure and the impure.

In contrast to Ladoo's extreme scepticism, the scatological image most often comes from a liberal-pluralist position, as it does in Chris Scott's brilliant novel *Antichthon*. Like *Not Wanted on the Voyage* and *The Handmaid's Tale*, *Antichthon* projects the representation of religion into another time when religious authority could immediately, not just vicariously, lacerate the dissenter. Because of this the repressive hypothesis can regain the kind of urgency that it did not always have in the 1980s. Scott allows Giordano Bruno the role of the body – arguing that life comes from putrefaction (14), affirming that flies have souls and that they will appear in heaven (104), and parodying medieval scholastic language about God: 'A worm segmented or a worm integral? A worm infinite or a worm temporal? A worm *in potentia* or *in essentia*?' (109).

Although the Archbishop of Venice, Lorenzo Priuli, and Pope Clement VIII also want Bruno to exist under the sign of filth in prison (172, 211) so as to degrade him, Scott reduces the anonymous authority of a dominant Catholic discourse to a material and human constituent in Priuli: 'Small tears of malice glittered on your cheeks, and around your mouth, pursed and venomous, there formed droplets of a grey effluvia – spittle that had dried in the mouth' (46). Scott's scatology takes Priuli lower than Bruno. Furthermore, these bodily signs become exactly that which Priuli must repress in order to maintain his faith:

'My faith is firm, but – *Christ's teeth!* for fifty years and more I was racked by a doubt, one doubt, an awful little tiny doubt, niggling, my lords, nibbling that's the word, *nibbling*, eating away my soul, nibble, nibble, nibble. *His* teeth, my lords. His *little* teeth, what became of them, eh? Those little pearls of Our Lord's innocence, His *milk* teeth, my lords. Nibble nibble. What happened to them? They fell out, yes, and then? When He rose on the third day, did they rise with Him, those little teeth? If so, how so? If not, why not? Nibble. That's where the rot sets in'. (46)

Outside of the strategies of mimesis (the attempt to make Priuli more convincing psychologically than Dostoevsky's Grand Inquisitor) are the problems of Christian history: How does a sixteenth-century archbishop settle the question of Christ's divinity and the bodily resurrection?

Milk teeth are only one of the many bodily ejecta which could carry the traditional doubt.[22] But the way that Scott has Priuli handle his doubt is more suggestive of a Gnostic than of a Christian settlement. According to Clement of Alexandria, Valentinus (the third-century Gnostic) denied that Christ ejected anything from his body: 'He ate and drank in a peculiar way and did not evacuate his food. For he had so great a power of continence that the food was not corrupted in him, since he himself was not perishable' (*Stromata* 3.59.3).[23] The orthodox Catholic settlement was to proclaim that Christ was all human and all divine in a mysterious hypostatic union.[24]

Religion 129

The problem of historicizing Priuli is compounded in the subjectivity of the novel since Priuli is a ghost speaking from Hell. Scott does not allow the reader to make a judgment on the materiality of the after-lives that the novel represents, but what is certain is that Priuli's discourse foliates the discourse of Bruno; specifically, Priuli's comment about 'rot' continues Bruno's concern with 'putrefaction.' Close to the end of the novel, when Clement VIII says, 'I am an old man gone in the teeth' (221), the material problematic resurfaces, but without self-conscious commentary. Mimesis without seam, it is presented as simple description, which by this time, of course, it hardly is. In a sophisticated fashion Scott thus extends a silent ideology of the body over papal infallibility and over any human representation of Christ. Instead of Clement VIII bringing Bruno crashing down to earth like (in Hippolytus's fable) Peter did to Simon Magus (211), and no matter how the historical Priuli and Clement VIII justified their use of torture, Scott brings the Catholic hierarchy down under the sign of Gnostic dualism,[25] while Bruno represents interpretive plenitude – reading both as a literalist and as an allegorist, almost as a liberal pluralist. Indeed, the strength of *Antichthon* is that each voice is answered with a counter voice.

Wayne Johnston's pluralism also makes much of counter-voicing. Usually Johnston undercuts the signifieds of religious language by replacing them with the scatological in *The Story of Bobby O'Malley*. When the young Bobby is a 'rebel of the pot,' his mother Agnes is 'sustained by faith alone' (7). When the toilet backs up in their house, Bobby's father Ted asks Agnes to pray that God grant what she calls 'the sordid miracle': 'If God can part the Red Sea, he can damn well plug this pipe' (13). The distant, holy, almost purely textual God is drawn into degrading proximity with excrement. Allegorically, Johnston divides Bobby between the Catholic mother, whom the young Bobby consciously imitates, and the secular father, with whom Bobby unconsciously identifies until he explicitly takes on Ted's persona as the narrator of his own life. Agnes euphemizes 'effluent' (12), has 'neutered the universe' (49) for Bobby, and tells him that Protestants do not wash (101). She particularly hates the cleaning of the septic tank because the process makes their excretions public. Ted, meanwhile, talks about confession as the disposing of the past and of the priest as 'a kind of garbage-collector' (165), echoing Rabelais's satire in *Gargantua*. According to Rabelais, monks are shunned because 'ilz mangent la merde du monde, c'est à dire les péchéz, et comme machemerdes l'on les rejecte en leurs retraictz, ce sont leur conventz et abbayes, séparéz de conversation politicque comme sont les retraictz d'une maison' (*Gargantua* 1.40.118; 'they eat the world's excrement, that is to say, sins; and as eaters of excrement they are cast into their privies – their convents and abbeys that is – which are cut off from all civil intercourse, as are the privies of a house' 1.40.125). In this way Ted regularly undercuts his wife's religious metaphors with material glosses. When Agnes attempts to explain Hell metaphorically, containing not actual flames but 'some "more subtle, but no less purgative agony,"' Ted makes Agnes's metaphor explicit: 'Like throwing up?' (102). Although the mother's metaphoricized Hell engenders Bobby's existential fears, the dead father's sceptical materialist voice can consistently be discerned in Bobby's voice – for example, when Bobby describes the 'visions' of his companion Gabriel. 'Squirming in agony, face and body coursing with divine wisdom, [Gabriel] might say: "John gets to blow the biggest frog." These rulings were not questioned. It was the will of God that John blow the biggest frog' (38). Scatology (the game of blowing through a straw into the frog's anus), religious instrumentality, and male adolescent cruelty are wound up in the sacred associations of names such as 'Gabriel' and 'John.' In the 'telling,' Bobby does not tell his mother's rosary; he tells his father's jokes.

iv

Although Johnston directs most of his scatology against Agnes, Bobby realizes towards the end of the narrative that he does not really understand his mother. Furthermore, Ted's last testament – 'What is more final than flushing the toilet? Do this in memory of me' (184) – nearly secularizes and naturalizes Christ.

Davies, who does want to naturalize Christian pluralism, often begins with a dialogic attack on Puritanism similar to Johnston's counter-voicing. *Fifth Business* begins with the terrible Puritan mother: 'Our privy set the sanitary tone for the village' (18). According to the Puritan interpretive standards of mother and town, the gravel pit where the dirty tramps live is Hell.[26] But what represents the world, the flesh, and the devil to Dunstan Ramsay's mother fascinates him. Because he believes that he has grown up lacking one whole side of his being, he trades in the Puritan mother for a more promiscuous mother (Mary Dempster), who is not so appalled by gravel pits and dirty tramps. In *The Manticore* Ontario Puritanism becomes even more fantastic and lacerating as David Staunton, at the suggestion of his grandfather, receives a purifying enema, Dr Tyrrell's Internal Bath, every Saturday to prepare for Sunday church services. Netty takes over the procedure and the role of the Puritan mother with her smegmal theories, telling David not to play with other boys: 'Probably they did not wash often enough under their foreskins. Netty was very strong on that ... "If you're not clean there, you're not clean anyplace"' (94). David learns the social power of the discourse linking evil with uncleanness; later he uses it. When, as a lawyer, he must defend a woman who blew her husband's head off while he was sitting on the privy, David tells the court that she had to perform fellatio even though her husband was notoriously dirty. Davies's mimetic purpose is to parody that rationalist theology which pursues filth up into its hiding places, but such purposes are complicated by Netty's unscientific postscript to her rather sound washing injunctions. She also warns David not to spit his brains out like Cece Athelstan, 'a man well advanced in syphilis ... certainly a victim of unchecked spitting' (94). Davies's evident fascination with such archaic mythologies of the unitary body (where the mouth has access to the brain, or the mouth represents the ejaculating penis in an unconscious discourse of homeopathic magic) make Netty, and not the rational psychoanalyst Dr von Haller, the repository of Deptford's bodily unconscious.

Perhaps it is not so surprising, then, that for Davies scatology can stand in for mystical discourse, since both have been made to seem archaic by scientific discourse. Like Munro's Del Jordan, who knows that to ask God to reveal himself in the United Church would be 'as inappropriate as farting' (*Lives of Girls and Women* 80), David Staunton knows the denominational sanctions that invite and prohibit spiritual language: 'In the Anglican church I nodded my head, as if to say "Quite so," or (in the slang of the day) "Hot spit!" whenever Jesus was named in a hymn. But in the United Church if Jesus turned up I sang the name very low, and in the secret voice I used when talking to my grandmother about what my bowels were doing' (*The Manticore* 88). This satire does not undermine spirituality; it attacks a rationalized public language by means of the privacies of body and belief.

In one sense, the dialectic in Davies's fiction is not so much between Dunstan and his mother, or David and Netty, but between the Protestant and the anus. The characters exist in the gulf between the two. Paul Dempster agonizes in *World of Wonders* because of the physical analogy that links kneeling for prayer and kneeling for Willard's sodomy. Having escaped the two private powers – the one which defines the blasphemy and the other which abuses him sexually – Paul solemnly spits at Puritanical Deptford and at the site of his rape by Willard. The material bases in Davies's pluralism are evident in that Paul cannot simply reject the old roles ideologically, but must reject them in a scatological ritual which according to Netty's earlier gloss involves more than saliva.[27] John Parlabane's diabolical scepticism in *The Rebel Angels* is consistently tied to filth. In *What's Bred in the Bone* Bella Mae's agony is less because her repression of one antagonist (the anus) is greater: 'You don't think [Jesus] wants to look at your bare B.T.M.' (77), and Simon Darcourt's belief is such that, while he is ready to grant excrement its place, he sublimates Ozias Froats's slides of feces into a vision of the New Jerusalem: 'They were of extraordinary beauty, like splendid cuttings of moss-agate, eye-agate, brecciated agate, and my mind turned to that chalcedony which John's Revelation tells us is part of the foundations of the Holy City' (110).[28] Not anal, though still scatological, is Hannah's parodic desire in *World of Wonders* to recoup the body for Protestantism by means of jokes about the river Pison, and her typology of Rango the monkey as 'natural, unredeemed man' (80) urinating in public.

Davies satirizes Hannah; nevertheless, he follows a similar pattern in his novels, especially in *The Rebel Angels*. With Uncle Yerko (whose real name is Miya Lautero or Martin Luther), Davies also revises Protestant historical origins in the Reformation. Like Luther, the luthier Yerko maintains a scatological innocence in his constant farting, yet Davies also gives him a pre-Reformation love of images. Yerko thus eludes Parlabane's sceptical attack on all metaphysics and on Luther in particular. But Davies trades the single-mindedness of the historical Luther's attacks for the broader Rabelaisian laughter that intends to bind all spiritualized voices in a democracy of the low image. The best example of this is when Darcourt talks about Froats's Sheldonian attempts to situate human personality according to excrement type. Darcourt calls excrement 'what is rejected, what is accounted of no worth to mankind. Filth therapy ... is astonishingly similar to alchemy in basic principle – the recognition of what is of worth in that which is scorned by the unseeing. The alchemist's long quest for the Stone, and the biblical stone which the builders refused becoming the headstone of the corner' (82). The discourses discernible here are the biblical (Ps. 118:22, and most importantly Acts 4:11 in which Christ is interpreted as the rejected cornerstone), an alchemical language no longer reputable to Froats, and a scientific language wherein the hypothetical basis of enquiry is overdetermined towards materialism. The low image does not so much deny the Christian or alchemical self as link a newer material ideology to these traditions. Despite the potential for extreme scepticism, the discourses of science and religion confirm each other in Froats's coinage, 'physiological predestination' (250).[29] Beyond the satire hinted at by the compensatory nature of Froats's scholarship, he comes off rather well in the novel as a researcher who is not cowed by the secularized Puritanism of public fashion.

In fact, by collating Christian theology, alchemy, and scatology Davies makes Darcourt echo comments that first appeared in Carl Jung's *Psychologie und Alchemie*: 'Die grobe Materialität des gelben Metalls mit seinem odiosen Beigeschmack der Währungsgrundlage ... machen die Verwerfung zwar begreiflich; darum ist es ja so schwer, den "lapis" zu finden, weil er "exilis," unansehnlich, ist, weil er "in via eiectus invenitur" ... Aber der "lapis in via eiectus" könnte auch zum "angularis" werden' (103; 'The gross materiality of the yellow metal with its odious fiscal flavour ... make ... rejections comprehensible enough – but that is precisely why it is so hard to find the lapis: it is *exilis*, uncomely, it is thrown out into the street or on the dunghill ... But "the stone which the builders rejected, the same is become the head of the corner"' 350). Although Maria is surprised that Froats buys excrement for his work, excrement achieves immense exchange value when, at the end of the novel, Froats wins the Nobel prize. Jung's syncretic recuperation of discredited languages in the figure of the collective unconscious is clearly Davies's – as Davies has often admitted – and religious recuperation has certainly had its fiscal rewards for Davies. If Sheldonian constitutional psychology did not merit the attention it once got, that may be the most potent levelling irony in Davies's attempt to shore up religious language with scientific discourse.

In Laurence's *The Diviners* the garbage collector Christie Logan is the leveller. He is both Morag's readopted father and a reconstituted Christ. Unlike Beckett's Christy in *All That Fall*, who offers free dung instead of eternal life, Laurence's Christie naturalizes the doctrine of original sin as original abjection, and his parody of Christ's language recuperates that language in a realist context: 'I *am* muck, but so are they ... When I carry away their refuse, I'm carrying off part of them, do you see? ... By their garbage ye shall know them' (39). The parody returns the spiritualized agriculture of 'By their fruits ye shall know them' (Matt. 7:20) to the lower world, and less obviously, it echoes more explicit comments of Christ's: 'Whatsoever thing from without entereth into a man, it cannot defile him; because it entereth not into his heart, but into the belly and goeth out into the draught, purging all meats. And he said, that which cometh out of the man, that defileth the man' (Mark 7:18-20). As Christ spiritualizes the body, so does Christie: 'I see what they throw out, and I don't care a shit, but they think I do, so that's why they cannot look at me. They think muck's dirty. It's no more dirty than what's in their heads' (39).

By uncovering Manawaka's repressed side, Laurence accommodates the Christian mythos to the Freudian mythos of body and repression. This process of accommodation is consistent throughout her novels. In *The Stone Angel*, Hagar's constipation acts as a counterweight to Rev Troy's spiritual clichés (40), and yet Hagar plays out the mythos of Christian communion. In *A Jest of God* the Dukes' 'mongoloid' son swears and uses scatological language during the sermon in the United Church, an unconscionable rebuke to the self-possessed language of Rachel and her mother, just as Rachel's momentary lapse into glossolalia is. Although Morag Gunn in *The Diviners* represses Ross McVitie's scatological puns on the line 'Ox and ass before him bow' (from the hymn 'Good Christian Men Rejoice' 80), she later opens into an identical language while seeking refuge during a dance:

> John of Ages
> locked for me
> let me hide
> myself in thee. (151)

Morag's metaphor for the writing process – divining – parallels the scatomancy of Christie, 'who divined with garbage' (394). By consciously identifying the writer with a revised, scatological Christ, Laurence acknowledges, in ways that Atwood and Findley do not, that the civilized self in the West (and Freudian 'I') are at least partially constituted through the Christian tradition.

This acknowledgment is even more pronounced in the novels of David Williams and in Brian Moore's *Black Robe*. In *Eye of the Father*, the descendants of Magnus Vangdal are each forced to find some way of revising the anal Eden that he bequeaths to them; Wayne and

Karen eventually secularize the roles of Joseph and Mary. Williams's materialization of the soul as squalid and smelly in *The Burning Wood* (118) is comparable to the dialogism of Rabelais when Tripet throws his soul up (*Gargantua* 116). Although native ejecta undercut the transcendental location of the soul for Joshua Cardiff in *The Burning Wood* and Jack Cann in *The River Horsemen*, those two characters erase the soul and then reinscribe, as their initials hint, a different sign of Christ.[30] In *Black Robe* Pierre Tallevant's statement – 'We're not colonizing the Savages. They're colonizing us' (22) – has no meaning in terms of political power, but Moore, like Williams, insists that it convey an ideological meaning for the Christian. The Jesuits must learn scatological languages in order to work among the indigenes, and this process of learning a new bodily culture enervates Father Laforgue's faith, creating a physio-spiritual problem that is compounded when he sees the rotting martyr, Father Duval. Filth becomes that which Father Laforgue must include in his new conception of faith, but Moore includes it much more provisionally and less easily than Laurence does. Laurence, Williams, and Moore represent twentieth-century accommodations of Christianity to material epistemologies, but their approach was already implicit in Augustine's distrust of classical aesthetics and his understanding of the rhetorical implications of the incarnation: 'Sie erzeugt einen neuen hohen Stil, der das Alltägliche keineswegs verschmäht, und der das sinnlich Realistische, ja das Hässliche, Unwürdige, körperlich Niedrige in sich aufnimmt' (Auerbach 76; 'It engenders a new elevated style, which does not scorn everyday life and which is ready to absorb the sensorily realistic, even the ugly, the undignified, the physically-base' 63).

Robert Cluett has documented the highly nominal nature of Richler's linguistic style (121), and in a precise play on words Cluett argues that Richler's language 'embodies the apparent future direction of *things*' (123, my italics). If Richler's syntax veers sharply away from function-word dominated language and towards lexemes, his scatology too revises traditional religious language, in his case the language of Judaism: 'These are the Days of Awe. Tomorrow is Rosh Hashonna, our new year, and like a week later it's Yom Kippur, when if you shit on anybody during the year you got a legal right to repent. And God forgives you' (*Joshua Then and Now* 65). The symbiosis between tradition and the body is the satirist's symbiosis. Although Reuben seems to be irreverent in saying these things (and the passage gave Richler much trouble when he spoke in synagogues), Reuben's irreverence is unconscious, as is his later summary of the book of Job: 'If you continue to believe in God, even when you're up shit's creek, it can pay off double at the window' (169). Here Richler combines three low languages – cliché, scatology, and the argot of the gambler, the latter of which is nicely sharpened by God's wager upon Job's righteousness. Reuben, however, unlike Agnes O'Malley, is Richler's norm. Judaism becomes important precisely *because* of its association with Reuben and with all that is low, so that whatever is overly spiritual or overly euphemized in the tradition is discarded by the satirist.

The Old Testament, with a strong materialist base in its dietary laws (Stern 322), is therefore not under as much epistemological pressure as the New Testament: 'Like if a guy is going to shit on you he usually leads with a quote from it ... The dirtier the sin, the sweeter the saying. The New Testament covers everything. I recommend it highly' (170).[31] The grown Joshua, interpreting the spirit of the Pentateuch strangely along Christ's lines, breaks the Mosaic law in Num. 5:1-5 (which was intended to isolate people with discharges) by kissing his sick homosexual friend Murdoch on the mouth.

This last is a revision of the artist-protagonist in *St Urbain's Horseman*. While Joshua merely notes that 'there seems to be an awful lot of washing up involved' in the Jewish tradition (*Joshua* 68), *Horseman*'s Jake Hersh has internalized categories of clean and unclean to the point where he can neither dispose of his excrement nor acknowledge it. Although his pluralist culture tells him that 'everything is holy' (*Horseman* 171), his tradition denies this. Pretending that the excrement is not his, he convinces himself that filth is always elsewhere, and Ormsby-Fletcher's child becomes the scapegoat for the plugged toilet. Contrary to normal satiric practice which makes the sinner pay, the scapegoat in the Old Testament was allowed to go free (albeit into the desert) after having been declared the demon *Azazel*'s while the pure goat was sacrificed. Like the satirist who creates an elite authorial persona, Jake's early shedding of responsibility nearly sabotages the intent of the Jewish tradition that Richler later intends him to reclaim.

v

These naturalizations of the Judeo-Christian tradition via the scatological image rely on a 'traditional methodology of biblical hermeneutics ... whereby the approximation of divinity through material figures was understood to accord with God's own intent' (McKeon 74). In the Protestant West 'the really real is asked for in time and space' (Tillich 71). Tillich claims that any natural object could become sacramental (106), although it is unlikely that he gave much thought to the *filthy* object. The difficulty with such metaphors, as McKeon notes, is that the analogy of 'material signifier and spiritual signified ... threatens at times to transform itself into an antithetical signifying relationship in which the priority of sense experience is felt to have not simply a pedagogic but an ontological force' (87). Erasure of the distinction between spiritual and secular callings among early Protestants often caused difficulties in signification, 'for it is sometimes difficult to remember which of the things compared is the most important. Was it grace or manure which was honored by the simile?' (Schlatter 197).[32] This is precisely the force that Nietzsche counts on when in *Also Sprach Zarathustra* he materializes and parodies the mass through the voice of an earthly prophet: 'Du willst uns doch nicht mit Reden abspeisen?' (520; 'You're not going to make us dine on speeches, are you?'). Later the ass's choric '*I-A*' (ie. '*ja*' 547; 'Ye-a' 322) kills with laughter the spiritualized human 'yea' in the mass. By the time of Ephraim Gursky's ten commandments in *Solomon Gursky Was Here*, it is more difficult to say whether Richler is satirizing Ephraim or sabotaging Judaism: 'Thou shalt not bow down to Narssuk, whose prick I have shrivelled, or to any other gods, you ignorant little fuckers. For the Lord thy God is a jealous God, visiting the iniquity of the fathers upon the children unto the third and fourth generation of them that hate me' (439).

The force of sense experience, which makes any incarnation a potentially unstable compound, can already be detected in Luther's 'physical creaturalness':[33] 'Ego miror, das man nit lanngst die welt vol geschissen etc. bis an den himel' (*Tischreden* #1259, 2.12; 'I marvel that man hasn't long since defecated the whole world full, up to the sky' 130). 'Ich habe der welt sat, so hat sie meiner wider sath ... Es ist doch, wie ich offt gesagt: Ich bin der reiffe dreck, so ist die welt das weite arschloch; drumb sein wir wol zu scheiden' (*Tischreden* #5537, 5.222; 'I'm fed up with the world, and it is fed up with me ... It's as I've often said: I'm like a ripe stool and the world's like a gigantic anus, and so we're about to let go of each other' 448). Luther's Augustinian humility about human effort and earthly phenomena could dismiss all ways of knowing but the scatological. Filth can redraw the line between the sacred and the profane (Davis 180), especially since conceptions of the human body are closely connected to the ways in which man represents God (Bottomley 24). The obscene, which has residual power in keeping with its social boundary status but out of keeping with its linguistic status, can potentially come to stand in the place of the unrepresentable divine so that religion loses its social valence and simply becomes, as it does for Georges Bataille, the encoding of the death drive (Kristeva 1987, 368–71).[34]

In *The Prince of Darkness and Co.*, where Robert Graves's mythopoeic desire for the primitive is only Philip Sparrow's desire to see blood flow (22, 140), Daryl Hine mocks this interpretation of the sacred, but Leonard Cohen takes it very seriously in *Beautiful Losers*, relying upon Luther in the process:

Homage to ... the Catechism which invited marginal obscenity and contributed to the maintenance of the lavatory as a thrilling temple of the Profane. Homage to the great slabs of marble with which the cubicles were constructed, to which no smear of shit could ever adhere. Here was enshrined the anti-Lutheran possibility of matter which succumbed easily to washing. Homage to marble in the Halls of Excrement, Maginot Line against the invasion of Papal Fallibility. (106)

This traditional use of scatological satire to deflate the pretensions of high religion also telegraphs what Cohen does to reduce Catherine Tekakwitha, the Iroquois Virgin, the moment he begins to imagine her. However, scatology cannot, despite Bakhtin, function entirely on a political level to demystify authority. Once the narrator begins to psychoanalyse his 'Lutheran' constipation – 'What unassailable bank in my psyche needs shit?' (40) – scatology trades the pedagogic for the ontological. The trope of constipation allows a focus on consumption – eating, drug addiction, taking in information – and destabilizes the confluence of Platonic (from *Symposium*) and Christian traditions of the human as container of an external divinity: 'Please make me empty, if I'm empty then I can receive, if I can receive it means it comes from somewhere outside of me, if it comes from outside of me I'm not alone! ... Please let me be hungry, then I am not the dead center ... I want to be fascinated by the phenomena' (Cohen 42). For Cohen consumption globalizes the Nazi economy of thanatos. The excremental and deadly extremes to which F. goes certainly belie Cohen's disingenuous comment that 'there are no obscene words ever' and Linda Hutcheon's reading of *Beautiful Losers* as Bakhtinian carnival (*The Candian Postmodern* 31). The scatological war against civil and religious boundaries begins rather benignly with, 'Is shit kosher?' (Cohen 95) and 'You have been baptized with fire, shit, history, love, and loss' (159), but by the time that F. and Edith bathe themselves with Mengele's soap made from human flesh, Kristeva's 'le *borderline* ... qui ... transforme l'abject en lieu de l'Autre' ('borderline patient' who 'transforms the abject into the site of the Other') cannot be considered a 'habitant de la frontière' ('frontiersman') or 'métaphysicien' (1980, 65; 'metaphysician' 54). The 'unavoidable alliance between shame, the obscene, and the sacred' in the process of setting things apart and veiling them (Huxley 13) certainly drives *Beautiful Losers*, but the extreme degradation that the characters undergo emphasizes (perhaps unintentionally) the social utility of Protestant individualism. Coded through the rejection of the scatological image, the social project behind the older Christian polemic of spirituality becomes intelligible: the choice in *Beautiful Losers* is between bodily discontent and thanatos.

Confirming this choice, but complicating our ways of speaking about it, Cohen hints that all the images of the social and of social boundaries may merely be verbal satellites spinning weightlessly around the central signifier of heroin ('shit' in the addict's argot). Religious and all other abjections would then have no significance in themselves. As a result, the erotic finality of Bataille's filthy explosion cannot seduce Cohen's (ultimately) civilized narrator: 'Does God love the world? What a monstrous system of nourishment! ... Tomorrow I begin my fast' (Cohen 42). What could seem a Gnostic response or at least St Catherine of Sienna's costive form of self-denial (Wright 24) may have as its subtext heroin withdrawal. More important, the narrator's final transformation into a movie destroys the mimetic contract which guaranteed that the narrator's persona represented a real world. The text moves towards pure word; the narrator's drive towards an object which is less and less available moves more and more eccentrically 'beyond pleasure' (184) into anal aggression (181-2, 189-91) and coprophagy (201-2), but neither spiritual repression nor an excremental drive to recover the body are any longer sufficient causes to explain the narrator's actions or the textual machine.

Rooke and Klein are less extreme in *Shakespeare's Dog* and *The Second Scroll*, but also respond to the limits of the repressive hypothesis and material signification. Hooker's vomit, in *Shakespeare's Dog*, leads him to theorize about the soul (32), inverting the order of the

Rabelaisian trope in which the metaphysical soul is deformed by the material signifier. Dirt and bodily anomaly evidently call attention to other levels of existence as Douglas (39) claims. The figure of the beast thus begins impossibly to think as if it had a human soul – 'Why Hooker?' (60) – but Hooker consistently refuses to make the grand cosmological claims that his namesake Richard Hooker made. In *The Second Scroll* the narrator's early attack on materialism is quite naïve: 'I brashly advanced *myself* as an example of spirituality – heckled only by the hybris of a Coca-cola belch – and damned all materialisms' (46). It is only by recovering the ex-temporized body in the Casablanca mellah and in Melech's analysis of the Sistine Chapel ('the flesh majuscule' 105) that the narrator can understand the double nature of his tradition: a (Jewish and Christian) tradition which, despite commandments to the contrary, is constantly representing God, even scatologically, and yet a tradition which refuses to finally trust natural representations. It refuses, as Greenstein says, the direct encounter (8). Despite the increasing will to glorify the body, the narrator cannot finally be shown Uncle Melech because Klein cannot finally allow any material signifier to stand in for the holy: 'It doffed the flesh that had been its first abode. Yet it persisted. It was the miracle of the Discarnation' (71).[35] Like Cohen and Rooke, Klein does not trust the scatological registers of twentieth-century material discourses – the soul is never simply a prison for the body – but neither does he intend to circle religious signification back to a naïve Puritan version of spirit; in the end the nature of representation itself, not just a particular religious discourse, comes under interrogation.

PART III

TWO STUDIES IN SCATOLOGY
AND LITERARY GENRE

Introduction

They attributed senses and passions ... to bodies ... Later, as these vast imaginations shrank and the powers of abstraction grew, the personifications were reduced to diminutive signs.

– Giambattista Vico, *Principii di una scienza nuova intorno alla natura delle nazioni*

If Mary Douglas is right to argue that dirt is the sign whereby people are excluded from participation in religious and social systems, my analyses in Part II – especially of religious materialism – have been intended to show how scatology is central to literary versions of social or religious patterning. Douglas would certainly agree that all symbolic systems, literature as much as religion, constitute themselves upon filth in some way. Or, following Vico's theory of mythography – which entails theories of mimesis and genre, of the subtle shifts between belief and sign, thing and representation – we might say that all symbolic systems require a 'prior' body from which to signify even if we do not take Vico's history of symbolism quite literally. Dirt, excrement, or the abject, then, are better spoken of as elements *within* the pattern which maintain the pattern.

I will not here attempt a broad defence of genre, but the next two chapters demand a few preliminary words. Jacques Derrida has enunciated the post-structural claim that genre falsifies any text. Ralph Cohen, defending genre, will therefore not say that a work belongs to a particular type, but will only cite the hermeneutic consequences of putting the work in that category (212). Attempts to isolate genres as if they were singulative systems that completely inhabit a text (for example Todorov's *The Fantastic* or Frye's *Anatomy of Criticism*) represent the victory of de Saussure's *langue* over *parole*, and are therefore extremely limited as tools to understanding the complex forces operating in particular texts and cultures. Reception theorists such as Jonathan Culler, with a looser version of *langue*, have done better – interpreting genre in the context of reader anticipation. This is roughly parallel to Marshall McLuhan's conception of genre as cliché, to Viktor Shklovsky's 'defamiliarization,' and to Roman Jacobson's application of frustrated expectation to poetic devices: 'The *langue* is a theoretical tool useful for explaining why and how *language* works,' and is not limited to intention (Eco 1987, 115, 118–19).

However, materialist and historicist critics know best what to say about reading habits. Fredric Jameson and Barbara Foley define genre as a social contract between a work and a particular public (R. Cohen 208; Foley 51).[1] Mikhail Bakhtin speaks of genres as historically determined languages (1981, 288),[2] and Hayden White's interdisciplinary studies of textuality show the presence of fictional genres even in historiography. 'Genre is the principle category by which we acknowledge the inescapable historicity of form itself' (McKeon 6), and as a counter-figure to Frye's heirophanic 'displacement,' Michael McKeon claims that genre 'emplaces' – it progressively specifies 'imaginative forms to the only locus of real meaning, the circumstantial and material reality of human experience' (10). He cites the key tension in the novel as that between 'the individual life and the overarching pattern[s]' (90) created by social, economic, scientific, and religious forces. Advertising, for example, markets even genre-breaking texts according to some category. The concept of 'genre' thus avoids the premature equation of the text (even the autobiographical text) with the ego of its author. If in Derrida's witty deconstruction of genre the desire to classify always manifests a fear of contagion (1980, 204), Maxmilian Novak extends and historicizes Derrida's logic to imply that the fear of genre also expresses a taboo; that taboo, we might add, is the interdiction of the avant-garde against traditionalist interpretations of culture.

'Mimesis inherently generalizes,' says Foley (65), but abstraction has its limits. As the exchange between Derrida and anthropology shows, even the most abstract of texts gesture back to the body, though I would hesitate to say just which taboos – speaking of one's mother-in-law or referring to excrement – Derrida means the reader to take as 'l'impureté, l'anomalie ou la monstruosité' (1980, 177; 'impurity, anomaly or monstrosity' 204). The uses to which an author puts scatology imply generic boundaries to a text, and this holds as true for the discourse that has come to be known as post-modernism as for discourses that rely on more traditional autobiographical conventions. Some theorists (Kroker, Calinescu, Lyotard, and Spariosu) are very reluctant to set post-modernism among other 'genres.' If post-modernism can be defined as 'anti-mimetic' (Calinescu 8), an 'incredulity toward metanarratives' (Lyotard xxiv, 37), or 'anti-allegorical' (Spariosu 61), post-modernism cannot generate a meta-narrative like *Bildung*.[3] Lyotard, however, clearly recognizes that post-modernism at most destroys the notion of a *grand* consensus, and still produces the 'petit récit' (98; 'little narrative' 60) or 'un *jeu* de langage' (66; 'language *game*'). I provisionally take as genre anything that calls itself or is called a genre, since each attribution of a category makes a historical claim. Thus, to simplify, those texts linked genetically by their refusal of a grand consensus I call post-modern. Unless we accept Kroker's (following Bataille's) melodramatic proclamation of the end of history, we may still speak of 'genres' even if we distrust the biological meta-narrative behind this trope.

Yet, according to Derrida's supplementary logic, my transgression occurs even earlier because post-modernism and autobiography overlap, so that all cases are already extra-legal. I nevertheless utilize the categories and set them against each other because of their argument about the relations between world and text (or body and text): the post-modernist has been accused of understanding the relations as wholly simulated, while the traditional autobiographer has been accused of believing in the possibility of a transliteration between the body and its other. But works such as Cohen's *Beautiful Losers* immediately exemplify the miscegenation that thwarts the study of genre. Even as the characters in the novel at points reveal their simulation by becoming interchangeable, the novel also relies on known details from the life of Cohen (his drug addiction most notably), and Cohen has made a more or less referential claim in an interview: '*Beautiful Losers* only sold one thousand copies when it came out. Then the landscape opens up as more people have a certain kind of experience' (Cohen in Twigg 57). Further complicating this refusal to stay on the level of the 'diminutive sign,' we might guess that 'a certain kind of experience' refers at least partly to the experience of media simulation.

In response to Derrida I would argue that here we have to do with history: to address a particular work as if it were completely co-extensive with a genre would confirm Derrida's suspicions, because such a supposition would incarcerate fiction prematurely in a ridiculously pure form of historical discourse; on the other hand, to exempt literature from genre by deconstructing genre is to exempt it from historical analogies and claims. If social structures are never exempt from taboos or codified laws, how can literature be wholly different? A refusal to speak of genres makes each text anomalous and ignores not only the impulses behind consumer categories, but also the absolute pervasiveness of parody – hosts and guests – in textual production. Since anomalous language operates upon the *conventions* of language, whether before or after J.L. Austin's 'serious' speech act, we may also expect that anomalous texts operate upon the *conventions* of language forms. If 'genres' do not belong to 'things in themselves,' genres at the very least belong to the reception of any speech act, to its historical context.

11

'Wen I de Small Man Sometime I Used to Eat Goat Shit': The Base and Written Self in Fictional Autobiography

Les autres forment l'homme; je le recite ... Je ne peints pas l'estre. Je peints le passage. (Others fashion man, I repeat him ... I describe not the essence, but the passage.)

– Montaigne, 'Du repentir' (Florio translation)

Seine Hauptklage war, das ... er durch einen Schleier von der Welt getrennt sei. Dieser Schleier zerriss nur in dem einen Moment, wenn beim Lavement der Darminhalt den Darm verliess, und dann fühlte er sich auch wieder gesund und normal. (His principal subject of complaint was that ... he was cut off from the world by a veil. This veil was torn only at one moment – when, after an enema, the contents of the bowel left the intestinal canal; and then he felt well and normal again.)

– Sigmund Freud, *Aus der Geschichte einer infantilen Neurose*

I forgot about constipation! Constipation didn't let me forget. Constipation ever since I compiled the list. Five days ruined in their first half-hours. Why me? – the great complaint of the constipated. Why doesn't the world work for me? The lonely man sitting on the porcelain machine. What did I do wrong yesterday? What unassailable bank in my psyche needs shit? How can I begin anything new with all of yesterday in me? The hater of history crouched over the immaculate bowl. How can I prove the body is on my side? ... Lost ordinary magic! The squatting man bargaining with God, submitting list after list of New Year's Resolutions. I will eat only lettuce ... Nothing helps, is that what you want me to learn? The straining man perched on a circle prepares to abandon all systems.

– the narrator of *Beautiful Losers*

i

We turn first to the fictionalizaton of a form in which the relation between body and text gestures at transparency, a 'real' form anticipated in the first references to manners books at the outset of this study. At the popular level of autobiography, the categorical claim of the autobiographer offers an almost unmediated translation of world into the text. What better way to refer to the world than by the sign of excrement: common to every body, the realist's old ploy, often private or censored (and therefore so convincingly the thing *outside* of the text); excrement appears to have been the last link between Freud's sadistic patient and the world. Even in detecting autobiographical lies or distortions, and especially in detecting omissions, the reader does not so much refuse the mimetic contract as confirm its premises, and as such, autobiography is a crucial link between literary studies and the more mimetic conventions of other disciplines, for example history. While it is premature to suggest as Karl Stich does that autobiography stands up against deconstruction, the rhetorical status of the genre depends upon the mimetic claim to 'worldliness,' and despite Paul de Man's warnings,[1] theorists such as Philippe Lejeune and John Paul Eakin correctly refuse to jettison the referential impulse entirely.[2] De Man argues that 'as soon as we understand the rhetorical function of prosopopeia as positing voice or face by means of language, we also understand that what we are deprived of is not life but the shape and the sense of a world accessible only in the privative way of understanding' (De Man 930). However, recent post-mortem intrusions into de Man's collaborationist past,[3] like researches into Frederick Philip Grove, make it impossible to ignore the private interest in the 'defacement' trope that de Man sets in contest with the 'voice from beyond the grave.' De Man's trope reveals a certain *autobiographical* ingenuity involved in the post-structural privation of the world, a calculated 'de-Manning' of World War II literary history. His theory of autobiography does not forget his personal past, even if he does.[4]

For Émile Benveniste discourse is, more broadly than for de Man or Stich, the arena in which man designates himself as a continuous *subject*, a 'unity that transcends the totality of actual experiences': 'Est "ego" qui *dit* "ego"' (260; '"Ego" is he who *says* "ego"' 224). Although the personal pronoun (in its referential shift with each individual speaker) does not take part in the same order of referentiality that other nominal objects do (218), Benveniste's mobilization of speech act theory to explain how each 'I' appropriates deictic markers ('here,' 'this,' 'now') for itself sets another kind of referential structure in place. In other words, the 'I' does not disappear in an autobiographical mask, but appropriates the speech of another to its own purposes (Benveniste 227), just as the adoption of a particular manner is not simply a disguise, but a method of becoming another. In fictional autobiography – the literary reorientation of autobiography, the representational claim is transposed to another level: no longer does the writer claim to report the affairs of a particular body, but rather claims a secondary artistic fidelity to certain types of experiences and bodies.

Because of this, the theoretical difference between a first person account and a third person limited omniscient account (or other third person forms for that matter) is not always a substantive difference. A strictly formalist definition such as Gérard Genette's autodiegesis (wherein the equation of narrator and character is the salient which distinguishes 'autobiography' from other texts) cannot, therefore, be maintained under pressure. We cannot *a priori* exclude novels such as *Under the Volcano, Yesterdays, Who Do You Think You Are?*, and *The River Horsemen*, which, though not in the first person, cross over significantly into the lives of their authors. As Lejeune says, 'Qui m'empêcherait d'écrire ma vie en me nommant "tu"?' (1975, 17; 'What would prevent me from writing my life's story and calling myself "you"?' 7). When Flo holds up a pair of stained shorts in *Who Do You Think You Are?*, glad to be able to signal decay and death, we cannot fully separate her act or her persona from Munro's mother who died of Parkinson's disease after a long illness, despite the autobiographical disclaimers that Munro and others employ.[5]

The third person 'alienation' of the narrative voice allows for more stable authorial ironies than does a first person voice, but it can also foster the illusion of a loss of agency. The mimetic level can accommodate both the discourse of fictional autobiography and theoretical discourse *about* autobiography, without forcing us (perhaps falsely) to follow Genette in differentiating mimesis from diegesis. An interesting case is Davies's essay 'In Pursuit of Pornography.' Davies's argument that a man's library is a portrait of the man – we must see *all* of a man's books, even his pornography to know him (264) – turns the library into a patient, with a conscious and a repressed self. But 'I' (unintentionally or intentionally) breaks down the rational tone of the objective authority psychoanalysing a culture even before the analysis is made. The elevated position from which the author looks at pornography (as evidence of certain social conditions) disintegrates as the subject matter comes to seem more and more a constituent of the writer's (and reader's) personal abjection, or, in other words, more and more a function of autobiography than of scientific investigation. Once the author says 'I' (and no writer can completely avoid this), the author, not any other matter, becomes the subject. 'There is now virtually no written form that has not either been included in some study of autobiography or else been subjected to autobiographical analysis' (Spengemann xii). We might go further: there is no writing which does not in some way disclose the subject. Works such as *The Collected Works of Billy the Kid*, with its photographs of a young Ondaatje in a cowboy outfit, and Cohen's *Beautiful Losers*, in which Cohen's final 'welcome to you who read me today' (260) parodies the forms of direct address, remind us that, despite the anti-realist constructions, post-modern texts carry biographies, however uneasily.

On the other hand, recent critical theory has taught us above all to be reluctant even to address the relations between the author's historical self and the textual representation of that self. 'Je est un autre,' Lejeune calls his book,[6] but we can get a much more emotionally charged sense of how opaque the mask of authorship is by looking at Ladoo's *Yesterdays*. There Tailor, whose name and whose habit of chronicling village 'affairs' (95) suggest that he is a persona for the author, unintentionally reveals something about his past to Ragbir:

'People shit is de wost kinda shit to smell,' Tailor said. 'Cow shit does smell nice. Horse shit does smell good too. Goat shit and sheep shit is nice shit to smell. But dog shit does stink like people own, you know boy Rag.'

'Korek.'

'You know wen I de small boy Rag, we de have a goat. Wen I de small man sometime I used to eat goat shit man Rag.'

'Wat make you stop?'

Realizing that he had said something about his past life, Tailor maintained a stony silence. (74)

The Base and Written Self 151

How are we to measure this confessional moment? Has Ladoo confessed a detail of his pre-Canadian past through a third person? Has he confessed in order to record the past or merely to shock his Canadian readers with the primitive? Is the relatively minor transgression of coprophagy a screen whereby Ladoo secretly confesses something unspeakable? More damaging to the *genre*, has he anything to confess at all? – couldn't he simply be playing with the reader who demands scandal? If Tailor makes a slip of the tongue, Ladoo, after all, does not speak: as the initial editor of his own graphic slips, Ladoo's cover-up can always precede even posthumous publication.

Instead of providing answers about Ladoo's life or attempting here what even full-scale biography has difficulty doing, I will limit myself mostly to fictional stagings of the autobiographical problem in order to see how particular authors address the problems of autobiography as a genre rather than by what complex processes they refer to their own lives outside of the text. For example, Ladoo's momentary autobiographical gesture addresses the problem of reportage and suppression, of how the written self represses and yet wants to confess filthy details about the body. Authorial practices can reveal particular lives – Eliot's dissociation of sensibility notwithstanding – but can only do so through a series of cultural and generic screens.

The example from *Yesterdays* suggests that everything said in Part I about personal and social histories – the formation of the self in reaction to filth, the doubling back into the country or the past to recover the body,[7] and the extreme scepticism which mistrusts even bodily signification – could be repeated as a background to how scatology constitutes the autobiographical subject. In fact, we could repeat each chapter from the rhetorical adoption of lower-class positions to the material reorientation of religious materials, so that each separate 'topic' becomes a simultaneous masking and divulging of the self.

If scatology can found symbolic systems by initiating a series of exclusions, we might expect it to function simultaneously as that system's base and as its photographic negative. In other words, without some reference to what is excluded neither the autobiographical subject nor the system within which he or she takes meaning can be intelligible, but the base reference threatens to destroy the logical integrity of the system simply by being present in the system's discourse about itself. We need not go to post-structuralism or post-modernism for versions of this paradox. In Canadian fictional autobiography a basic constituent of the written self is filth, which forms a 'base' self in both senses of the word. In *World of Wonders, Lives of Girls and Women,* and *The Story of Bobby O'Malley,* the authors create a 'base' self which is at once the fundament of the written self and the excremental version of the self that is rejected in the founding act.[8] 'Paul' in Davies's *World of Wonders* inherits a double body when he climbs inside the card-playing machine, 'Abdullah.' Echoing the Odyssean ruse, Paul calls himself 'Nobody,' and although the interior smells of urine, Abdullah becomes a hermetically safe body, a respite from Willard the 'arse-bandit' (61). Magnus, with the transcendence brought about by retrospect, a name change, and the actor's mask, ties his (oral) historical self-explanation to the disappearance of filth. During a performance he entertains the idea of throwing a full chamber-pot into the royal box (110), but his adoption of Sir John Tresize's persona prevents so gross a gesture; instead, Magnus learns how to say '"kiss my arse" *with class*' (181). Like St Augustine – 'I stank in Thine eyes' (*Confessiones* 2.23) – Magnus has come a long way from his 'foul' past, but we might expect that the transcendent location of the narrating self in Augustinian autobiography (Spengemann 1) would be negated by scatology in both of the two central topoi marking the fictional autobiographer's base self: these topoi are 'the scatological body as dead self' and 'confession as purgation.'[9] By pursuing these and other scatological peculiarities (such as those marking the suppression of information and the mechanism of projection) we can see how a particular 'thematic' can signal the world and yet dismantle the very structure that makes theme intelligible.[10]

ii
The Dead Self

'À [la technique punitive] de reconstituer l'infime et le pire dans la form du savoir' (*sic* 1975, 255; 'It falls to the punitive technique ... to reconstitute all the sordid details of a life in the form of knowledge' 219), asserts Foucault, connecting biography, the history of manners, the human sciences, and criminology. As readers of confessional autobiographies know, such attempts at making not only a crime but an abject narrated life answer to the knower (God, or a later converted self) occur long before the eighteenth century. In the twentieth century, confessions of a dead self are necessarily more oblique and less pious. Munro's *Lives of Girls and Women* obviously exposes a trauma about the self and not about the lives of cows when Del Jordan reports her own overbearing and pollutive reaction to the dead cow. She wants to 'pee on it, anything to punish it' for being dead (38), and later realizes that 'to be made of flesh was humiliation' (48).

Not uncoincidentally in the same chapter, 'Heirs of the Living Body,' Del is able to define her status as a writer and to distinguish her own voice from the voice that her aunts want her to imitate, the dead historical voice in Uncle Craig's manuscript. Dead Uncle Craig is something like a dead cow, an abject version of the self; this must be so because Del senses enough of a personal stake to refuse to see the body of her relative. What is this but confession? On the other hand, Del's pleasure at seeing that Uncle Craig's manuscript (posthumously given into Del's care) has become waterlogged requires a less communitarian explanation. The fate of Uncle Craig's body signals her own body; the fate of Uncle Craig's composition signals nothing about her own compositions. Why? For Del, at least, the fate of the written self must evidently be distinguishable (almost romantically so) from the abject fate of the body, and the written self is for her less a question of shared discourse than (also romantically) of individual 'style.' These premises are not treated ironically in 'Heirs of the Living Body,' but Munro does interrogate them in the 'Epilogue.' Until Del begins to theorize about the relations between her life and her text, writing is stable and distinct from the body, an early separation that may grow out of the problem of gender: Del cannot afford a great deal of fellow-feeling when her anxiety of (at this point) male influence is paramount.[11]

The scatological association of the self with the dead body is less stable in Johnston's *The Story of Bobby O'Malley*. The O'Malley septic tank is 'the size of a coffin' (13), and the sewage hose used to empty the tank becomes the first vortex for Bobby's existential fears: 'It'll suck ye right inside, an' no-one'll know ye ever lived' (14). 'My father told me to remember that I got older every time I flushed the toilet. I imagined what it was like inside the tank ... "Dark and foul" my father said, "dark and foul"' (15). The retrospective narrator understands the bathroom as the site of disillusionment and of the beginning of Bobby's fears that his father will desert the family. In the bathroom, Bobby's father tells Bobby that he is going bowling when he really plans to see Harold's mother. Bobby, sensing a repeated deception, forces his father to let him help plan elaborate bowling strategies in the bathroom.

But there is a certain speciousness about speaking of time, process, and beginnings in autobiography. Can the written event be isolated outside of its retrospective emplotment? Given the later associations of the father's apparent suicide and the toilet, it is not by chance that Bobby begins his own story with sewage and the dead self. On the day that Bobby follows his mother around, hoping to find clues to the secret of her being, he wants to depend upon a Freudian epistemology in which identity is marked materially and scatologically by repression: 'I hoped that, when no-one was looking, she would give herself away – pick her nose, or scratch her backside, or put a roll of candy in her pocket and walk out without paying' (155). Johnston is not hesitant to admit the limits of this epistemology when Bobby's mother does not give him the required sign and Bobby fails (perhaps inevitably given his epistemology) to understand her. Johnston, inverting Augustine, 'converts' Bobby out of the priesthood and into secular society. However, in Geoffrey Harpham's reading of Augustine, the mode of conversion – particularly as a species of writing – can never include a prior state. 'The fact that we are never free from impingement by the "word of another" leads to [a] quarrel with Vance (and with almost every other reader of Augustine's), this time in his claim that conversion can be assigned to a definite temporal moment ... No moment of consciousness is "pre-conversion." Nor, we must remember, does the subject ever achieve a "post-conversional" condition' (Harpham 48). Harpham argues that the always-prior condition of language (the word of another) is too near the meaning of Augustine's conversion (impingement by the word of another) to allow for proper conceptual differentiation. Spengemann analyses Books 1 to 9 of the *Confessiones* in a similar way: 'While the protagonist believes that he is going to the Manichees to find the truth, the narrator knows that he really went in order to become disillusioned with them' (Spengemann 8). While the protagonist of *The Story of Bobby O'Malley* believes that he is gravitating towards the priesthood because his mother knows the truth about the world, the narrator knows that he went in order to become disillusioned with the church. The retrospective Bobby, who relies on Ted's epistemology, does not for a moment believe in Bobby the potential vicar of Christ. A primary justification for autobiography is the representation of change through time, but the 'new' self always shows up 'back there' (at almost every moment) in the graphic past to make teleological sense of the 'old' self. The 'panopticon,' we might say, is not the exclusive tool of the state or a religious tradition, but also a tool in counter-epistemologies and sceptical surveyors of penal architecture.

This is important in novels such as *Fifth Business* where self-making and myth-making are inextricably bound. Filth runs counter to miracle and myth, and it is the image of the rotting corpse that Dunstan Ramsay must best in the case of his brother Willie's 'stubborn retention' (58) of urine. Urine signals death because if Willie cannot expel his waste he will become it;[12] but the autobiographer's deck is already stacked against urine and death: by presenting Mary Dempster's role in Willie's cure first (before Ramsay's 'conversion' to her and before a rational explanation) Ramsay's temporal rhetoric favours the miracle as an objective event.

This is true in *The Story of Bobby O'Malley* as well. The early association between the mother's puritanical embracing of sterilization and Bobby's isolation very quickly signifies that Bobby has adopted the maternal persona, but ought not have. Yet the presentation of 'Bobby' – in formalist terms Johnston's *machine* – has already ensured that the puritanical self is merely a screen for the apparently *later* (but already planned) secular conversion. The real issue is the provenance of the father's filth (not the mother's hygiene) in Bobby's father-bound voice. Indeed, autobiography presents to psychoanalysis a need for a conception of 'screen memory' that can account for the retrospective encoding of experience. While 'screen memory' is usually a trope for how retrospective analysis can unlock a repressed past, scatology in *The Story of Bobby O'Malley* has never really been repressed, and rather shows us how the retrospective act itself skews the earlier memories towards its own teleology. To maintain the unity of the autobiographical subject, the late conversion must be shown by the autobiographer *in potentia*. Although lives may change, prolepsis prevents those changes from being fully mirrored in narrative. Therefore: sewage in the beginning.

Sewage in the beginning is located in the father at the end, and the emphasis on scatology marks Bobby's attempt to recapture his father's sceptical mode of expression, indeed, to become Ted O'Malley by turning Ted's eight-chapter outline of the innocently titled *Our Memoirs* into *The Story of Bobby O'Malley*. Bobby discovers that his father has apparently been flushing the familial autobiography down the toilet as each page was completed. The dead self thus circumscribes a greater area than it does for Del, extending even into writing. On the back of the outline, Bobby finds several pencilled notes:

'What is more final than flushing the toilet? Do this in memory of me' and 'The book is a pound of flesh on every page' (184). The deformation of Christian language suggests an alternative to the hagiographic models of the gospels, under which Agnes has tried to set Bobby's life. Ted's dialogic recasting of religious language informs the novel at its deepest level, and the toilet becomes the medium of Bobby's secular conversion. Bobby takes the videotape of his father, his mother's hair (saved from her premarital celibacy), and the St Joseph's beard that he was once forced to wear – relics all – and burns them in the toilet:[13]

> The bowl was blazing as if hell itself was backing up inside the pipes ... On my knees I had to keep my face back from the flame and reach around it with my arm to flush the toilet. Eyes burning from the smoke, my forehead hot, I somehow found the handle and pushed it down. As the water rushed in, the flames started going round and going out at the same time. The water ate in from the outer edge until only the core of flame was left, an island getting smaller, going round and round and down. Finally, there was just one central spark which, with the water at the bottom, seemed to turn inside out, then vanished. (186)

Without the transcendental location of self driving traditional autobiography, which because of its spiritual program is no longer available to Ted, the possibility of ontological defeat becomes a potential trap for Bobby. Given the likelihood that his father's death was suicide, the relations between central sparks and authoritative models of the self have implications beyond rhetoric. To return Bobby's 'life' to the scene of the body, Johnston has him get drunk and then purge his insides into the same toilet. For Johnston the repressed self asserts itself against Bobby's rational self: 'It's probably true that, as Little Laurence said, I paused between regurgitations to communicate a marked, if heretofore well hidden aversion to clerical life' (189).

Thus Bobby's life; not thus the writing of it: the demands for artistic coherence are such that any single text describes a state, not a process. To the scandal of referentiality, Bobby's scatology insists that the aversion never was hidden, and that even a conversion to the body requires a 'transcendent' narrator, one who can see eternal patterns at work. It would be inaccurate to say that Bobby has abandoned all systems.

iii
Confession

These scenes near the end of *The Story of Bobby O'Malley* also rely on another topos in the abject identification of the self: confession as scatological. The association between purification and purgation, much older than Rabelais's satire against monks, perhaps helps to explain Freud's sadistic patient and his literal-minded need for enemas.[14] 'I lack the confessional spirit' (*The Manticore* 23), says Davies's often cruel David Staunton, 'my nature is a retentive, secretive one' (43). The cliché of 'dumping on someone' (Findley,*The Telling of Lies* 18) is a popular and offhanded version of this, but the topos becomes more central in works such as Williams's *Eye of the Father*, where Wayne Goodman must acknowledge that the pollutive sins of the grandfather exist in his own personality before the narrative can come to a comic resolution. Likewise, Smart's *The Assumption of Rogues and Rascals* builds towards a confession of inner abjection, but the triple evacuations of excrement, child, and writing conveniently allow Smart to claim experience as more important than literary structure. The scatological implications are shifted away from the lonely, the pollutive, the forced, the haemorrhoidal, towards the relational, as the act of excretion is transferred from the writer to the baby through the metaphor of the necessary diaper.

Although I hesitate to equate any sign directly with a moral function, there are hints that a depersonalized scatology or a lack of scatology can point to an incomplete confession. In Grove's *A Search for America* Philip's 'lack of condescension to everyday slang' (3) seems modified when he enters the foul-smelling lavatory in the basement of the restaurant where he works (41). Throughout his autobiography, Philip implies that he is in the process of both dirtying himself in America and giving away terrible secrets about himself, yet someone else always seems to either be responsible or provide an alibi for his shortcomings. The structuring of the moment of descent is symptomatic of Philip's (and perhaps Grove's) maintenance of a transcendental version of the self: Philip assimilates the lavatory to an epic pattern of descent into the underworld, so that he retains his aristocratic bearing (and alibi) in a formal sense. A more thoroughgoing elision occurs at the end of *The Telling of Lies*. Findley has his detective, Vanessa Van Horne, 'confess' her own role in the 'collective lie' (288) that contributed to Calder Maddox's murder. Her confession rings hollow because she is not implicated in any bodily, material, or personal way. The novel tends towards a moral dimorphism between class authorities and innocent victims.

While conclusions based on absences are at best hypothetical, some writers have more consciously enacted instances where the repression of filth points to problems in autobiographical reportage. Hagar, in *The Stone Angel*, wets her sheets every night for several months, but does not 'remember' this in her narrative (73–4); Laurence's disclosure of this through Doris changes the shape of the narrative from Hagar's autobiographical sense of herself as a victim to a more ambiguous structure in which writing is not circumscribed by the first person. For this instance we might rename the 'panopticon' as the tool of consciousness, self-scrutiny. In *Running in the Family*, Ondaatje's sisters are so embarrassed that for fifteen years they will not speak of their grandmother Lalla urinating behind the bushes on Parents' Day (124). The gap in the autobiographer's reportage in both cases is exactly that which the self represses in order to become civilized, and in order to have access to record-keeping languages.

iv
Dirty Shadows

Compared to the problem of the gap, projection is more easily identified. David Staunton dreams of wiping the filth off his father's (Percy Boyd Staunton's) face and uncovering there his own face as a child (*The Manticore* 98). Elsewhere, Adrian Pledger-Brown draws up an appropriate heraldic device for the Stauntons and then calls it '*anitergium* ... a trifle, a sketch, something disposable. Well actually the monks used it for the throwouts from the scriptorium which they used for bumwipe' (237). Although the former image is 'psychological' and the latter is 'external' to David, their symbolic collusion in an autobiography points to the teller's sense of abjection. Davies plays these projective signs against David's tendency to disavow evil. For example, David reduces his own role in an incident of vandalism by emphasizing how Bill Unsworth defecates on somebody's photographs: 'As he struggled, red-faced and pop-eyed, and as he appeared at last with a great stool dangling from his apelike rump, I regained my senses and said to myself ... "Why is he doing that?" The destruction was simply a prelude to this. It is a dirty, animal act of defiance and protest against – well, against what?' (168) In Davies's Jungian scheme, projection of course heralds the beginning of self-knowledge, as the subject separates himself from the shadow. Scatology thus becomes the signal cue for self-construction, and Dr von Haller interprets David's dream of his father's backside as an unmasking of David's *internalized* authorities, especially the one nominated 'Judge Staunton.'

Father, fear, bear; Davies is unwilling to fully dematerialize them into a Law of the Father or into David himself, 'devourer' of witnesses (278). Even so, it is not clear at the end of the narrative whether a real bear or an archetype has confronted David in the dark cave. In any case, David's 'second birth' (evidently meant as a psychoanalytic representation of the child filling the birth canal with meconium) involves David's recognition that the stinking backside belongs not to his father or to a bear, but to himself: 'The terrible stench that filled the tunnel was my own' (304). The fluidity of exchange between internal and external is a basic psychoanalytic principle, but this process of creating symbols of the self (even out of one's excrements) is at once basic to and disruptive of autobiography. If excrement, which more than anything ought to refer to real things and actual deeds in their chaotic, unidealized existence, if even excrement inevitably takes the guise of one more symbol of the self, then the aspect of autobiography that promises to refer to the world is compromised. If excrement cannot even signify the world, what can?

The problem of how reportage is affected by projection is increased for Davies by the time of *What's Bred in the Bone*, the fictional biography of Francis Cornish. 'The Looner,' who farts loudly and masturbates in public, is not only a figure for what exists before manners, but as Cornish's older brother and indeed the original Francis Cornish, the Looner specifically becomes the 'first self' for the other, later Francis. Once the hidden filthy double is discovered, he becomes a central feature in Cornish's anachronistic art.

This can hardly surprise us, given what we have seen of doubling back, but who among the literate narrates the Looner's history? Other private histories in the novel press towards the same question. At the beginning of the novel Cornish avoids shaking hands: 'Said he could smell mortality on his hand when it touched somebody else's. When he absolutely had to shake hands with some fellow who didn't get his clear signals, he would shoot off to the washroom as soon as he could and wash his hands' (6–7). By the end we know why Cornish's compulsive behaviour occurs. Before he to all intents and purposes killed Jean-Paul Letzpfennig, Cornish had to shake Letzpfennig's 'unpleasantly damp' (420) hand, and Cornish 'wished he could wash the corpse-sweat from his right hand' (421). Darcourt reports Cornish's words in the first instance (6-7), but who vouchsafes the unspoken scatological details of the second? In yet another scene, Cornish's schoolfellows 'catch a frog, stick a straw up its cloaca, and blow it up to enormous size. As the frog swelled, there was a delightful apprehension that it might burst. There was an even more splendid hope that the boy who was blowing might, if enough funny things were said to him, stop blowing for a moment and suck and then – why, he might even die, which would richly crown the fun. Frank's eyes were on the frog, whose contortions and wildly waving legs pierced his heart with a vivid sense of the sufferings of Jesus' (96-7). We might say that the language divides neatly between the cadences of a good-humoured aristocrat and the limited sensibilities of young boys, or in a different vein, that Davies here strangely reverses Bakhtin's dialogic so that the myth of the incarnation is confirmed by what we would expect to read parodically – a suffering frog.

But again, who or what narrates? Apparently a filmlike machine that the daimon Maimas and the angel of biography, the Lesser Zadkiel, have access to. The biographer's problem, especially in a post-phenomenological age – of being limited only to Cornish's external contacts with the world – initially seems exactly opposite to that of the autobiographer, but Davies, unlike Cornish's biographer Simon Darcourt, requires Cornish to think and sense in the first person. The quirky use of Maimas and Zadkiel implies a lack of confidence in the omniscient narrator, the traditional formal solution to the problem of insider knowledge. Maimas and Zadkiel, instead of solving the problem in a new way, are *dei*, literally *ex machina*, and their omniscience – limited to Francis Cornish – thus produces autobiography in the third person even though they claim not to know the full truth about Cornish. Darcourt rationalizes theology (including Maimas and Zadkiel) as a type of medieval psychological science, while Davies apparently means to criticize Darcourt by means of Maria Cornish, who refuses to modernize her language. Italicized, outside of the main narrative, Maimas and Zadkiel approach the old, omniscient narrator; yet, inside of the main narrative, they are nothing more or less than Francis Cornish to the point where they paradoxically confirm Darcourt's rationalizing against Davies's irony. In this *reductio*, the

The Base and Written Self 161

scatological details of the private body push the narrative towards a singulative point of view and, what is more crucial in the wake of discourse theory, towards a singulative vision: that of Davies, call him Maria Cornish (who picks up her archaic language from other Davies novels), call her Simon Darcourt (who with qualifications adopts her terms), call him Maimas and the Lesser Zadkiel (who appear as soon as Darcourt speaks their names), call them Francis Cornish (whose thoughts are accessible to daimons and angels), call him Davies (for whom anachronism and the precivilized Looner are the substance of art). We are left with the same problem of projection, not just in the characters, but in the formal choices of the author.

Scatological details, initially worldly gestures that separate the text from the world, just as often trap, or at least bracket, the world phenomenologically within the pattern of one self. We revisit, one last time, the interrogative mood of this chapter: 'Qui est-ce qui *dit* "Qui suis-je?"' (Lejeune 1975, 119; 'Who is it who *says* "Who am I?"' 8). The bodily details that structure the 'inside' of a narrative are used in such a way that they cannot help but dismantle the system of 'external' references.

12

Post-Modern Decomposition: Guaranteeing the World of an Indeterminate Text

Don't despise things.

– Saraceni in *What's Bred in the Bone*

Es gab überhaupt keine Dinge in Grenouilles innerem Universum, sondern nur die Düfte von Dingen. (There were no real things at all in Grenouille's innermost universe, only the odors of things.)

– Patrick Süskind, *Das Parfüm*

L'écriture, c'est ce neutre, ce composite, cet oblique où fuit notre sujet, le noir-et-blanc où vient se perdre toute identité, à commencer par celle-là même du corps qui écrit. (Writing is that neuter, that composite, that obliquity into which the subject flees, the black and white where all identity is lost, beginning with the very identity of the body that writes.)

– Roland Barthes, 'La mort de l'auteur'

The Romantic creator, as originating and original source of meaning, may well be dead, as Barthes argued years ago, but the creator's *position* – a position of discursive authority – remains, and increasingly is the self-conscious focus of much contemporary art.

– Linda Hutcheon, *A Theory of Parody*

i

If in discussing autobiography I appear to have succumbed to the logic of Paul de Man – asking for Newton's autobiography and then feigning surprise when scatology disappoints a solar system of the objectified self – I hope it will become clear that I mean this reading to take place within the ambidextrous (if I may coordinate human bodies with celestial) theory of Lejeune, who notices that writing is to some extent always an alibi, but that this does not automatically make autobiography non-referential. Barthes's *'mort de l'auteur'* and his later sense of textual pleasure,[1] like Baudrillard's recent discussions of the media, depend on a sliding non-systematic form of reference and contain assumptions about mimesis that are clearly at odds with the dominant assumptions in most fictional autobiographies. But if scatology lets the autobiographer articulate a scepticism which destroys the referential certainties within the *Bildungs* genre, it is worth asking several questions of the post-modern: Is scatology as a trope then inherently allied with post-modern scepticism? Or does scatology undermine the conventions of even sceptical and ironic genres? In other words, instead of here blaming post-modernism for its political significations as Jürgen Habermas, Fredric Jameson, Terry Eagleton, and Barbara Foley do,[2] I want to extend Linda Hutcheon's 'on the other hand' – arguing, like she does, that post-modern texts question referentiality and subjecthood, but only from *within* history and the subject (Hutcheon 1988b, 19).

What is post-modernism? For many theorists, post-modernism sets itself equally against modernism and realism (Lyotard 75; Pache 76; Kroker 15; Hutcheon 1988, 4, 149; Bowering 1982, 79–81). Theorists often come up against the difficulty that the specific techniques used to define post-modernism – the pleasure of the fragmentary, the blurring of genre boundaries, the blurring of boundaries between art and life, the distrust for totalizing languages, the play on surfaces, and scepticism about 'depth' – are not new. Some theorists, as a result, expand the definition to the point of inutility: Arthur Kroker locates the crisis of representation in St Augustine, calling him the first post-modernist and equating Augustine's 'closing of the eye of the flesh' with Bataille's 'pineal eye' (Kroker 28). Lyotard insists that post-modernism precedes modernism, and is in fact modernism in its nascent moment (79) – when modernism breaks with the real 'à presenter qu'il y a de l'imprésentable' (1982, 364; 'to present the fact that the unpresentable exists' 78) and before modernist fragments project a nostalgia for realist totalities. Postmodernism thus becomes a synonym for all avant-gardes.

An alternative theoretical strategy involves defining modernism narrowly and totally as a pure break with history (Hutcheon 1988, 4) and as an escape into the world of symbol. This approach emphasizes modern architecture (Hutcheon 1988, 26), and de-emphasizes contingency in modernist literature. In a modernist text such as Sheila Watson's *The Double Hook*, the language is often entirely double: 'Coyote made the land his pastime. ... He breathed on the grass. His spittle eyed it with prickly pear' (22) or '[James] smelt the stench of Coyote's bedhole' (43). The language is purely symbolic (since Watson does not put a literal faith in Native mythology) and yet edged with bodily contingencies. The symbolic language makes discourse (not reality) the primary constituent of the 'novel,' creating serious opacities for those not familiar with the compressions of Imagism. It is therefore true to say that the principle of order is 'not in the sequence of historical time or the evolving sequence of character ... as in realism or naturalism; [modernist writers] tend to work spatially or through layers of consciousness, working toward a logic of metaphor or form' (Bradbury and McFarlane 50). Yet the consistent attribution of filth to the creator Coyote implies a primary 'real' world antecedent to the text; this invalidates the associated claim that the modernist novel flees from 'material realism' or that 'language ceases to be what we see through, and becomes what we see' (Fletcher and Bradbury 401). Both the metropolitan language of modernism and the dirty farmyard in *The Double Hook* qualify each other's precedence. The characters are eventually redeemed by the old Christian symbols (spoken anew by Felix), but to focus only on this would be to ignore the historical contingency of incarnated characters who are at the mercy of Canadian settlement patterns.

My purpose, however, is not to affirm or create a particular definition of post-modernism. Some elements, such as the emphasis on surfaces, can seem deceptively simple, especially to those critics who make political arguments against certain *styles* of representation.[3] But I would be hesitant to jettison any of these definitions: even Kroker is useful in showing that simulation was not invented in the 1970s or by Beckett.[4] Since many of these definitions are included in Hutcheon's claim that post-modern texts question referentiality and subjecthood, and since this claim marks what I see as post-modernism's most insistent historical departure, it is her definition that I will rely on the most. Hutcheon does not allow Richard Rorty's and Michel Riffaterre's contention that the referential status of fiction is entirely different from the referential status of history (1988, 143, 148): 'The familiar humanist separation of art and life (or human imagination and order *versus* chaos and disorder) no longer holds' (1988, 7). I suspect that these 'separations' reappear (if in altered form) in post-modernism, but my scope is quite limited: if autobiographical scatology (intended to be stable) eventually decomposes assurances about the narrated world, it is conversely possible that post-modern scatology, often intended as a destabilizer, also unintentionally guarantees a stable system of references.

ii

Post-modernism does not entirely succeed in overcoming structuralist binaries, but in each case we must initially agree with Hutcheon that post-modern scatological parody can destabilize older authoritative narratives. Mary Douglas argues that 'dirt was created by the differentiating activity of mind, it was a by-product of the creation of order' (161). Thus the ritual pollution described in Leviticus signifies both the chaos before creation and the dissolution to come, while the taboos were intended to support the Genesis narrative of an ordered creation. Theorists of parody emphasize how scatology destroys the founding narratives of Western culture – Jewish, Christian, Platonic, all of them patriarchal. Kristeva (1982, 4; 1987, 368) and Kroker (134) follow Bataille's sense of parody articulated in 'L'anus solaire': 'Il est clair que le monde est purement parodique ... Le globe terrestre est couverte de volcans qui lui servent d'anus. Bien que ce globe ne mange rien, il rejette parfois audehors le contenu de ses entrailles ... répandant partout la mort et la terreur ... Je suis le Jésuve, immonde parodie du soleil torride et aveuglant' (I.81–6; 'It is clear that the world is purely parodic ... The terrestrial globe is covered with volcanoes, which serve as its anus. Although the globe eats nothing it often violently ejects the contents of its entrails ... spreading death and terror everywhere ... I am the *Jésuve*, the filthy parody of the torrid and blinding sun' 5–9). When Cixous argues that female writing cannot be defined because it is 'against theory,' that female language wrecks 'les cloisonnements, classes et rhétoriques, ordonnances et codes' ('Méduse' 48; 'partitions, classes, and rhetorics, regulations and codes' 256), she too uses scatology: 'pulsion orale, pulsion anale, pulsion vocale, toutes les pulsions sont nos bonnes forces' (52; 'oral drive, anal drive, vocal drive – all these drives are our strengths' 261). Even theorists who have no interest in post-modernism acknowledge the dislocating power of the grotesque (P. Thompson 18).

In Canadian post-modernism, as in John Barth's *Giles Goat Boy* (with the Mathematical Psycho-Proctocologist Max Spielman) or in Thomas Pynchon's *The Crying of Lot 49* (with the W.A.S.T.E. mail system), scatology parodically devalues cultural conventions. Leon Rooke, for example, deflects the reader's gaze from the classic Shakespearean text and its attendant chain of the writer's metaphysical authority, focusing on what was evidently repressed – Shakespeare's dog's life. The material and grotesquely sensual dog's autobiography trades the high ritual agony of kings for the sniffing of turds, and thrusts a grotesque body upon The Greatest English Writer Of All Time, who has unceremoniously been banished to the periphery of the text. Moreover, Rooke's formal inversions trade the well-made plot for intimate descriptions of Hooker at stoole, and Hooker not always prepared to find a systematic coherence in his actions: '"Why did you leak there?" she said. "Oh I wish I understood you accursed dogs." I kept quiet. If I had to give brain to every act, as she did hers, I'd soon be knitted up like a stew!' (125). Since Old John Shakespeare predicts the imparking of the world (44), the only way out of systematic enclosures, it seems, is to live as a dog.

If Rooke's Hooker can undermine the English cleric who turns the caprice of a divorce-eager king into pious order and good ecclesiastical government, dog nevertheless has his own implied principles of order: 'Man's upright and he takes his news from that' (33), says Hooker, of course hinting that dog is four-footed and 'takes his news from that.' At one level, *Shakespeare's Dog* must therefore necessarily be the simplest of inversions: the 'smooth and impenetrable surface' of the classical body (Bakhtin 1984, 317) exchanged for the filthy body.

This occurs biographically and discursively. The image of the classic, quoted Shakespeare is broken up by the knowledge that it eventually takes 'a dog's wide learning' to make Shakespeare a 'play-spinner' (47) – Shakespeare reduced to the sum of Hooker's gathered knowledge.[5] The images inherited from biblical discourse are refracted through matter: a 'dog returning to his vomit' is no longer mainly the vehicle of a metaphor or mainly proverbial, but is treated mimetically as a sensual *event*. Rooke satirizes (and reverses) traditional Judeo-Christian cosmology in which spirit animates inert matter by fiat, parodying, as we have seen in Chapter 10, metaphysical explanations of the soul. Arguing from vomit, the tangible insides, Hooker postulates that fifth bodiless 'element' – the quintessence or 'soul' (32). This is a crucial moment in the education of Rooke's Shakespeare, who is something of a sceptic.

Crucial for *us* is Rooke's substitution of vomit for soul at the original moment. Even though Hooker does not trust human materialism, the material and mimetic qualities of filth have the central role here in administering a shock to Christian metaphysics. Of course, this mimetic centre does not cover all there is to Rooke's post-modernism. The parodic inversion of Proverbs does not so much reverse the spiritualizing tendencies of Jewish folk wisdom as write another account over or beside Proverbs. Rooke's sense of scatological representation writes over the past in two divergent ways: the imitative and the fabular. On the one hand, by describing the treading of phlegm underfoot (91), Rooke clearly strives for historical accuracy about the difference in bodily minutiae between the sixteenth century and the present. Erasmus, in *De civilitate morum puerilium*, says that 'the polite way is to catch the matter from the nose in a handkerchief, and this should be done by turning away slightly if decent people are present. If, in clearing your nose with two fingers, some matter falls on the ground, it should be immediately ground under foot' (275). Rooke's mimetic gesture thus argues against Eagleton's claim that history is what 'post-modernism must at all costs efface' (68). On the other hand, the fable of origins comprised in 'why Shakespeare came to London' (to save Hooker from the Regarders) depends upon a tactical disregard for history. These contradictions – referential parody and destabilizing parody – are not the poles of post-modern discourse, but the nucleus.[6]

Like Rooke to Shakespeare, Findley gets to Noah 'first,' before the original collectors and the priestly redactors. 'Middenites' (*Not Wanted on the Voyage* 22) and 'the rain of Onan' (130) thus get material significations 'before' they are systematically politicized and moralized by Judaism and Christianity as 'Midian' and 'onanism.' Findley's central focus is on how a new dispensation allegorized the master drama of the world's salvation, and Findley applies filth as a solvent for the transcendent battle between Yaweh and Lucifer. Late in the novel, a demon grows hot and bright in its nether regions, while Lucy holds its paws the way a mother might hold the hands of a child having 'a difficult moment on the pot' (301). This parody of toilet training domesticates the demonic realm, and although we might be tempted to read the scene as a slaughter of the referents (both of Christian dualism and of realism), the parody of mother and child also has a humanizing effect. Indeed, fabular scatology paradoxically becomes a kind of realist ploy; the gap made by the dispersal of transcendental meaning is 'always already' filled by more 'natural' subjects – little demons on the potty, and cats. When Mottyl, the cat who narrates, discovers the dead dog Bip with his crown of flies, she prays for him and leaves her 'heat-infested traces' nearby (56–7). The adoption of a cat's point of view does *not* disperse the human subject. The animal in fact fulfils the anti-ideal emphasis of liberal humanism and the broadening egalitarian scope of the civilized self. The characters in *Not Wanted on the Voyage* and *Shakespeare's Dog* are marked as to whether they care for or mistreat the dirty beast-narrators. As in *Shakespeare's Dog*, the fabular in *Not Wanted on the Voyage* therefore does not destroy history even though Findley's social history – that of the late-twentieth-century animal rights – is less self-conscious than Rooke's.

The realist confidence that matter, particularly filthy matter, is more authentic than a religious code, and the humanist confidence that the thing is more honest than the miracle appears often in Findley's work. As if to guarantee honesty, Findley has Vanessa Van Horne lose control of her bladder while weeping for her dead father in *The Telling of Lies*. Weeping, it seems, can be feigned, abject urination cannot – very much a referential faith. Reference is much more complex in *Famous Last Words* because Mauberley, Ezra Pound's text, cannot always be taken as analogous to a real person. Against Lieutenant Quinn's defence of Mauberley's mythological writing, Captain Freyberg attacks with the fury of historical reference: 'It's not the Trojan War I don't believe in ... it's the Trojan horseshit' (150). Freyberg's serious critique of fiction as devious and false is made all the more powerful because of Mauberley's implication in Fascist plotting and, by extension, in Dachau.

But Freyberg's desire, according to Quinn, is for blank walls. This is another sort of aestheticism, which admits the filthy in human beings, but does not allow for the soiling of walls and pages. The scatological terms of Freyberg's denunciation of Mauberley – 'He's beginning to smell, isn't he' (149) – initially work *against* Freyberg. Mauberley, after all, has been smelling since the beginning of the novel, where we first saw him in rotted underwear fleeing the Allies (4). The 'smell' there served to humanize Mauberley according to the dictates of Findley's novelistic representation (as opposed to Pound's arcane poetic dialect). Findley shifts Pound's Mauberley from a satiric figure to a character for whom we can feel bodily sympathy, especially given the wholesale transgressions against his fastidiousness. In other words, for the length of Mauberley's dispossession Findley gives him a body which suggests victimhood. Such an attribution is heavily referential in a humanist direction – even Fascists have feelings. Scatology therefore becomes Findley's material concession to Freyberg's overstable sense of historical reference. If Hutcheon shows how post-modernism 'de-natures' (1989, 2), we can see in these references how it 'natures.' But, of course, Mauberley's ahistorical status puts all this in post-modern brackets, since we know that despite the traces of a real body Mauberley is always only *figura*. *Famous Last Words* is post-modern not because it erases reference, but because it places human affect and the body very consciously within the context of what can only be a simulated reality and a simulated subject.

iii

Here we are no longer precisely dealing with the scatological corrosion of master narratives. Rooke and Findley both point us in two directions: first, the 'text' reaches so far into the 'world' that it infects the world with its own radical disembodiment; in other words, the world is no longer the world, but becomes a tangent to itself. Conversely, the references to filth could become *so* corrosive that they not only destroy ideal structures, but also the realist faith in matter. In theory we can distinguish between the two directions. The first phenomenologically brackets the world within a somewhat ideal theory of discourse. In the second, 'heterogeneous matter' is so repulsive that it resists 'not only the idealisms of Christians, Hegelians, and surrealists, but even the edifice building of traditional materialists ... Bataille precisely recognizes that the *fall* of the elevated and noble threatens the coherent theory of allegory itself ... At the *end* of reason, at the *end* of man, at the *end* of the Cartesian pineal gland (the supposed seat of consciousness) there is only organism and a simultaneous fall, a simultaneous death' (Stoekl xi–xiv).[7] Bataille says that Gnosticism, for example, attributes 'la création de la terre où a lieu notre agitation répugnante et dérisoire à un principe horrible et *parfaitement illégitime*' ('Le bas matérialisme et la gnose' I.223; 'the creation of the earth, where our repugnant and derisory agitation takes place, to a horrible and *perfectly illegitimate* principle' 47). Taking heresiological polemic quite literally, Bataille maintains that a being obsessed with matter and bestiality 'ne peuvent se soumettre en effet qu'à ce qui est plus *bas*, à ce qui ne peut servir en aucun cas à singer une autorité quelconque' (I.225; 'can only submit to what is *lower*, to what can never serve in any case to ape a given authority' 50).

Phrased in this way, both directions seem anti-mimetic. In practice, however, the case is not so simple. William Gibson's 'designer bodies' might initially seem to be a pure instance of the first direction. Gibson's heroes in *Neuromancer* and *Count Zero*, with biochips implanted in their brains, operate for much of the novels in virtual realities where the 'très vieille mystification, qui consiste toujours à placer la Nature au fond de l'Histoire' (Barthes 1957, 196; 'old mystification, which always consists in placing Nature at the bottom of history' 101) no longer operates. Many accounts of how post-modernism de-natures the world rely on disembodiment. In 'What Is an Author?' Foucault follows the Barthesian model by placing the text while refusing to place a biological subject in the author function. Lyotard calls the self a post for messages (15), while Kroker, somewhat curiously given his reliance on Bataille, argues that virtual technologies and the philosophy of the sign mean not only 'the end of the fantasy of the Real' (15), but also that simulations triumph over rationalization (272). For Kroker the post-modern is a state in which everything is decentred and disembodied as the inner (pineal) eye opens to simulated experience (73-4). 'We will never in future be able to separate reality from its statistical, simulative projection in the media' (Baudrillard 1988, 210) seems at first to describe Gibson's texts, and David Porush (the best commentator on Gibson) notes that in cybernetic theory the self becomes a message of the self (1989, 374-5).

However, as Hutcheon shows, post-modern practice is not always identical with post-structural theory.[8] Big corporations are the radical forces in Gibson's novels, creating new virtual environments so that the characters can go places where their bodies cannot. Deconstruction is accomplished not in the literary arena, but by genetics and computers. In virtual realities, apparently, the pull of mimesis is powerful, but entirely deceptive: Neuromancer, the artificial intelligence or 'AI,' almost seduces Case into accepting the virtual reality as all that is the world, a complete shadowland in which Case can have whatever he did not *really* get. However, if the science-fiction writer reconciles us to new technologies, scatology in Gibson's work is inherently conservative, gesturing back, almost nostalgically, to the 'past' biological unity of the individual human body.[9] Gibson follows the logic of colloquial usage which makes the posterior – 'We wait for him, pick him up, get his ass to Hosaka intact' (*Count Zero* 23) – a metonym for the entire human being, and excrement the basic constituent of language and identity: 'You poor stupid shit. Poor stupid dead shit' (*Count Zero* 144).[10] In one sense, of course, all texts signal the deferral of the body, but Gibson counters scatology and human affect against the post-biological model – to maintain something like the traditional humanist subject.

This technique is so grounded in conventional referentiality that we might almost suspect that Gibson is a realist masquerading as something else. But in his AIs, some of whom have citizenship (*Count Zero* 78), we see a more complicated form of reference. The amoral AI in *Count Zero* (the result of Neuromancer's conjunction with Wintermute) manipulates characters, including Christopher Mitchell who is convinced to leave Maas Biolabs. It is not only this echo of Pynchon that makes the novel post-modern, but that the AI may be read as a computer deconstruction of the humanist subject; the AI operates from out in space as a disembodied power that overarches individual functionaries and makes its presences felt in human bodies. Thus far the structure resembles Foucault's analysis of discursivity, and when the characters use the metaphor of *vodou* to speak of the AI's disparate subprograms, the description very much resembles Lyotard's performativity principle: '"Vodou isn't like that," Beauvoir said. "It isn't concerned with notions of salvation and transcendence. What it's about is getting things *done*"' (76). Of course, the anachronistic language of *vodou* and the explicit force of will interrupt the notion that the subject has been dispersed. Speech act theorists would not deny that the text as text disperses the author, but would insist that to jettison the positions of sender and receiver is to mystify discourse. While we do not know what sort of body or will the AI in *Count Zero* is, we do know that its artistic tendency is to parody the boxes of Joseph Cornell: the AI creates 'an arrangement of brown old maps and tarnished mirror. The seas of the cartographers had been cut away, exposing the flaking mirrors, landmasses afloat on dirty silver' (226). This art is an art of garbage, fragments, a W.A.S.T.E. system in which the artist does not try to put the world back together.

Marly Krushkhova in fact guesses that even the AI is 'someone else's collage,' into whom has been 'spilled, somehow, all the worn sad evidence of a family's humanity' (227). Sender and message, both coded through refuse, are filthy and to some extent 'human' without reversing textual disembodiment in any simple way. If the territory is now rotting on the map (Baudrillard 1988, 166), shreds of the real (including bits of old maps in the Cornell box) nevertheless tell us that a territory is still there as ordure, even if we virtually ignore it. Even if the AI is not some body, the art of garbage tells us that there is more than a *point* of sending, and Gibson eventually reveals the hidden sender of messages to at least one receiver who completes the biological model of the speech act. Marly's tears indicate that the receiver is not 'un homme sans histoire, sans biographie, sans psychologie' (Barthes 1968, 67; 'a man without history, without biography, without psychology' 59).

Gibson qualifies post-modern theories of disembodiment by staging a bodied speech act, but the second direction of post-modern theory – that towards 'heterogeneous matter' – cannot as easily be recuperated to mimesis. The texts of Kroetsch and Ondaatje can serve as examples. In *Badlands*, the archaeologist William Dawe convinces the members of his expedition to strip off their clothes and underclothes, mix them with flour and water so that the last of the dinosaur bones 'might go out of the canyon dressed and proper and secure' (226). By this process signs are dressed up, while human beings appear to turn naked and animal. The civilizing process thus accretes under, around, and over the early product of evolution (the dinosaur), while the 'highest' and 'latest' product dissolves, losing its cloak of civility in inverse proportion to the dressing up of the ancestor. This rhetorical theory is explicitly literary in Kroetsch's later novel, *Alibi*, which parodies Freudian, Jungian, and modernist interpretations of the body. Dorf, the narrator, serves as proxy for a man he has never met, Calgary oil baron Jack Deemer, who in best modernist fashion collects collections. Commissioned to find the perfect spa, Dorf undergoes spa doctor Manuel De Medeiros's 'severely critical examination' of his rectum (121, parodying Freud's 'discovery' of the anal roots of sadism) only to learn what he already knows: 'You hate the desire that makes you love' (123). De Medeiros points Dorf further back to a Grecian spa which consists not of water, but of mud – 'the blackest black pit' (164): 'I couldn't quite immerse myself in that stinking thick mud where all the sick and the maimed did their suffering and their hoping. And their pissing and their bleeding and their farting' (165). In this enlarged collective anus, a man who turns out to be the famed 'smelly woman' (137) takes Dorf back to a magical world of ritual mud-masks through which the frail body is made whole and luminous and eternal. But Dorf is unable to transplant this collective to his new North American spa. His faith in traditional signification founders on opening night – he is apparently raped in the dark of his own healing place. When he subsequently attempts scatomancy, his anus cannot divulge the sign of the crime: 'My stool was perfectly formed this morning, making a sickle-moon where it fell' (234). In post-modernism, all writing and interpretation become pathetic fallacy: not even the body signifies. Dorf's hermit existence on an island and the desecration of the printed word, as Dorf daily shreds his diary into the privy, suggest a complete scepticism about deciphering bodily symptoms; in place of the balanced polarities of Frye's 'bush garden,' Dorf finds only bush. He finds this not only by reversing the geographical fantasies of Donne or Henry James – going west – but by examining waste.

Left hands, headless chickens, and the seeping out of bodily fluids in Ondaatje's *The Collected Works of Billy the Kid* too signal the disappearance of the rational grids (including prose) that cover experience. The last moments of manic activity before death are filthy, whether they belong to Charlie Bowdre 'giggling' and 'pissing into his trouser legs in pain' (12) or to a flower's 'sweat like lilac urine smell' (56). Tom O'Folliard drinking urine in the desert (50), Billy having sex with Angela on the toilet (68), and Billy urinating down his legs onto his horse (76) draw attention to how Billy and his men (intentionally and unintentionally) have transgressed the boundaries of civilized life. Rational, non-scatological orders appear only where things are dead:

if you cut the stalk ...
the flower gets small smells sane
deteriorates in a hand (56)

In *Coming through Slaughter* the policeman Webb, like Kroetsch's Dorf, finds excrement unreadable. To him, Crawley's report about 'the tail of shit' (30) is tangential to the search for Buddy, but to Buddy (and to Ondaatje), the things (mostly 'filthy') that don't *mean* are the substance of art: 'the wet slime from toilets, grey rub of phones, the alley shit on his shoe when he crouched where others had crouched, tea leaves, beer stains off tables, piano sweat, trombone spit, someone's smell off a towel' (40). Buddy's songs therefore seem to be formless and genre-breaking. From Buddy's comments on the rational analysis of relationships – 'I shat those theories out completely' (113) – it is clear that in taking up the prehistory before jazz recordings Ondaatje makes scatology stand for the absence of maps and signs, even materialist ones. Scatology defines the moment after theory.[11]

But what are we to make of Stephen Tatum's reasons for calling Ondaatje's Billy the 'richest' (Tatum 149) treatment of the legend of Billy the Kid? 'Ondaatje's Kid, no saint or Satan, kills plants with his urine, fornicates on an outhouse floor, vomits in the desert during a hang-over' (Tatum 143). He is 'a human being caught in a maelstrom of biological and political circumstances' (Tatum 151). Clearly, for Tatum a particularized body is more authentic than documented history. As a repeated affront to civilization and even sanity, Ondaatje's scatology is destructive of order, but Tatum's almost realist, certainly referential faith is not simply a misreading. What Tatum understands is that Ondaatje has not completely defected from order, but has been substituting a less programmatic order for traditional character motivations. Even if post-modernism purposefully distorts history, it does not escape history or mimesis. The gypsy-foot whores who carry on their trade around raw sewage (119) certainly signal the history of slavery and perhaps even of Buddy's reified enslavement. When Buddy describes his music, he uses a modernist hierarchy of forms: 'Every now and then my note like a bird flying out of shit and hanging loud and long' (129).[12]

Buddy's very inscrutability, once it is converted to language, becomes a system in the text, so that excrement becomes a trope for the pretextual world, becomes an alibi or pretext for the 'real' thing. This is not just because Buddy parodies a primate marking system which Hooker and Mottyl might be familiar with, but because even the enunciations least susceptible to analysis are formal rather than heterogeneous. Ondaatje says as much about Buddy through Frank Lewis: 'We thought he was formless, but I think now he was tormented by order, what was outside it' (37).

Even *Running in the Family* with its built-in Dorfian gaps does not escape mimesis. The massive gaps in Ondaatje's story of himself corrode the notion of historical continuity even if we hear the names and deeds of Ondaatje's parents and grandparents. When the narrator's father urinates 'into darkness and mysterious foliage' (187) or when the ants attack the father's novel left on the bathroom floor (189), we are invited to feel that experience consists of a few animal markings but of very little order: 'No sweeper for weeks. And nature advanced ... If you stood still you were invaded ... A whole batallion was carrying one page away from its source ... It was page 189' (189). The 'magical' conjunction of 189 and 189 is, however, finally ambidextrous: on the one hand, it suggests that anything can get into a text, and that texts very easily decompose, especially under the sign of the body (the bathroom and 'sub-animal' nature); further, that autobiographies are always fictional since miracles and even miracles, as unprepossessing as the magical conjunction of numbers, must be stage-managed. On the other hand, this latter evidence of fictionality is paradoxically also a sign of history: the illusion that anything can get into a text requires very careful planning (and the unusual cooperation of a publisher). As such, it overwhelmingly signals the presence of the author. 'Donner un Auteur à un texte, c'est imposer à ce texte un cran d'arrêt' ('To assign an author to a text is to impose a brake on it'), says Roland Barthes (1968, 65) who, so the critical commonplace goes, did not fail to append a proper name nor to copyright 'La mort de l'auteur.' When 'Ondaatje' shows up in *Coming through Slaughter* or in the final photograph of *The Collected Works of Billy the Kid* we take this as direct autobiography only at our peril. Such a technique is partly confessional and referential because of who authorizes the 'intrusions,' but only partly, because once the author becomes a *character*, his chosen surrogate is hypostatically separated from the referent. Yet when the author manipulates page numbers, he acts *only* as a composed subject and not as a surface feature of the text. On page 189 then, for a moment, we had the referent of Ondaatje's discontinuous autobiography.

iv

Leonard Cohen's *Beautiful Losers*, which is surely an early instance of post-modernism (Hutcheon 1988a, 27), may be taken as its most comprehensive case because his text moves in both directions – towards disembodiment and towards heterogeneous matter – at once. When we first run across the narrator – 'I am an old scholar, better-looking now than when I was young. That's what sitting on your ass does to your face' (3) – we might expect Bakhtin's dialogue of the face with the buttocks (1984, 434) to follow. It does not, mainly because

F., the narrator's teacher, has spent much of his life not merely subverting the high, but attempting to confuse all hierarchies of high and low, outer and inner, good and evil. Bakhtin's jubilant folk wisdom still maintains such distinctions in the faith that if birth and decomposition are at the *heart* of things themselves, then a low humane parody can always restore egalitarianism against priests and party members who *superficially* style themselves as high. F., conversely, says, 'We've got to learn to stop bravely at the surface. We've got to learn to love appearances' (4). To the (stylistic) patchwork question, 'Do you think I can learn to perceive the diamonds of good amongst all this shit?' F. replies, 'It is all diamond' (9). The fallout of this anti-depth education is the narrator's repeated question: 'Are the stars tiny after all?' (5). According to bodily surfaces, the thumbless narrator is really F., who blew his own thumb away during a mistimed terrorist bombing. If surfaces are the whole story, 'appearances,' including confusion between individuals, need no longer be 'saved' by explanation. These are the initial stages of the narrator's disembodiment which drives him into a Total Fast and eventually turns him into a movie of Ray Charles. These are also post-modern games of the type that trouble a theorist such as Jameson, who comments on the 'facetiousness' (1984b, 370) of post-modernism.[13]

Yet F. is more than a decadent master willing to try any aphorism on his pupil/himself. The narrator discovers that his wife, Edith, was created by F. using the Pimple Cure, 'bosom aggrandizers,' and perhaps the 'Sphincter Kit' (171). 'Her buttocks' says F., 'were my masterpiece' (176), and he criticizes the narrator for improperly exercising his buttock muscles: 'A very selfish development and a factor in your bowel predicament' (170). In this way F. represents the commodification of the body, a process that the narrator both desires (he is pleased with Edith's beauty) and despises (he wishes that she were a product of 'nature,' he hates to hear of her production). This commodification is at once a disembodiment, since it substitutes a simulated body for the original, and a signal of the presence of heterogeneous matter, since the substitution implies a disgust for the first body. Moreover, F. is also a representative of the Creator – at one point elaborating upon his initial, he says, 'Call me Dr Frankenstein with a deadline' (186) – who can neither be pleased with the original chaos nor be enchanted with his creations, and consequently always pushes further 'beyond pleasure' (184). The narrator, post-pleasure, recognizes the force of the question, 'Where do we go next?' 'Once you ate shit. How can I live in the world beside all your damn adventures' (16). These 'adventures' lead to an orgasm during which F. and Edith bathe themselves in Mengele's human soap while F. reads a post-erotic litany parodying extremist pornographic magazines – 'Not Models! Actual Photos of Male and Female Sex Organs and Excrement ... Men masturbated to death. Cannibalism during Foreplay. Skull Coition' (181–2) – culminating in a description of the torture of Brébeuf and Lalement (183).

Heterogeneous matter with a vengeance, Cohen's 'end of man' includes what Bataille's does not: a mimetic process in which matter signals not its own 'heterogeneity,' but real historical atrocities. One response to these horrors is an equally exorbitant sign of *care*:

– I injured the waterfall with urine. Pray for me ...
– I soiled a loincloth. Pray for me. (221)

But these aching confessions by the Iroquois appear among less innocent confessions:

– I long for a human morsel. Pray for me ...
– I got the yellow out of a worm. Pray for me ...
– I killed a Jew. Pray for me ...
– I tortured a raccoon. Pray for me ...
– I prayed for a famine lesson. Pray for me.
– I dirtied on my beads. Pray for me. (221–2)

Furthermore, it is not always clear where the Confessor Tekakwitha's preferences lie, since her masochism allies her with Edith. The equation of Tekakwitha's asceticism with institutionalized twentieth-century sado-masochisms seems to collapse historical forms into each other. There may be no way, in *Beautiful Losers*, of isolating the *meaning* of the narrator's suffering or transformation – the text is not Jewish, Christian, anti-technological, or even nihilistic (given the post-climactic Part 3) in Bataille's explosive sense.[14] The parodic reinterpretation of Tekakwitha's religious devotion should then lead to simulacra if Cohen seamlessly replaced the belief in historical difference with a sense that the imaging of history in language finally effaces all past events.

However, even if Tekakwitha's and the narrator's Total Fasts become ambiguous and extreme simulacra, neither all referents nor even a moral position have been completely destroyed. The scatological confessions are deflected from Iroquois culture towards European history by 'I killed a Jew.' Historiography has often been the place in which the powerful organize the facts to confirm those narratives which give them their positions, so Cohen's redirection of history is not necessarily synonymous with 'collapse.' Cohen avoids the kind of forgetfulness which would presume that because the writer gives us bodily details we have somehow got an accurate transcription of Iroquois voices. Such built-in scepticism about historiography cannot be called mimetic, but paradoxically might be called an extension of realist practices since the realist uneasiness with respect to idealized narratives extends to a scepticism about the way even the 'real' has been abstracted into singulative narratives and ideological forms.[15] Historical commentary might also invite us to see the narrator's constipation as a parody of Luther's *Turmerlebnis*, when Luther discovered on the privy that the just shall live by faith: 'Nothing helps, is that what you want me to learn? The strain man perched on a circle prepares to abandon all systems' (41).[16] In both the parody of the Iroquois and of Luther, the past returns to comment on the present historical moment: on anti-Semitism, on sadism, on the complexities of post-Reformation scepticism about religious and other systems of order.[17] History, Cohen implies, is always partially simulated for present purposes, but this knowledge only allows us a sceptical distance from the multiform past instead of exhausting it.

Cohen's historiographic parodies force us to reconsider what I earlier called his drive into pure word. The catalogue of unclean and mortifying practices, if it transgresses the bodily limits created by most systems of social mores, does not entirely trade mimesis for pure surface. 'L'interieur du corps vient ... suppléer à l'effondrement de la frontière dedans/dehors' ('The body's inside ... shows up in order to compensate for the collapse of the border between inside and outside'). Skin becomes transparent, a weak boundary, and gives way 'devant la déjection du contenu. Urine, sang, sperme, excrément viennent alors rassurer un sujet en manque de son "propre"' (Kristeva 1980, 65; 'before the dejection of its contents. Urine, blood, sperm, excrement then show up in order to reassure a subject that is lacking its "own and clean self"' 53). Despite Lyotard, the obscene is precisely *not* the 'unpresentable.' 'Fuck her on the moon with a steel hourglass up your hole' (13) – language loosed from its referents – may be called 'unpresentable,' 'facetious,' or (to be more literal) 'weightless,'[18] but it does not belong to the final orgasm because F.'s climax exactingly requires that the reader be able to imagine the obscenities *embodied*. If language entails the loss of the object (Kristeva 1982, 41), it still keeps the object in mind. Cohen imagines possible bodies and follows documented history: *The Jesuit Relations*, the history of Nazi Germany, the history of pornographic discourse. If Edith's acne recalled Tekakwitha's pre-Enlightenment face (pock-marked by the Plague), it was F.'s 'famous soap collection' (142) that 'cured' her.

The commercial surface of and in *Beautiful Losers* is thus not glib, but terminally blemished. Elias anticipated the scepticism about depth, and the fallacies created by analysing human beings as containers. Most 'inner' processes, he argued, are touched by society (259).[19] Other theorists have been less measured: 'La psychanalyse met fin à l'inconscient et au désir, tout comme le marxisme met fin à la lutte de classes, en les hypostasiant et en les enterrant dans leur entreprise théoretique' (Baudrillard 1977, 16; 'Psychoanalysis puts an end to the unconscious and desire, just as Marxism put an end to the class struggle, because it hypostatizes them and buries them in their theoretical project' 89). For Marcel Détienne, quoted in Michel de Certeau's *Arts de faire*, Greek stories about *metis* 'say exactly what they do ... There is no need to add a gloss that knows what they express without knowing it, nor to wonder *what* they are a metaphor of. You ask what they "mean"? I'll tell them to you again' (80).[20] Baudrillard and Détienne want to foreclose on particular types of speech, but Cohen's novel is not post-interpretive, and history has not collapsed simply because F. wanted to blow things up. 'Are the stars tiny?' is finally neither nostalgic nor anti-historical: it depends for its effect on the interpretive knowledge that the stars could not possibly be tiny. Appearances are important ruses in the novel, but the Pimple Cure and constipation require social and historical interpretation. As such Cohen moves the lexis away from ontological arguments towards the level of game, but not towards a game without parameters. When we come the long way round to the live author's claims that the source of *Beautiful Losers* was 'a certain type of experience' (interview with Twigg 57), or when Cohen calls *Beautiful Losers* both an expression of his chemico-mental state on Cos in 1965 and prophetic of his difficulties a year or two later (Harris 55; Lumsden 72),[21] we are strangely in the territory of autobiography and *Bildung*, where invented selves impinge upon some body: not that we could make a realist equation between Cohen and the narrator, not that

Cohen hasn't made a career of adopting poses, but that instead of being loose among the surfaces of signs, even the most exorbitant text is anchored to another discursive post and *body*, that shifting depth which Adrienne Clarkson, following convention, still calls Leonard Cohen.

Epilogue:
New Detours to the Symbolic

Mais tout ceci se peut raporter à l'estroite cousture de l'esprit et du corps s'entre-communiquants leurs fortunes. (But all this may be referred to the narrow suture of the Spirit and the body, enter-communicating their fortunes one unto another.)

– Montaigne, *'De la force de l'imagination'* (Florio translation)

L'argot est un langage de haine qui vous assoit très bien le lecteur ... l'annihile! ... a votre merci! ... il rest tout con! (Slang is a language of hatred that knocks the reader out very nicely ... annihilates him! ... completely in your power! ... he just lies there like an eightball!)

– Louis-Ferdinand Céline, *Entretiens avec le professeur Y*

i

Only for a moment. 'As late as 1930, four-letter words made visual on the printed page seemed portentous ... Most "four-letter words" are heavy with tactile-involving stress. For this reason they seem earthy and vigorous to visual man' (McLuhan 1964, 116). The offhanded way that 'late' and '1930' roll off McLuhan's tongue, as if *Ulysses* and *Lady Chatterley's Lover* changed the cultural landscape in an evening, makes McLuhan seem urbane (almost as if he claims personal responsibility for the 1960s), but it does not make him an accurate commentator on the Canadian ethos. Yet the 1955 Céline quote also seems too extreme in the opposite direction. Hodgins's Madmother Thomas keeps 'pog mahone' ('kiss my arse' 335) as a reserve fund against the world, and she never spends it – possibly because she, like her mother who bequeathed the words, knows that they will not really knock anyone out for long.

From lampoon to autohagiography, all writing transgresses the boundaries between word and world (especially writing which confusedly gives the metaphor 'tongue' for print, or a translation which slips too easily from 'con' to 'eightball'), but scatology is a special case, allowing us neither to approach it dispassionately as only a textual feature or emotionally as just the sign of hatred. In *Histoire de la sexualité* Michel Foucault attacks the Freudian repressive hypothesis by speaking of the massive increase in *discourse* about sexuality; as the least-sophisticated writer knows, sexual language can incite a physiological response. I would argue that at the moment of physiological response the separation of world from word is fogged over, if not erased. Here the arts are fluid because the word-picture does almost what the picture does. The same is true of metaphysics: the moment of faith closes the gap (existentially, if not theoretically) between the sacred text and the world it represents. The same is *not* true of scatology. Like the gap between musical notation and music, or like the gap between the richness of the odorous world and the poverty of language in Süskind's *Das Parfüm*, scatology as a language may never get near the referent.[1] This means that the growth of scatology in English-Canadian literature is not merely a return of what has been repressed, a slap at Victoria or Presbyterians as Irving Layton imagined, but another convert to the ever-widening sphere of abstract knowledge and the proper self. One who writes about excrement is not necessarily less repressed than one who ignores it. Yet scatology, unlike discourse about music (but like some musical forms) has often been suppressed. On the popular level, it has evidently been felt that slang *can* knock the reader out. Literary theorists have insisted that even when the sign displaces the world, the duplicitous sign refers to a real body (Howells 125, 130; Foley 18; Cixous 1980, 252) and to the subject who deploys the language (Foley 97).

At its most basic level, scatology functions as a trope for the 'world' in a narrative text which abstracts itself, mimetically, from the world. Scatology does indeed gesture at the world (as realists and modernists in their destruction of romance or romanticism or Victorianism always suspected), but scatology is also unavoidably rhetorical, thus, in its own way, even ideal.

Epilogue: New Detours to the Symbolic 183

We have seen that Canadian post-modernists too retain the old model of signification, mimesis, in which excrement signals a 'real' chaotic world. Like Kristeva, if less explicitly and only partially, they too declare an alliance 'à l'Idée, au Logos, à la Forme, à la vieille Europe' (Kristeva 1983, 54; with 'the Idea, the Logos, the Form: in short, the old Judeo-Christian Europe' 1984, 235). If we pursue scatology in enough detail, from one angle post-modern texts begin to appear curiously referential and stable, very much at ease in the world. These texts bring more and more of the human body into the order of language, perhaps expanding the practices we call 'civilized.' The effect is somewhat like Miss Manners's approach to etiquette: she no longer fully believes in the conventions, but she still uses them and passes them on. Rooke's Will Shakespeare makes this clear in his despair: 'Begone Hooker ... Better you had followed a maggot to its nursing or a turd to its disintegration' (101). The passage owes something to the world because Will and Rooke are able to formulate an 'inner' emotion by fixing on 'outer' processes. But these processes have already been treated by past writers as signs appropriate to 'despair,' so Will's use of the topos is conventional. The death's-head conceits, the rather elegant way decomposition is *worded*, eventually limit the despair. They call attention to a civilized voice even if Will is sutured onto biodegradable matter, and call attention to a collective logos in the reader who activates the conceit.

I offer two contradictory conclusions. First, the untranslatable body is what makes metaphors possible. In particular, Atwood, Gibson, Munro, and Richler show, through scatology, how the high prices of racist discourses, multinational economies, and male discourses about clean and proper women are registered in the body. At the same time, writers such as Haliburton (consciously) and Ondaatje (less consciously) naturalize economic or political practices, just as others – Chris Scott and Laurence respectively – use scatology to discredit or bolster earlier discourses about the 'soul.' In other words, for all of these writers, the filthy body both precedes and follows the text.

Second, scatology is a language; matter in a text is never completely heterogeneous or corrosive, but as part of a sign system, represents historical depths. This is why writers such as Davies and Laurence can rhetorically include lower-class positions without a literal investment in those positions. I intend not a working-class criticism of such an appropriation, but a description of the elasticity of the Word, which doesn't necessarily emancipate, but which removes some of the rhetorical barriers to emancipation. The etymologies of words sometimes used to describe scatology – 'obscene' (ill omen) and 'graphic' – bear my double conclusion, declaring themselves at once inside of and beyond signification. My sympathy, I confess, is with those displaced souls who when they are confronted by a thing search for words, and when they are confronted with a word look for things. Too many theorists, who recognize that one must take the body into any account of texts, emphasize one of these conclusions over the other. Bataille says that 'l'abjection ... est simplement l'incapacité d'assumer avec une force suffisante l'acte impératif d'exclusion des choses abjectes (qui constitue le fondement de l'existence collective)' (quoted in Kristeva 1980, 70; 'the Abject is merely the inability to assume with sufficient strength the imperative act of excluding things, and that act establishes the foundations of collective existence' 1982, 56). But even if one wants to deconstruct sociology, language puts the neurotic (not autistic) frontiersman into a social context at the moment when he theoretically wants to fall into decomposition. A distinction between unorganized or amoral experience and the moralistic interpretation of experience (M. Davis 93) oversimplifies a dialectic that Montaigne knew was, and still is, more complex. MacLennan tries to insist upon the ontological primacy of the 'real' world when he depicts World War I: 'Some had stood up to their necks in cold water stained with blood and human excrement while they waited for hours to crawl a few yards closer to Passchendaele ... Words are human and have a history and this had none' (309, 312). But MacLennan must have had some faith that words can register suffering, and he would not have wanted to dislodge his description from the historical context of conscription battles in Quebec.

We might, then, sympathize with Descartes, for whom matter was constantly telling things not about matter, but about consciousness. If he displaced the old location of the soul up higher into the 'pineal' gland where Bataille could mock it, he was not alone.

According to Kristeva we cannot get rid of the impure, but we can 'le faire être une deuxième fois, et différemment de l'impureté originelle. Répétition en rythme et en chant ... L'écrivain: un phobique qui réussit à métaphoriser pour ne pas mourir de peur mais pour ressusciter dans les signes' (1980, 36, 49; 'bring it into being a second time, and differently from the original impurity. It is a repetition through rhythm and song ... The writer is a phobic who succeeds in metaphorizing in order to keep from being frightened to death; instead he comes to life again in signs' 28, 38). The strength of this formulation is that despite the emphasis on the individual origins of abjection Kristeva acknowledges language as a symbolic system deploying subject positions. The model that 'repetition' appoaches is that of a feedback loop. The writer metaphorizes his or her impurity; later the textual mechanism is perceived as too empty of the world; the next phobic brings in new impurities; but those also, living for a while as symbols, come to seem too abstract; and so on. Because of this process, it is naïve to place (as many theorists have done since the 1960s) an unqualified value on the widest possible variety of bodily practices, on 'restored ... animality' (Foucault 1965, 75), or on some other guarantee of heterotopia. Instead of a single thesis of what scatology *means* in the English-Canadian novel, each appeal to the filthy body requires, finally, a separate aesthetic, historical, and discursive explication.

ii

Still, at the end of a study such as this we cannot ignore the vast growth in scatological discourse that the Canadian novel is symptomatic of – the shift from *To Him That Hath* (1921), in which Patricia Templeton can shock her mother by saying 'Rot!' (71), to *Beautiful Losers*. Changes in obscenity laws are partially responsible, but they may be effect rather than cause. Narratives that cannot accommodate scatology are becoming obsolete, and are increasingly consigned to the dump of anachronism. Kristeva's comment on Leviticus – 'Le corps ne doit garder aucune trace de sa dette envers la nature: il doit être propre pour être pleinement symbolique' (1980, 121; 'The body must bear no trace of its debt to nature: it must be clean and proper in order to be fully symbolic' 102) – may be inverted to correspond with the latter half of the twentieth century. The body must signify its debt to nature: it must include the foul and abject in order to be fully symbolic. We see this when writers such as Laurence or Atwood parody the disembodiments of, for example, romantic poetry or travel writing: 'What the hell is this crap? "I wandered lonely as a cloud." This Wordsworth, now, he was a pansy' (*The Diviners* 63); '"Throwing up in the Sun," [Rennie] thinks briefly. Tippy would say everything's raw material, you just have to know how to work it in' (*Bodily Harm* 98). Duddy Kravitz's apprenticeship in language is to save obscenity even when passing through the censors. Mrs Cox wants to change the boys' language without seeming Victorian or other than them: 'You only use those words for their shock value and that's silly, because you can't shock me ... Do you know what a penis is?' Duddy's answer takes the form of feigned innocence: '"Sure," Duddy said. "A penis is a guy that plays the piano"' (21). Duddy goes Mrs Cox one better by adding her 'correct' word, 'penis,' to the list of what needs to be repressed and by simultaneously recuperating its obscene value for the boys via insinuation and wordplay (just as Richler does with Mrs Cox's name). In *Joshua Then and Now* Richler gives us two versions of an event to show that only before the interior censor clicks on do we get accurate ideological and emotional representations:

'... And then I said,' McMaster droned on, as the Sony whirled, '"Look Colucci, you dumb dago, you North End asshole, I don't know what you got with anybody else in No. 4, but you can stuff that envelope where the monkey put his fingers." Cut. Stop. Correction. And then I said, "Look Colucci, you are dissimulating, you are not a credit to your people, like Dante or Mayor La Guardia, I don't know what arrangements you have with other officers in this station, but I do not accept emoluments, and therefore please put that envelope back in your pocket." Is that better?' (301)

'The alliance between literature and excrement has been consolidated since the former began to identify itself more and more with the violation of a system' (Enzensberger 34). McMaster, a policeman, is especially cognizant of laws and standards of expression, but his impulse as a writer and a bigot is to break the rules.

Do these satires against disembodiment herald the devaluation of language as a mode of existence? Tillich claims that 'the word as breath, as sound, as something heard, is a natural phenomena' (98). Davies's Kinghoven goes further:

'You're all mad for words. Words are just farts from a lot of fools who have swallowed too many books. Give me things! Give me the appearances of a thing, and I'll show you the way to photograph it so the reality comes right out in front of your eyes. The Devil? Balls! God? Balls! Get me that Fat Woman and I'll photograph her one way and you'll know the Devil made her, then I'll photograph her another way and you'll swear you see the work of God! Light! That's the whole secret ... Let there be light! Who said that? I said it!' (*World of Wonders* 87)

Kinghoven's scepticism about the high does not stop him from taking more than a princely role while he assures his auditors that mi-

Epilogue: New Detours to the Symbolic 187

mesis, and perhaps creation, is all fakery. Magnus, however, spends much of the narrative trying to find the proper way of arranging his life in language. Even if he is a master illusionist and even if he feels dismay when writers begin to name certain acts, Magnus's deepest impulse is to bring into being a second time in language the true impropriety of his rape by Williard: 'It was something going in where I knew only that filthy things should come out, as secretly as could be managed' (34). Kinghoven praises and devalues all art as a mode of existence divorced from things; Magnus, alternatively, turns writing into a repository for the impure, and he thereby changes the makeup of the sphere of culture. In *World of Wonders*, as in other postwar Canadian novels, there is little room for an unqualified 'high' language, but the system of words has by no means been dismissed. Rather, one language has been displaced by another.

One of the functions of Bakhtin's polyglossia was to confront high languages with their repressed bodies. Scatology limits the idealization of particular narratives, including that of Magnus's great success and including, I think, that of Bakhtin's bodily utopianism: the new detour to the symbolic is through the abject. Scatology does not destroy allegory or hermeneutics, but makes a different route, through the minutiae of the body instead of Platonic ascent or Christian asceticism, to what is outside of the text.

However, that scatology almost always defines itself against idealized bodies and idealized narratives exposes a limit to my study. The problem is enunciated in a different context by Michael McKeon: 'Medieval romance, in which the antecedents of our "history" and "romance" coexist in fluid suspension, becomes "medieval romance," the product of an earlier period and increasingly the locus of strictly "romance" elements that have been separated out from the documentary objectivity of "history" and of print, the technology to which it therefore owes (at least in part) both its birth and its instantaneous obsolescence' (McKeon 45). I say little about romances such as O'Hagan's *Tay John* and Kinsella's *Shoeless Joe* because they nearly evade scatology. In *Tay John* scatology is only found in the 'historical' sections and then only in abbreviated form: 'I think these railway men must have their brains in their bowels' (181); '"Lady, yer cawn't sing with yer buttocks"' (196). The latter comment is thrown at Ardith Aeriola before O'Hagan transforms her from railroaders' mistress to romantic heroine. In *Shoeless Joe* J.D. Salinger equates writing (as a job) with a farmer's barn-cleaning (92), and after Kid Scissons wears his baseball out, he practises 'with rocks and frozen horse turds' (145). Scatology enters these romances only momentarily on behalf of the disillusioning bits of world that must be overcome for the story to approach a higher realm. Scatology, I claimed early on, stands for the past, but once it is recuperated in the epistemological reversal that we have seen in Chapter 3, scatology becomes *all* of the present while romance, less scatological, functions as the obsolete immediate past ('Victorian') or, at most, as a failed mimetic move. The nearest affinity of scatology is with ironic modes.

It would be false to conclude that romances and, on the other hand, post-modern texts are actually realist texts in disguise, or that no texts really undermine material signification. McKeon speaks of the tension in ideology between the 'will to engage what is problematic' and the 'will to naturalize' (233); the resolution of these tensions inevitably varies. Just as the basic constituents and the realist meaning-gestures of fictional autobiography cannot be completely exploded by internal scepticism, so spiritual romance cannot fully be explained by what it represses. In a different way, the post-modern need to refer to the world does not completely secure post-modern epistemologies to a referential model. In Ondaatje's *Running in the Family*, after a wild pig steals the soap that kept the narrator 'aristocratic' and 'feeling good all through the filthy hotels of Africa,' he imagines the creature 'returning to his friends with Pears Transparent Soap, then all of them bathing and scrubbing their armpits in the rain in a foul parody of us' (143). Too anthropomorphic, this parody of human *cleanliness* is also *too* amenable to the theory of the liberal humanist expansion of the civilized self to be admitted as evidence of my claims. What were the pigs thinking? Had they found sufficient strength to give up slang, hoping, even without opposable thumbs, to educate their bodies in the rudiments of courtesy? Or were they laughing at the young sons of nobility, Erasmus, Miss Manners, the whole crew? Their cloven-hoofed bodies, though they don't exist, trouble me.

Notes

INTRODUCTION

1 All references, except direct quotations, are to the English translations of foreign language texts.
2 Although Elias starts with the Middle Ages in order to get at later developments, the Middle Ages should obviously not be literally understood as 'origins.' For example, euphemisms for toilet (itself a euphemism) were in force in medieval times: garderobe (i.e., wardrobe), necessarium, necessary house (Wright 47). Francis Barker, in *The Tremulous Private Body*, locates the beginnings of the modern separation of public and private realms in the English revolution, and suggests in particular that Milton's *Areopagitica* interiorized censorship, emphasizing private copyright over Jacobean collaborative writing. Julia Kristeva in *Pouvoirs de l'horreur* attributes this movement into private guilt to Christ. The English revolution does represent a codification of the privatizing tendencies in copyright law, and Kristeva is also correct to suggest Christ's importance for the interiorization of the 'abject' that accompanies the interiorization of Jewish ritual law. However, when one traces scatology, such 'cruxes' proliferate: Ezekiel's scatological transgression (Ezek. 4:12) in the sixth century BC, for example, personalizes the abject even though his enactment was intended as drama. To insist upon a particular moment is to prematurely simplify the process.
3 In Richler's children's book *Jacob Two-Two Meets the Hooded Fang*, Jacob confronts exactly this when he is constantly reminded of his disgusting nature. He is called to court by Justice Rough for 'peeing without lifting the seat' (18). Even when he merely forgets to euphemize (by mentioning that his older brother is 'doing his dump' 30), he gets into trouble.

4 Elias is much less total in his explanations than his critics make him out to be. Bullough ignores Elias's comment that the growth of shame is not explicable by one social factor, but that changes in technical apparatus cannot be explained simply on a scientific level (Elias 139–40); Adams completely misreads Elias as a Freudian primitivist. For a better analysis of Elias's ideas, see Stephen Mennell's book-length study, *Norbert Elias: Civilization and the Human Self-Image.*
5 Della Casa is much less forward, counselling his pupil to avoid scatological and base speech. Although he gleefully reports sexual malapropisms, he regularly uses circumlocution, and he criticizes Dante for failing to observe the propriety of noble speech for noble occasions.
6 Although the writers of books on manners present idealized worlds, they cannot be dismissed simply as prudish distorters of actual culture. Even as the voices of conservatism they can be in the avant-garde of cultural change: many cities have recently adopted by-laws requiring owners to remove their pets' feces from public areas; Ford advocates some swearing so that women can gain access to male language (64).
7 'Good education demands ... to close up and limit the body's confines and to smooth the bulges' (Bakhtin 1984, 322). The emission of bodily substances and speech about them are 'bulges' in Bakhtin's sense.
8 Semiotics must be interdisciplinary to look at methods of signification (Eco 115). The refusal to cross disciplines is one of the ways in which literary studies have been depoliticized and marginalized (Said 1983, 146–53). Mennell notes that Elias's interest in the body has interdisciplinary sources: Elias studied both medicine and philosophy, and was disturbed for many years by 'the discrepancy between the philosophical-idealist and the anatomical-physiological image of man' (Elias quoted in Mennell 7).
9 Lucy, another signing chimpanzee, urinated on one of her keepers and 'signed "funny" in a self-congratulatory way' (Linden 97). For her, 'dirty' and 'leash' were always associated, as were 'dirty' and 'cat' (113). Linden says that, for the outsider, swearing is the most dramatic way in which the signing chimpanzees appear human (114). Critics have questioned the methods and results of these experiments: See Martin Gardner, 'Monkey Business,' *New York Review of Books* 20 March 1980: 3–4.
10 See, for example, Said's criticism of functionalist theories which pay too little attention to the text's materiality (1983), 148). 'For the critic, texts are texts not as symbols of something else but as displacements (Frye's vocabulary is useful here) of other things; texts are deviations

from, exaggerations and negations of, human presence' (147). Although Said overstates his case, his work is a good corrective to less wordly theories of literature.
11 In her study *The Body in Pain* Scarry cites the McGill Pain Questionnaire (which gathers the seemingly random words of patients into diagnostic sets) as an instance of how the human voice is a reliable instrument for 'exposing even the most resistant aspects of material reality' (1985, 8).
12 See John Sutherland, *Offensive Literature: Decensorship in Britain, 1960–1982* 21–8; and Alec Craig, *The Banned Books of England and Other Countries* 133.
13 Not unrelated to this is Robert Cluett's computer analysis of prose styles and parts of speech. He identifies a movement, over the last one hundred years 'away from ornament towards utility and matter' (169).
14 Again, this is a comment that Kayser makes about the grotesque (31).

CHAPTER 1

1 'The tip-tilted outhouse looking like a child's parody of the leaning tower' (114), Laurence's direct copy of Steve's artwork in Sinclair Ross's *As For Me and My House*, is what bothers Hagar the most about the home that she and Bram share.
2 For a parodic history of the topos of Christy, the quaint old hired man, see F. Scott Fitzgerald's letter to Maxwell Perkins (ca. 1 June 1925), *The Letters of F. Scott Fitzgerald*, ed. Andrew Turnbull (Harmondsworth: Penguin, 1963) 204–6. We might add Beckett's Christy from *All That Fall* and Laurence's Christie to a scatological post–World War II extension of Fitzgerald's list.
3 'Smell must be civilization's first casualty,' says Carlyle Sinclair in Mitchell's *The Vanishing Point* (133) as Mitchell reactivates Sinclair's lost sense on a Cree reservation. On the elimination of smell in literate societies, see Marshall McLuhan, *Understanding Media: The Extensions of Man* 136. In 1929 scientist J.D. Bernal predicted that in the future smell would have a 'less primitively emotional role than now' (39). For a connection between a heightened sense of smell and decivilization, see Judith Thompson's play *White Biting Dog* (20).
4 Compare a less sympathetic variant in R.V. Krafft-Ebing's *Lehrbuch der Psychiatrie*: a patient believes that the smells and odours of his neighbour's greasy cooking are getting into his skin and that excrement is falling from his ceiling (Enzensberger 22).

5 More recently, environmental groups in North America have been pressing for the adoption of a 1.6-gallon toilet tank instead of the typical 3.5-gallon tank (*Winnipeg Free Press* Tues. 26 July 1990: 27).
6 On the discipline involved in getting French schoolchildren to sit, not climb and squat, on toilets, see Corbin 174.
7 See also Elizabeth D. Harvey, 'Property, Digestion, and Intertext in Robertson Davies' *The Rebel Angels*,' and Patricia Monk, 'Somatogyping, Scatomancy, and Sophia: The Relation of Body and Soul in the Novels of Robertson Davies.'
8 On the varieties of new Canadian social histories, see George S. Kealey, 'Introduction,' *Class, Gender, and Region: Essays in Canadian Historical Sociology*, ed. Kealey (St John's: Canadian Journal of Sociology, 1988) 1–7.
9 Gregory the Great, who recommended bathing (Wright 24), and Christchurch Monastary at Canterbury with its elaborate water supply system (26) represent the modern in a medieval world, against St Benedict, St Jerome, and St Francis who all considered bathing as a sign of affectation (24). Da Vinci's plan for Ten New Towns (including spiral stairways 'to prevent unsanitary misuse of landings' 53) and Sir John Harrington's 1596 invention of the flushing water closet (71) represent a renaissance to Wright that finds its fulfilment only in the eighteenth century. Along the way there are famous regressions, as Anthony à Wood recounts of Charles II's courtiers: 'Though they were neat and gay in their apparel, yet they were very nasty and beastly, leaving at their departure their excrements in every corner, in chimneys, studies, colehouses, cellars. Rude, rough, whoremongers; vaine, empty, careless' (Wright 76).
10 To put a point on the obvious hierarchical change that Bataille is attempting, compare Bernardus Silvestris's twelfth-century comment in the *Cosmographia* that man's head is purposely placed so that it is far from the bowels and regions of decay.
11 I refer to Lévi-Strauss's proposed play, 'L'apothéose d'Auguste,' in which Augustus very clearly represents the civilized anthropologist: 'Auguste n'apercevra pas qu'il est devenu dieu à quelque sensation rayonnante ou au pouvoir de faire des miracles, mais quand il supportera sans dégoût l'approche d'une bête sauvage, toléra son odeur et les excréments dont elle le couvrira' (438; 'Augustus would realize that he had become a god, not by some radiant sensation or the power to work miracles, but by his ability to tolerate the proximity of a wild

beast without a sensation of disgust, to put up with its stench and the excrement with which it would cover him' 432). Academia, of course, has its own rhetorical techniques which preclude such returns, and register distance from origins: Lévi-Strauss uses pseudo-mathematics at the same time as he discusses a myth of auto-chthonic origins in 'La structure des mythes,' *Anthropologie Structurale* (Paris: Plon, 1958; *Structural Anthropology*, trans. Claire Jacobson and Brooke Grundfest Schoepf, Garden City, N.Y.: Doubleday, 1963, 225). To this we might compare Paracelsus's more naïve version of the same scientizing stance when he insists that he did not get his (rather chthonic) knowledge from a urinal. 'Manual Concerning the Medicinal Stone of the Philosophers,' *The Hermetic and Alchemical Writings*, Vol. 2, ed. Arthur Edward Waite (1984; rpt. Berkeley: Shambhala, 1976) 104.

CHAPTER 2

1 Pineo and Porter have shown how a rural background is often a greater debility to occupational attainment than ethnic status (391). On the connections between class and country or town origins in Canada, see Dennis Forcese, *The Canadian Class Structure*, 3rd ed. (Toronto: McGraw-Hill Ryerson, 1986) 33–7.
2 It is unclear whether Ostenso was aware of the etymology, or whether genre closes its own circuits, so that the realist naming of the process can, even inadvertently, register the real work involved. See Raymond Williams, *The Country and the City* (New York: Oxford UP, 1973) on the testing of language about farming – in particular the pastoral – against experience. Williams takes language as a material *activity* in an attempt to expand materialist conceptions beyond sense apprehensions and positivism; *Marxism and Literature* (New York: Oxford UP, 1977) 30f.
3 Haliburton (13) criticizes the Bluenosers, Frances Brooke the French Canadians (60, 167) for being too lazy to manure their crops. Although Moodie usually resists scatology, she is proud of fields 'plentifully manured' (421). The Romans, notes Theodor Rosebury, deified Stercus because of the invention of manuring (111). Alain Corbin notes that agriculturists distrusted attempts to deodorize dung (213).
4 For the inability to see the comic in the grotesque because of civilized values, see Philip Thompson, *The Grotesque* 55. For the taboo against choosing a urinal immediately next to another man (when other urinals

are available), see R. Dale Guthrie, *Body Hotspots: The Anatomy of Human Social Organs and Behavior* 191, and Barrington Moore, *Privacy: Studies in Social and Cultural History* 60–1.
5 In 'The American Scholar,' just prior to proclaiming 'the new importance given to the single person,' Emerson writes of how Swedenborg 'showed the mysterious bond that allies moral evil to the foul material forms' (*Selected Essays*, ed. Larzer Ziff, Harmondsworth: Penguin, 1982, 103). The correspondences between Emerson and David Canaan are many.
6 For David Canaan as artist, see David Williams, *Confessional Fictions: A Portrait of the Artist in the Canadian Novel*. For outhouses, see Ray Guy, *Outhouses of the East*, Photographs by Sherman Hines (Halifax: Nimbus, 1988).
7 See Albert and Theresa Moritz, *The Oxford Illustrated Literary Guide to Canada* (Toronto: Oxford UP, 1987), and *The Oxford Companion to English Literature*, ed. William Toye (Toronto: Oxford UP, 1983). See also Rosmarin Heidenreich, *The Postwar Novel in Canada: Narrative Patterns and Reader Response* 14–15, on the structures in the text that imply a desire to affirm threatened rural norms.

CHAPTER 3

1 McKeon's book is of obvious importance for this study, but his structure is the inverse of the one implied by the scatological image. His medieval romance sources imply idealist origins for the novel genre, origins which naïve empiricists criticized with the 'truth' of history; the empiricists in turn came under attack from an extreme sceptical position. The difference between attitudes to genre in the eighteenth century (Defoe defining himself against romance) and the imagined history of the self in twentieth-century novels owes something to historical changes (since both modernists and post-modernists have tended to define themselves against realism). Because 'origins' in the Canadian novel are so often posited as filthy, the second move is a civilizing or idealizing process which only 'later' comes under sceptical attack. In the extreme version of this third move – 'the parodic maneuvers of extreme skepticism' (McKeon 115) – my categories for the first time properly coincide with those of McKeon.
2 On the scatological roles of pigs, particularly on the differences between town versions and country versions of the pig, see Stallybrass and White 45, 49.

3 A similar historical revisionism, by means of the repressive hypothesis, also marks D.G. Jones's renovation of Archibald Lampman's voice – 'We cared/little for Arcadia its/ elementary joys, its excrement' – in 'Kate, These Flowers ...' *15 Canadian Poets 2*, ed. Gary Geddes (Toronto: Oxford UP, 1988), as well as Margaret Atwood's revision of Susanna Moodie in *The Journals of Susanna Moodie* (Toronto: Oxford UP, 1970).
4 Compare Morag's knowing irony in *The Diviners* when she reports on the town dump's name change from 'Nuisance Grounds' to 'Municipal Disposal Area.' Morag's attitude towards garbage is not at all different from the attitudes that initiate the name change.
5 While he was a book reviewer for the *Toronto Daily Star*, Davies himself enacted the process of 'recovering' excluded scatology, praising Wright's *Clean and Decent*, John Pudney's *The Smallest Room*, and Reginald Reynolds's *Cleanliness and Godliness* (11 June 1960, reprinted in *The Enthusiasms of Robertson Davies*, ed. Judith Skelton Grant, Toronto: McClelland and Stewart, 1979): '*Clean and Decent* has changed my notions of plumbing and history' (191). 'You don't want to read about sewage? I am grieved but not surprised' (193).
6 For the outhouse as a symbol for leaving behind 'the effete, deodorized, decaffinated East' (8), see Silver Donald Cameron, *Outhouses of the West*, Photographs by Sherman Hines (Halifax: Nimbus, 1988). One of the euphemisms for outhouse – 'house of Parliament' (Muriel E. Newton White, *Backhouses of the North*, Cobalt, Ont.: Highway Book Shop, 1972, 18) – suggests precise political satire.
7 There are even hints of a North/South axis to the coding of scatology. Nick Sluzick prefers to spit rather than speak in *La petite poule d'eau* (19, 27), and he plans on moving farther north once he feels that there are too many people settled near the Water Hen River.

CHAPTER 4

1 See also McLuhan's metaphor – the city as middenheap in *From Cliché to Archetype* (New York: Viking, 1970) 65. The scatological element in the modern wasteland topos may owe something to nineteenth-century attempts to run city sewage systems on town lines. See Wright 90, 144.
2 Compare Rabelais's report of Fabrius dying because he held a fart in while he was in the presence of the emperor Claudius. *Pantagruel* Book 4.17.489.
3 Kristeva puts the abject on the boundary of man and animal (1982, 12), while Murray Davis shows how excrement is used to signal the sub-

human and bestial (138–9). Mennell finds the ability to identify with animals in the increasing reluctance of people to eat such things as animal testicles. See also Corbin on the decline of animal perfumes such as musk, civet, and ambergris (73–4).
4 For Nazi reactions to literary scatology, see Jost Hermand, *Stänker und Weismacher*.

CHAPTER 5

1 See Michael McKeon (150–9) on the shifting epistemology in the concept of 'honour' when the post-medieval English aristocracy shored its ranks by means of practices such as the sale of honours, surrogate heirship, and name-changing.
2 In Hindu culture the head (Brahmin) does the thinking and praying, while the despised parts (Harijan) carry away the waste (Douglas 123). Secular society complicates such symbolic markers, but does not do away with them: Douglas cites a study of Canadian mental patients in which hospitalization marks a threshold of toleration. As long as the patients are not hospitalized, their aberrant behaviour is tolerated, but once they are hospitalized they are avoided as taboo (Douglas 97).
3 'The axis of the body is transcoded through the axis of the city' (Stallybrass 145). Freud 'brilliantly imagines the splitting of the Subject, but then he proceeds to suppress the social terrain through which that splitting is articulated' (Stallybrass 153). Compare Freud's *Aus der Geschichte einer infantilen Neurose, SE*, Vol. 17, especially pages 95–101.
4 For example, if we use job status as a criterion, a number of the characters under discussion would belong to what Wallace Clement in *Class, Power and Property* calls the 'resource proletariat.'
5 In *Not Wanted on the Voyage*, Mottyl's voice is even more humane than that of Shakespeare's dog. Findley combines Mottyl's integrity with excremental concerns. See especially Mottyl's search for her missing kitten in the latrines (315–16).
6 On the association of offal with the food of the poor, see Mennell, *All Manners of Food: Eating and Taste in England from the Middle Ages to the Present* (Oxford: Blackwell, 1985) 312.
7 On the relations between Grove's life and his autobiographical poses, see David Williams, *Confessional Fictions* 44–54.
8 Compare the advertisement for soap as a 'Kit for Climbers' (Ewen 45). The ad showed climbers scaling a mountain up to 'Heart's Desire.' Ewen notes the irony inherent in an attempt to evade mass life (to

'climb') while one is dependent on a mass-produced commodity – 'a sort of mass pseudo-demassification' (45).

9 'The inexpungeability of aristocratic nobility' is a romance convention, but 'the stories of successful younger sons of the nobility tended to be accommodated to the progressive plot-model of the career open to talents' (McKeon 213, 219). This creates a high degree of confusion 'between "restorations" and "original raisings"' (McKeon 220).

10 On modern reactions to the moralizing qualities of the fable, see Thomas Noel, *Theories of the Fable in the Eighteenth Century* (New York: Columbia UP, 1975).

11 Godard argues her case using *The Rebel Angels*, not *The Lyre of Orpheus*. Nevertheless, she, as I do, intends her claims to hold good for the bulk of Davies's writing. Her analysis of the competing voices in Davies's work is quite valuable, except for the claim that Davies includes 'no single authoritative vision of truth' (75). Although Davies repeatedly undercuts authorities, the authoritative position from which he does so can be educed from any page of his writing or from any interview. Godard seems to approach this conception when she notices a censorship that occurs in his writing, but she implies that the censors are external to Davies (Godard 78). Not only are there always clear hierarchies in Davies, but it is even doubtful whether there are competing voices (Cluett 107). Rather, ideas generally compete within a single voice. Although Davies wants Hulda Schnakenburg to speak with the inflexions of 1980s youth culture, he ends up giving her the voice of a 1960s teenager – 'it kinda grabs me' (27) – or the voice of a seventy-five-year-old British-inflected Upper Canadian English professor: 'Fat lot of good that'll be' (26). Davies only avoids anachronism when he becomes scatological: 'They don't know shit about music' (26).

12 See *The Rebel Angels* 32. Compare Freud's *Charakter und Analerotik* (1908) *SE*, Vol. 9, 169–75.

13 'De mortuis nil nisi bonum' ('Of the dead, nothing but good') is attributed to Chilo. The statement has nothing scatological about it until Davies translates it into his idea of the speech of the lower classes.

14 According to Barker, 'Pepysian corporeality' and, later in the argument, Rembrandt's 'The Anatomy Lesson of Dr Nicholas Tulp' (1632) assign the 'spectacular body' to a 'secret half-life': 'This spectacular visible body is the proper gauge of what the bourgeoisie had to forget' (24–5). (See also Stallybrass and White 83.) Barker ends his book with Caspar Barlaeus, who wrote poetry in praise of the same Dr Tulp that Rembrandt commemorated. Apparently Barlaeus became afraid to sit because he thought that his buttocks were made of glass; Barker finds

'something at once risible and haunting about a poet of the bourgeois class who thought his body was made of glass' (Barker 115). It does not help Barker's argument that he relied on an expuraged version of Pepys and that he did not compare 'The Anatomy of Dr Nicholas Tulp' to 'The Anatomy Lesson of Dr Deyman' (1656), where the corpses recall Bergiani's and Mantegna's Christs, or to 'The Descent from the Cross' (1633), where Christ's body is the focus of most of the gazes and where the apostle recovering the body (presumably John) has his face in close proximity to Christ's pubic region. Barker, so careful about political and class nuances, does not notice the subtle lessons of religious irony which might, in a painter like Rembrandt, enter even secular anatomy lessons. On the other hand, the expurgated version of Pepys makes Barker an inadvertent commentator not on the seventeenth century, but on the nineteenth and the first half of the twentieth century.

15 For a corresponding analysis of the aristocratic elements in Davies's prose style, see Cluett 97–8. The hierarchizing of academic and non-academic language by means of scatological attributions to a lower class shows up even in writers who seem to be apologists for popular culture. Marshall McLuhan speaks of Joyce and Pound renewing language that is fouled a million times a day in normal use (*From Cliché to Archetype*, New York: Viking, 1970, 115).

16 Corbin refers to turn-of-the-century Praisian society, but his statement is also an accurate reflection of the Canadian prairies between 1920 and 1970. Older excretory patterns tend to obscure the line between man and animal.

17 A different balance may be observed in the scepticism of *Yesterdays*. Although much of Ladoo's intensely scatological novel takes place among a low class, the two wealthy men (the lawyer and Pandit Puru) are also represented scatologically – the one farting, and the other picking his nose (91–2). Ladoo collapses the image of social differentiation into a single class.

18 According to de Certeau, 'marginality is today no longer limited to minority groups, but ... is becoming universal. A marginal group has now become a silent majority. That does not mean the group is homogeneous' (xvii).

CHAPTER 6

1 This holds for most ethnic groups except Natives, but Pineo and Porter's research design is limited to testing for job status rather than for the less measurable effects of discrimination.

2 For the rhetorical sources of Canadian immigration policy, see Porter (61) and Terence Craig's introduction to *Racial Attitudes in English-Canadian Fiction, 1905–1980* – particularly the words 'lower breeds' and 'lower race' that Craig quotes from a 1920 essay by Andrew MacPhail.
3 Jost Hermand describes the effects of Nazi policy on German literature: 'Die Nazis brauchten daraus nur noch die Folgerung zu ziehen, die "Hässlichkeit" der expressionistischen Asphaltliteratur in blasphemischer Überspitzung auf die schmutzige Phantasie jener semitischen "Wüstenbewohner" zurückzufuhren, deren "stinkiger Atem" fast die gesamte deutsche Kunst verpestet habe. Als sie daher 1933 die Macht antraten, brach eine Periode der kulturellen "Sauberkeit" an' (11; 'The Nazis only had to draw the conclusion, to suggest that the "ugliness" of expressionist Asphalt-literature was a blasphemous attempt to outdo the dirty fantasies of those semitic "desert-dwellers," whose "stinking breath" was said to have infected nearly the whole of German art. So when the Nazis came to power, a period of cultural "cleanliness' broke upon us'). On the unsettled nature of the German language in reference to urination, see Enzensberger 59. Enzensberger also attributes the discovery of soap to the Teutons (14) in what must be a fabular fiction since soap was apparently already used in Sumer (Valérie-Anne Giscard d'Estaing, *The World Almanac Book of Inventions*, New York: World Amanac, 1985, 163–4). One of the initial Nazi attempts to degrade the Jews was to force them to clean the streets (Nathan Ausubel, *Pictorial History of the Jewish People*, New York: Crown, 1953, 255). Scatological degradation of the Jews was, of course, hardly news in Europe. On the British demonization of the Jew by means of porcine and excremental imagery, see Stallybrass and White 54.
4 One Canadian writer on immigration during the 1950s argued that the English, Germans, and Dutch were interchangeable since they had the same cleanliness standards (Porter 69).
5 The discourse of Anglo-conformity was not always subtle: 'Learning English and living under the British flag may make a British subject in the legal sense, but not in the real sense, in the light of national history and continuity. A few such people can easily be absorbed – over a large area many thousands can be absorbed. A little dose of them may even by variation do good, like a minute dose of poison in a medicine. But if you get enough of them, you get absorbed yourself. What you called the British Empire turns into the Russian and Galician Empire. I am not saying that we should absolutely shut out and debar the European

foreigner, as we should and do shut out the Oriental. But we should in no way facilitate his coming.' The words are Stephen Leacock's, from *Economic Prosperity in the British Empire* (Toronto: Macmillan, 1930) 196. Leacock follows with an account of how the desirable British immigrant ought to be integrated into the Canadian economy.

6 Richler even broadens his racial critique: the policeman McMaster speaks Harry Stein's lower-class language (so appealing to Jake Hersh), but, like Stein with women, he reduces the French, changing *Monsieur* to 'mon-sewer' (266). This occurs even though Richler is generally not sympathetic to Québécois aspirations. Québécois literature is outside of the parameters of this study. However, we might note that the French response to English-Canadian hegemony can be coded through scatology, as it is when Hubert Aquin's narrator in *Prochain épisode* speaks of 'la vomissure décantée de notre histoire nationale' (71; 'the vomit of our national history' 53).

7 See David Williams, 'The Indian Our Ancestor: Three Modes of Vision in Recent Canadian Fiction,' *Dalhousie Review* 58 (Summer 1978): 309–29, for other forms of the myth of reconciliation.

8 Diet and hygiene conventions are likely the causes for Burdener's perception.

9 Ladoo's ironic tone makes it unlikely that the doctor is performing a rectal and vaginal examination.

10 On the problem of parody, racial stereotyping, and fossilized cultures, see the exchange between Robert Kroetsch and Andrew Suknaski in 'Ethnicity and Identity: The Question of One's Literary Passport,' *Identifications: Ethnicity and the Writer in Canada*, ed. Jars Balan (Edmonton: Canadian Institute of Ukrainian Studies, 1982).

11 On Ladoo's social critique and Creole linguistic markings, see Clement H. Wyke, 'Harold Ladoo's Alternate Worlds: Canada and Carib Island.' Wyke calls Ladoo to task for his 'unsteady world' and 'haphazard depiction.' However, the destabilization is quite purposeful; in fact, the only criticism that might be made of Ladoo in this respect is that he is so single-minded in his semiosis that he narrows human complexity to a simple scatological obsession. Of course, these were also the criticisms traditionally levelled at Swift and Pope. On Ladoo's biography, including the role of race, see Peter Such, 'The Short Life and Sudden Death of Harold Ladoo.'

12 Sir Reginald Morton (Wacousta) recalls pursuing a wounded deer in the Scottish Highlands, a deer that led him to his faithless lover, Clara Beverly.

13 Both E.J. Pratt and his source in *The Jesuit Relations*, Christophe Regnaut, underestimate these traditions when reporting how the Natives drink de Brébeuf's blood. See *The Jesuit Relations and Allied Documents*, ed. S.R. Mealing (Toronto: McClelland and Stewart, 1963) 69.
14 Contrast the tears in *Wacousta*, which signal either British losses at the hands of the Natives (186, 195) or gratitude for narrow escapes (65).
15 On the strong Orange representation among the forces that put down the Northwest Rebellion, see Hereward Senior, *Orangeism: The Canadian Phase* (Toronto: McGraw-Hill Ryerson, 1972) 71–91. In Senior's account, Orangeism is much more complex than in Wiebe's novel. The strong emphasis on moral rectitude (Senior 8) did not preclude occasions of religious tolerance on a practical level (9, 88), nor did it preclude a tongue-in-cheek, albeit militant, scatology, as is evident in one charter oath: 'May we never want a Williamite to kick the ... [sic] of a Jacobite! and a ... [sic] for the Bishop of Cork!' (quoted in Senior 3).
16 On the question of European marginality, see Seija Paddon, 'John Ashbery and Paavo Haavikkof: Architects of the Postmodern Space in Mind and Language,' *Canadian Review of Comparative Literature* 20:3–3 (Sept.–Dec. 1993): 409–16.
17 To Erich Auerbach figural use of the Old Testament suggests a key antagosnism in the Christian world-view between things and their meaning: the Christianizing of the Old Testament involved 'einen Deutungszusammenhang ... sehr weit von seiner sinnlichen Grundlage' (54; 'a meaning far removed from its sensory origins').
18 In *Wacousta* Ellen Halloway's slovenly eating among the Ottawas is likewise a sign of her fall from civilization.
19 For generalized statements on the Trickster, see Paul Radin, *The Trickster: A Study in American Indian Mythology* (New York: Schocken Books, 1956), and Franz Boas, 'Introduction,' *Traditions of the Thompson River Indians*, James Teit (1891; rpt. New York: Kraus Reprint, 1969). Radin has come under attack from anthropologists who believe that the Winnebago culture that he studied was anomalous and not representative of Amerindian attitudes towards the Trickster. However, the more one looks at Amerindian myth as *literature* rather than as field report, the more convincing Radin's account of the Trickster's satire becomes.
20 Compare Brown's comments on the 'massive structure of excremental magic' in archaic man (*Life against Death: The Psychoanalytic Meaning of History* 299).

21 In *The Rez Sisters* and *Dry Lips Oughta Move to Kapuskasing*, Manitoba Cree playwright Tomson Highway explicitly disperses the Ojibway Trickster Nanabush's scatology and subversive jokes among Native women and men. American Laguna writer Leslie Marmon Silko's Coyote in 'Toe'osh: A Laguna Coyote Legend' (*Modern Poems*, 2nd ed., ed. Richard Ellmann and Robert O'Clair, New York: W.W. Norton, 1989, 840–2) is scatological, as is the Trickster-narrator in American Blackfoot writer James Welch's *Winter in the Blood* (New York: Penguin, 1974).

22 For Cree shamanism and the historical Fine-day, see David G. Mandelbaum, *The Plains Cree: An Ethnographic, Historical and Comparative Study* (Regina: Canadian Plains Research Centre, 1979) 160–70, 363–70, and the historical Fine-day's own account, posthumously edited by Adolph Hungry Wolf, *My Cree People* (Invermere, B.C.: Good Medicine Books, 1973). For a general theory of shamanism, see Mircea Eliade, *Shamanism: Archaic Techniques of Esctasy*, trans. Willard R. Trask (New York: Harper and Row, 1958). Despite Eliade's reductive dualism of sacred and profane, this is still a worthwhile study.

23 Porter is careful not to confuse high occupational levels with political power in Canada, since Jewish representation on the boards of Canadian corporate institutions has been small (Porter 88).

24 This complication appears in Métis writer Beatrice Culleton's *In Search of April Raintree*, where April uses the social criteria of White society to lord it over her younger sister Cheryl, and in Highway's *Dry Lips Oughta Move to Kapuskasing*, where Ojibway/Cree men suffer under White prejudice and yet subjugate the women on the reserve.

25 In this regard Klein's 'Political Meeting' is of special interest. The scatological 'body-odour of race' (*15 Canadian Poets x 2* 96) evoked by the orator's (Camillien Houde's) reference to French suffering under English-Canadian conscription can only be ambivalent when it is reported by a Jew who has little reason to trust Houde's *Parti National Social Crétien*. Richler has in recent years been similarly resistant to Québécois nationalism.

26 On the role of epic in relation to culture, see Bakhtin. Bakhtin overstates the monologism of the epic, but the discussion is nevertheless important in that it codifies how someone from the margins of a culture would see epic representations of that culture and the aesthetic resolutions of the culture's tensions.

27 Klein does so in a strange combination of scatological invective and anti-materialist doctrine: 'Ezra Pound senses no compunction of his aesthetic conscience when he fertilizes the poetic field with his genius and with adjectives manurial ... What today is heralded as imagist is no more than a reactionary reversal to the rebus intelligence, a degradation into the concrete, an acceptance of the nous of the noun' ('Worse Verse' from *The McGill Daily* 29 Oct.–10 Dec. 1927, *A.M. Klein: Literary Essays and Reviews*, ed. Usher Caplan and M.W. Steinberg, Toronto: U of Toronto P, 1987, 151–2). Again: 'One does not award the Nobel Prize to the coiner, no matter how gifted, of an epigram' ('T.S. Eliot and the Nobel Prize' 12–26 Nov. 1948, Caplan and Steinberg 270). The anti-Semitism of Pound and Eliot may of course also be subliminally at stake here.

CHAPTER 7

1 A Marxist, Foley makes an interlinked series of attacks on post-structuralism, addressing the practice of post-modern novelists who continue 'to invoke discursive contracts that [are] decidedly fictional or non-fictional' (14), and situating post-structuralism historically in 'advanced monopoly capitalism' which makes a fetish of the text (18). Her most telling criticism is that non-referential theories concentrate purely on textual features without acknowledging the reader/author axis (51). 'A positivist epistemology lurks not far beneath the surface of the non-referentiality criterion: the only realities, it seems are palpable "facts," and if a discourse cannot refer to those, it has no referent at all" (47).
2 For precise examples of how 'personal' micro-narratives support the macro-narratives of social or religious history, see McKeon, particularly 212–17.
3 For associations between filth, imprisonment, and torture, see Atwood's 'Footnote to the Amnesty Report on Torture' (*Modern Poems*, 2nd ed., ed. Richard Ellmann and Robert O'Clair, New York: W.W. Norton, 1989, 801), *Bodily Harm*, Pat Lowther's 'Chacabuco, The Pit' (*15 Canadian Poets x 2* 366), and Elaine Scarry's *The Body in Pain* (18).
4 In a letter Godfrey refutes ideologically polarized representations of African society by describing a middle class that predated the Portuguese landing in 1471, a middle class created by North African trade in gold and slaves (printed in *Man Deserves Man* 195).

5 See Roland Oliver and Anthony Atmore, *Africa since 1800*, 2nd ed. (London: Cambridge UP, 1972) 229–30.
6 See Godfrey's letter in *Man Deserves Man* for the ways in which the Nkrumah government's rhetoric simply reproduced the utilitarian discourse of British colonialism. The letter was written one month before a 1966 military coup took advantage of Nkrumah's visit to Hanoi, deposing him and sending him into exile in Guinea.
7 See also the 'escuz ... breneux' (5.15.785; 'shit-smeared crowns' 5.15.633) of the Furrycats in *Pantagruel*, from whom Bakhtin probably got his metaphor.
8 Kristeva makes exactly this point about Greek democracy and the 'discovery' of the tyrant's abjection in Oedipus (1982, 88).
9 See McKeon 138. Edward Walker in 1653 writes, 'The Curtain being drawn they were discovered to be Men that heretofore were reverenced as Angels" (quoted in McKeon 152).
10 See Shell's *The Economy of Literature* on the connection between coinage and the Greek tyrant, who was the middle term in the classical Greek polity between aristocratic rule and democracy.
11 In order to sell hygiene products, companies create a whole range of bodily areas that are newly made to appear dirty. Ewen reports a 1922 Pepsodent ad directed at parents and children: '"Shall They Suffer as you did from Film on teeth?" Implying that film on the teeth was known about, much less suffered by parents, the ad conveyed the message that the needs of the child were better understood by industry" (Ewen 145). Baudrillard too arrives at a version of the commodity-self: 'Les hommes de l'opulence ne sont plus tellement environnés, comme ils le furent de tout temps, par d'autres hommes que par des *objets*' (1970, 17; 'Men of wealth are no longer surrounded by other human beings, as they have been in the past, but by *objects*' 1988, 29). Baudrillard's proposed confusion between 'mass man' and the Western 'self' eventually leads him to prematurely theorize the disappearance of the subject. Compared to Ewen's dialectical self, Baudrillard's analysis appears overly mystical.
12 One of the reviewers of *The Civilizing Process* book notes that new market conditions have undermined both classic and Victorian forms of civility (Seigal 125).
13 Clara also voices a more traditional economic satire dependent upon Freud. Of her son Arthur's hoarding of excrement she says, 'Maybe he'll grow up to be a banker' (144).

14 See Foucault's *Histoire de la sexualité: la volonté de savoir*, and Baudrillard's 'Oublier Foucault' 94.
15 According to Kroker art enhances 'capital accumulation,' which is in its 'last, purely aesthetic phase: the phase of designer bodies' (*Postmodern* 18).
16 There are medieval punishments too. Dingleman advises Duddy not to pursue money as if he has 'a hot poker up his ass' (141). Compare this to the anal punishments suffered by misers in medieval art or in the work of Heironymus Bosch.
17 See also Freud's *Aus der Geschichte einer infantilen Neurose* 84, and *Charakter und Analerotik* 173.
18 Brown claims that 'all values are bodily values' and that if money were not excrement, it would have no value (293).
19 Compare Rosebury on how Vespasian increased revenues via public urinals. 'Does this money stink?' Vespasian is reputed to have asked his son. After the son's negative reply, Vespasian explains, 'And yet it comes from urine' (Rosebury 124).
20 Interestingly, Bataille in 'La notion de dépense' and Baudrillard (1988, 34–5) do not challenge Freud's reading.
21 Despite the similarities as systems of symbolization, the translation from language to money is a complex process. See Shell's discussion in *The Economy of Literature* 3–6.
22 In his fever Moddie's miser sleepwalks to where his gold is hidden and asks Max Weber's question, 'Will this save my soul?' (69). The problem is a formal one for Moodie as well: as in Emily Bronte's *Wuthering Heights* money is never far below the surface of the Victorian woman's version of the romance plot, and gendered inheritance laws constantly set the narrative in motion. Saving one's soul at times therefore seems subordinate to getting a share of the inheritance.
23 See Shell, *Money, Language and Thought: Literary and Philosophical Economies from the Medieval to the Modern Era* (Berkeley: U of California P, 1982) 5–23.
24 In this connection it is worth looking at Robin Matthews's *Canadian Literature* 93, 158, despite the shrill nationalism which obscures the depth of Canadian–American interrelations.
25 See Robert L. McDougall's 'Introduction' to the New Canadian Library edition of *The Clockmaker*.
26 This is also true of Haliburton's attitude towards America. Of Jefferson's declaration, Slick says, 'He gave the British the but-eend of

his mind there' (130). The document is lowered to the level of the everyday, the homely, the practical, but it is not demystified in any way.
27 This describes what happens in *Black Robe*, where the Algonkian leaders insult each other scatologically even if they cannot control the council's decisions. The abuse blows off steam and simultaneously keeps power from solidifying in any one individual.
28 Bataille's translator, Allan Stoekl, detects a similar connection between Bataille's words and his politics. Stoekl connects the Fascist orgy to the orgy which is forced by heterogeneous matter in Bataille's work (Stoekl xvii). For example, in 'La notion de dépense' Bataille collapses together two of Freud's interpretations of feces – as money and death (366). Any 'gift' thus unconsciously signals loss, destruction, and death, so that a potlatch economy celebrates death, not the social process of wealth redistribution. What the potlatch is only meant to do in 'Le labyrinthe' is 'éclairer la nuit, un instant' (I.441; 'to illuminate the night for an instant' 1985, 177).

CHAPTER 8

1 Rational hygienic explanations often occur long after a particular custom (for example, the restriction on spitting) has been adopted (Elias 156). Shame, in particular, must be a social agent because many things that are dangerous to human beings do not inspire shame in the way that bodily smells do. Elias contrasts poison gas to passed gas (158), which contains no known pathogens (Guthrie 194). Unlike his successors Elias does not, however, argue that shame is explicable by a single social factor such as class status (Elias 139). It should also be noted that Pasteur's work dignified disgust for bodily ejecta, and his work became the main reason that guano was substituted for human excrement as fertilizer (Corbin 224).
2 On miasmic theories of putrefaction, on attempts to deodorize excrement, and on the opening of the sewers, see Corbin 28, 55, 123, 212. Melville, Moodie's contemporary but better versed than she in science, clearly takes miasmic theory seriously in 'The Affidavit' chapter of *Moby Dick*. For the De Mille reference, see *The Dodge Club* 30.
3 Moodie spoke of the cholera as a visitation of God (*Letters of a Lifetime* 226). Geoffrey Bilson, in *A Darkened House: Cholera in Nineteenth Century Canada* (Toronto: U of Toronto P, 1980), argues that there was no general support for the water-borne theory until the 1880s (Bilson 3),

and by then cesspools began to be eliminated in favour of closed sewage systems (Corbin 224). *Mark Hurdlestone* was published in final form in 1853, though written, Moodie says, in 1838–9 (*Letters of a Lifetime* 123). *The Literary Garland* serialized a shorter version of the same plot, 'The Miser and His Son: A Tale,' which does not contain Juliet's visits to the infectious poor, beginning in June 1842.

4 For examples of how science emplots its narratives, see Hayden White, 'The Fictions of Factual Representation' in *The Literature of Fact: Selected Papers from the English Institute*, ed. Angus Fletcher (New York: Columbia UP, 1976) 21–44, and Francis Barker's analysis of Rembrandt's 'The Anatomy of Dr Nicholas Tulp.' On the connection between the quantifying premises of the empirical sciences and those of the monied interest, see McKeon 188.

5 On microbiological distinctions between odours, see Rosebury xiv, 170. Patrick Süskind's parody of the *fluidum letale* notwithstanding, even the respective valences of high and low may not simply be social. The higher one goes in the atmosphere, the less microbes there are (Rosebury 32). The analogy does not hold for the body, where anus and mouth have the greatest concentration of microbiological life.

6 See Douglas 29–31. She argues against this doctrine, suggesting that Hebrew purification laws were instead ways of ordering the categories of creation (53). In its twentieth-century incarnation, medical materialism appears as a faith in the power of science to erase past discourses about the body. Thus Floyd Dell claims that modern sanitation will make disgust an unnecessary didactic aid in toilet training. 'Objective' and 'unemotional' toilet training will also happily lessen interest in scatological humour on the part of young people, besides eliminating homosexuality (Dell 89)!

7 'Among all those [kinds of food] forbidden us, only pork and fat may be imagined not to be harmful. But this is not so, for pork is more humid than is proper and contains much superfluous matter. The major reason why the Law abhors it is its being very dirty and feeding on dirty things. You know to what extent the Law insists upon the need to remove filth out of sight, even in the field and in a military camp, and all the more in cities. Now if swine were used for food, market places and even houses would have been dirtier than *latrines*, as may be seen at present in the country of the Franks. You know the dictum of [the sages], *may their memory be blessed: The mouth* of a swine is like walking excrement' (III.48.598). 'With regard to *circumcision*, one of the reasons for it is ... the wish to bring about a decrease in sexual inter-

course and a weakening of the organ in question, so that this activity be diminished and the organ be in as quiet a state as possible. It has been thought that circumcision perfects what is defective congenitally' (Moses Maimonides, *The Guide of the Perplexed*, trans. Shlomo Pines, Chicago: U of Chicago P, 1963, III.49.609).

8 The main difference that distinguishes present reappearances has been the adoption of scientific rhetoric – thus the advertiser tells us that Buckley's contains the oil of pine needles or that Listerine 'kills germs.'

9 In Munro's work, too, bacteriology is a social tool: 'Don't come near me, I'm full of germs' ('A Queer Streak' 229) is Trevor's distancing tactic from Violet when he begins to think that her family problems make her unfit to become his wife. Clearly, Elias's thesis can explain behaviour just as much after Pasteur as before.

10 On the necessity for microbes in order to maintain life, and on the sorry state of germ-free animals, see Rosebury 43–50.

11 Corbin explains that 'two opposed conceptions of air, dirt, and excrement' are connected to the present 'ecological dream' (232). In one conception excrement is homologous to pollution, while in the other conception excrement, a 'natural' fertilizer, is homologous to soil and to greening.

12 See William A.R. Thompson, *Black's Medical Dictionary* (London: Adam and Charles Black, 1976).

13 Gibson's matrix may be compared to the lack of excretion in scientist J.D. Bernal's earlier and more cerebral prediction of escape from the body in *The World, the Flesh, and the Devil*. Bernal predicted that man's final state would be a brain immersed in cerebro-spinal fluid. As well, the cultural past in Gibson's work is signified by technological waste, for example by 'the guts of a television so old it was studded with the glass stumps of vacuum tubes' (48).

14 This is Marshall McLuhan's formula in *From Cliché to Archetype*.

15 See Chapter 12 for the ways in which Cohen moves beyond play.

16 See Arthur Kroker's analysis of Canadian technological humanism in *Technology and the Canadian Mind: Innis/McLuhan/Grant* 14, 56–72.

17 A *New York Times* article approaches Hawking's progressive motor-neuron disease thus: 'It is perhaps significant, then, that Stephen W. Hawking, a physicist whose insights about gravity and matter are changing the way we look at the universe, should have attained his intellectual stature while his body was failing him, atrophying, shaping him increasingly into a cerebral being' (23 Jan. 1983, 16).

Notes to pages 97–102   209

18 In *World of Wonders* it is 'poetry and wonder which might reveal themselves in the dunghill' (287).
19 See I. Bernard Cohen, *Revolutions in Science* (Harvard: Belknap, 1985). The volume of blood, when Harvey measured it against the volume of food intake, could only be accounted for by return through a circuit.

CHAPTER 9

1 Schweichart, in looking at the problems of female identification with male protagonists, refuses to make what she calls a false choice between emphasis on difference and emphasis on essential humanity (43), thereby avoiding a facile negation of the simultaneously autonomous and inclusive self created by male and female writers. Linda Hutcheon similarly claims that female writing is not more conservative than male writing – it's just that 'you can assume selfhood ("character formation") or "subjectivity" only when you have attained it. Subjectivity in the Western liberal humanist tradition has been defined in terms of rationality, individuality, and power; in other words, it is defined in terms of those domains traditionally denied women' (1988a, 5). Catherine Stimpson makes this the key term in the feminist quarrel with 'the death of the author' (Stimpson 366–7). Meanwhile, Peter Schwenger notes that the importance of the penis to the male is rarely reflected in literature. He suggests that this is because the female tends to be put in the place of the body in literature, and the male in the place of the rational self.
2 'Happy virgin!' ... She does not weigh down sluggish limbs with an imprisoned embryo; she is not depressed and worn out by its awkward weight ... When the belly swells from its wound and sensual dropsy grows, the woman's exhausted health hangs by a hair. The raised skin is so distent and misshapen that even though the mother may be happy with her burden, she becomes ashamed ... How describe the tears shed at the moment when the muscles relax to release the prisoner and procure relief for the viscera? A way is forced violently through the passage and a being, perhaps lifeless, brought to life' (sixth-century poet Fortunatus quoted in O'Faolain and Martines, *Not in God's Image* 138). Aunt Moira's 'gynecological odor' (34) and Naomi's constipation during pregnancy (195) in *Lives of Girls and Women* belong to this pattern.
3 Both K.P. Stich who speaks of Woman's equivocal ascendancy over Man ['Grove's Stella,' *Canadian Literature* 113/114 (Summer/Fall 1987):

258–62] and Robert Kroetsch who speaks of Niels's belief that 'he can attach the right woman to the word "wife"' ['Narrative Patterns in Ethnic Writing,' *Canadian Literature* 106 (Fall 1985): 68] hint at these problems.

4 See O'Faolain and Martines 137–43. Some medieval feminists such as Christine de Pisan also guarded the discourse of female holiness (N. Davis 126–7), likely because it was one way that women, despite their gender, could attain the sphere of rationality and power that Hutcheon refers to. Douglas puts forward a similar explanation for the emphasis on virginity in early Christianity (157). In response to the power of this discourse, Trotula, an eleventh-century woman doctor from Salerno, passed on 'remedies for a damaged maidenhead' – special baths, suppositories, and leeches – which would tighten the vagina and/or induce bleeding on the wedding night so as to simulate the breaking of the hymen (O'Faolain and Martines 142–3).

5 See also Roman Jakobson, 'Supraconscious Turgenev,' *On Signs*, ed. Marshall Blonsky (Baltimore: Johns Hopkins UP, 1985) 303–7.

6 Ondaatje has mentioned his debt to Smart's experiment in his 'Afterword' to the 1989 edition of O'Hagan's *Tay John*.

7 See O'Faolain and Martines xiii, 120, 207f; M. Davis 88; N. Davis 124.

8 For the anal birth, see *Über infantile Sexualtheorien* 219, and *Aus der Geschichte einer infantilen Neurose* 77–8, 82. Analysing Senatspräsident Schreber's memoirs, in which Schreber speaks of drawing female buttocks on his body, Freud draws the identical conclusion (*Psychoanalytische Bemerkungen über einen autobiographisch beschriebenen Fall von Paranoia [Dementia Paranoides]* 32–3.) For an analysis of Freud's social axis, see Stallybrass and White 153f.

9 The function of religious taboo, according to Kristeva, is to avoid letting identity sink back into the mother (1982, 64).

10 In Kristeva's understanding, the avant-garde (notably Joyce and Céline) expands 'the limits of the signifiable,' producing feminine-gendered texts which carry the signification of the body or 'semiotic' against the symbolic order (C. Burke 112).

11 On Islamic taboos against intercourse during menstruation, see O'Faolain and Martines 113, and 'The Cow' in the Koran. Compounding these taboos is the prohibition against allowing the Koran to come into contact with unclean substances (Charles J. Adams, 'The Islamic Religious Tradition,' *Religion and Man*, ed. W. Richard Comstock, New York: Harper and Row, 1971, 567), which effectively separates the female sphere from the sphere of the holy.

12 While it would be a mistake to equate Rabelais's extensive and hyperbolic corporeality with misogyny, it is just as naïve to dismiss (like Bakhtin does) the violence in some of Rabelais's attacks as simply anti-mimetic play and anti-romance satire. This violence is perhaps best exemplified when Panurge cuts up the genitalia of a bitch in heat and, by sprinkling it on a woman who has refused his advances, calls in the dogs to punish her (*Pantagruel* 2.22.242f).

13 For a concise and powerful version of an underground female discourse, see Atwood's poem, 'Marrying the Hangman' in *Two-Headed Poems* (Toronto: Oxford UP, 1978) 48–51.

14 See Ewen (148) for examples of how advertisers operate under the sign of sexual difference when advertising products such as the feminine douche.

15 See, for example, how her brother Stephen's language moves from simple scatological references (108), to the same references mutated in Pig Latin (180), to apotheosis of slang in the language of mathematics: 'You surd!' (230). As mentioned, Charlotte Ford in her book on manners advocates swearing as a means of access to male language.

CHAPTER 10

1 Weber contrasts the moral isolation in Calvinist theology with the communal laxity created by the 'relative moral helplessness of Lutheranism' (126). The privatization of sin, guilt, and confession, however, is a general feature of the Protestant Reformation above any denominational differences.

2 About this history of novelistic mimesis, the two most important historians of the novel, Ian Watt and Michael McKeon, have agreed. McKeon's Marxist ideology, however, immediately allows him to uncover the romance constructions and their generation in social ideology – which Watt ignored.

3 Eco leans towards Abelard's 'post-modern' sentence, 'Nulla rosa est' (*Postscript* 1), avoiding Aquinas's comments on the immateriality of the soul.

4 See *Totem und Tabu*, where Freud insists that every prohibition points to a desire. Washing thus becomes a compensation for taboo violation (829–33). An interesting footnote to Atwood's pumice is that the Roundheads apparently did not favour soap. Cromwell had a heavy tax on it (Wright 240).

5 For additional versions of Atwood's Puritan persona, see also *The Edible Woman*, where Ainsely leaves rings in the bathtub 'which the lady down below regards as a violation of her shrine' (59), and Atwood's short story 'The War in the Bathroom' in *Dancing Girls* (Toronto: McClelland and Stewart, 1977). A possible internal countermovement in *Cat's Eye* to Atwood's rhetoric occurs in Mr Hrbik's criticism of Elaine. He criticizes her for being able to draw objects, but not life: 'God first made the bowdy out of dirt and after he breathed in the soul' (*sic*, 291), he says. It is not clear whether this epistemology is a confirmation of Atwood's artistic persona or a self-directed critique.

6 These are not entirely new developments in Canadian literature. In E.J. Pratt's 1943 poem, 'The Truant,' man rebels against a figure who is called 'the great Panjandrum' and who appears as an Archon, but who has a number of features that tie him (as the Gnostics would have) to Yahweh. The Panjandrum intends to reinforce the old hierarchies, but his scatological invective against man undermines his separateness, his 'height':

> The ALL HIGH swore until his face was black.
> He called [man] a coprophagite.

7 See Bakhtin 1984, 147. The bishop-elect of fools rode through the crowd during the Feast of Fools and threw dung at the people in parody of the real bishop's censing. On the biblical sanction for the Feast of Fools – the Magnificat's 'He lifteth up the beggar from the dunghill to set them among princes' (1 Sam. 2:8, Ps. 113:7) – see Enid Welsford, *The Fool: His Social and Literary History* 200.

8 This new marking of what is human constitutes Derrida's system, given the transgression 'beast' that appears in 'La loi du genre' and in 'La structure, le signe et le jeu dans le discours des sciences humaines,' *L'ecriture et la différence* (Paris: Seuil, 1967; 'Structure, Sign, and Play in the Discourse of the Human Sciences,' *Writing and Difference*, trans. Alan Bass, Chicago: U of Chicago P, 1978, 278–93). This beast confirms Elaine Scarry's comments: 'Enough instances occur to make it reasonable, when in the presence of nonmaterialist or antimaterialist recommendations about language, to wonder whether there is not some piece of the material world lending those recommendations substance' (1985, xxii–xxiii).

9 See 2 Kings 6:25, 10:27, 18:27; Job 20:7; Ezek. 4:12, 15; Mal. 2:3; Phil. 3:8, for example. Also see Kristeva 109 on *so'im*, 'excrementitious.'

10 See Irenaeus 1:4:2, two Valentinian fragments ('E' and 'H') in Bentley Layton, *The Gnostic Scriptures* (Garden City, N.Y.: Doubleday, 1987) 239, 245; and Kurt Rudolph, *Die Gnosis: Wesen und Geschichte einer spätantiken Religion*, Leipzig: Koehler & Amelang, 1977; *Gnosis: The Nature and History of Gnosticism*, trans. Robert McLachlan Wilson (San Francisco: Harper and Row, 1983) 72.
11 This is one aspect of medieval theology that Erasmus satirizes in *Encomium Moriae*: 'Shall we be permitted to eat and drink after the resurrection? We're taking due precaution against hunger and thirst while there's time' (154).
12 See also the carving of 'Satan and a soul' pictured in T. Tindall Wildridge's *The Grotesque in Church Art* (London: William Andrews, 1899) 89.
13 'Wenn das argumentum nit hilfft quod christianus est sine lege et supra lege, so weise man ihn flugs mit eim furtz ab' (*Tischreden* #469, I.204-5; 'When the argument that the Christian is without the law and above the law doesn't help, I instantly chase him away with a fart' 78). On the Devil as Luther's middle term between anality and justification by faith, see N. Brown 206-25.
14 For samples of Luther's, see his discussion of a dog who had become 'Lutheran' and shit into the grave of the bishop of Halle (*Tischreden* #5418, 11 April-14 June 1542), or Luther's citation of Count Hoyer of Mansfeld who, though a 'papist,' satirized relics: 'in quodam loco hett der 11000 junckfrauen brunntzschirbel zum heilthumb geweiset' (#3785, III.612; 'in a certain place the chamber pots of eleven thousand virgins had been exhibited for healing' 28 Feb. 1538). On the other hand, Luther rejected the medieval tradition that women's private parts were putrid (*Not in God's Image* 197).
15 Mather's role was not nearly as clear-cut as Atwood implies. He defended a literalist belief in demonic appearances, and his writings almost certainly led to the Salem trials, but he also argued against accepting spectre evidence. Nevertheless, Atwood is right to suggest that witches were assigned the role of 'illegitimate' bodily impulses. See *Not in God's Image* 207f.
16 This divorce of religious signifieds from the scatological signifier in the twentieth century of course enters secular culture. Since taboos on scatological language are still in place, but since they no longer have a strong supporting ideology, writers on manners have difficulty explaining to a pluralist audience why scatological discourse should be suppressed at all. Elizabeth Post suggests that the decorum is about

place, not about language: 'There is nothing really objectionable in these words – they are universally used and understood and as [the child] grows older he will develop a natural modesty about his bodily functions' (291). The appeal to nature neatly obscures the social construction of obscenity. The more sophisticated Judith Martin gives an even more evasive answer: 'The person who grows up saying "I'm going to have a bowel movement now" is not going to have much of a social life' (334). The appeal to the social is a thinly disguised appeal (again) to nature (this time as an eternal social verity).

17 Compare the bathroom scenes in *Ulysses* or the scatological imagery of Eliot's 'East Coker,' which also undercut modernist approaches to myth.
18 On other ways in which Mrs Bentley gains sympathy, see Evelyn Hinz and John Teunissen, 'Who's the Father of Mrs Bentley's Child? *As for Me and My House* and the Conventions of Dramatic Monologue,' *Canadian Literature* 111 (Winter 1986): 101–13.
19 For *Mrs Blood* as a parody of the grail legend, see Hutcheon, *The Canadian Postmodern* 6.
20 Saliva is extremely defiling to the Brahmin (which Bisnath claims to be): the orthodox Brahmin throws food into his mouth or pours it in (Douglas 33–4).
21 As regent of the eastern quarter, Indra may again be under scatological attack. See Benjamin Walker, *The Hindu World: An Encyclopedic Survey of Hinduism*, Vol. 1 (New York: Praeger, 1968).
22 Compare Freud's patient in *Aus der Geschichte einer infantilen Neurose*, whose first religious doubts concerned 'ob Christus einen Hintern gehabt habe' (79; 'whether Christ had had a behind' 71). Freud interprets this as standing for a repulsion from the father who stood for God and the law (87). Interestingly, the same Gnostic problem reappears in Carl Jung's later analysis of God's hind parts in *Antwort auf Hiob* (381–2).
23 According to Layton, this passage may play on a double meaning in John 6:27: 'Jesus answered them ... do not labour for (or digest) the food that perishes, but for the food which endures to eternal life' (Layton 239).
24 See Aquinas, *Summa Contra Gentiles* 4:38–9 for example.
25 In Irenaeus's system, Simon Magus is the heresiarch responsible for Gnosticism.

26 Rev Andrew Boyer's sermon paralleling the tramps' pit to the Jewish Gehenna is not simply a mythical connection as Dunstan supposes. Gehenna was originally the Valley of Hinnom near Jerusalem and at a later date was thought to have become the city's rubbish heap. See 'Hell,' *A Theological Word Book of the Bible*, ed. Alan Richardson (London: SCM Press, 1957).
27 Daniel attempts a broader denunciation in *Black Robe* when he metaphorically spits on Jesus (12).
28 Excrement for the first time came under a microscopic gaze in the seventeenth century. Compare Anthony van Leewenhoek's fascinated 1683 description of his own excrements, quoted in Rosebury 13–16. Religious paradises are usually represented as free of filth, despite the sensate and material nature of popular utopias such as Cockayne (Manuel 80–1). Thomas Aquinas's heaven and the 'not-decaying, not-rotting' Zoroastrian paradise reported in the Manuels' *Utopian Thought in the Western World* (38) are cases in point. In contrast, one of the reasons that the 'underworld' from which the two daimons speak in Davies's *The Lyre of Orpheus* seems so contrived is that Davies forgoes the traditional associations of the anus with the daimonic. The closest that the novel comes to the daimonic is in its evocation of the past, the prompter's substage hell in Hoffman's nineteenth-century theatre (458).
29 Paracelsus, who figures prominently in *The Rebel Angels* and who is a father of modern chemistry because he argued that external agents and not an imbalance of humours caused disease, may be one source for Davies's physiological predestination. In *The Archidoxies*, Book 2, Paracelsus says that all kinds of bodies arise out of the four elements according to their predestined conditions.
30 Compare also Luther – 'ego sentis animam non extrinsecus accedere, sed ex materia seminis creari' (*Tischreden* #5230, V.18; 'it's my opinion that the soul isn't added from the outside but is created out of the matter of the semen' 2–17 Sept. 1540) – and Paracelsus: 'spirit grows out of the sperm, or out of the seed' (*The Archidoxies* 5.40–1). Bakhtin cites 'De flatibus' in the Hippocractic anthology in a similar vein: 'The spirit penetrates in a more or less large quantity. This is obvious from the fact that many persons belch when eating and drinking' (quoted in Bakhtin 1984, 356). A version of this trope appears in Irving Layton's rewriting of Plato's *Symposium*, 'Socrates at the Centaur' in *Canadian Literature* 112 (Spring 1987): 16–17:

> Inwardly I laughed
> to see them swallow the hook I'd baited
> with their own vanity, their faces made
> suddenly grave from that self-importance
> every possessor of a soul feels
> between one evacuation of his inflamed
> bladder and the next.

31 The referential difference between Old and New Testaments may be very easily illustrated by looking up 'dung' in a biblical concordance.
32 Jae Num Lee believes that the scatological metaphor in English Restoration satire was often mean to instil 'a theocentric rather than homocentric perspective' (Lee 47), but he deals only with authorial intent, not with the epistemologies of discourse. Francis Bacon uses the view of nature as 'God's other book' to divert attention onto matter: 'The relationship between spiritual and material study ceases to be one of the hierarchical superordination and becomes one of analogy. This change may be sensed, perhaps, in the careless ease with which Bacon employs the model of divine authority as though it were a rhetorical figure ... The familiar language of spiritual events finds its highest function to rest in signifying a more present reality of material success' (McKeon 66).
33 This is the designation that Auerbach applies to Shakespearean representation in *Mimesis* (275).
34 Theodor Rosebury, a popularizer of science uneasy with religious repression, also makes Bataille's naïve equation of divinity with the obscene. Since both the unclean and the holy require ritual ablutions, Rosebury disingenuously wonders whether the Hebrews execrated or worshipped swine (73). Such confusion comes from the separation of social categories from both religion and the obscene: elsewhere Rosebury imagines that the language can be 'detoxified' of obscenity once we become objective in our approach to excrement (189). To criticize Bataille and Rosebury is not to deny that there are cases in which scatological abasement (without a social purpose) has become linked to religious observation. See Havelock Ellis, *Studies in the Psychology of Sex* 57-9.
35 See also Barbara Babcock on the relation between Negativity Theory, and 'reversible world,' and religion, 'perhaps the most explicitly negativistic of all symbol systems' (18).

INTRODUCTION TO PART III

1 See also Foley 36-8. Although Foley's comments apply initially to mimesis, the way she speaks of mimesis and her etymological play on types of filiation suggest that she has genre in mind as well: 'Mimesis inherently generalizes' our social existence, and in this way creates cognition through 'analogous configuration' (68, 65).
2 Bakhtin is important not because of his generic attempts to distinguish between epic and novel (as if the novel could never retain elements of the tribal encyclopedia), but because we can apply his description of the novel's multiplicity of voices to the novel's multiplicity of genres.
3 'Postmodern literary texts will take an anti-allegorical stand, either by building and then destroying allegorical structures within their own fictional framework or by postulating a world of simulacra without depth, center, or meaning, where events are governed not by necessity or causation, but by pure chance' (Spariosu 61). Lyotard argues that the traditional meta-narratives driving the accumulation of knowledge – (1) the philosophical evolution of a 'world of spirit' or (2) the emancipation of 'the people' – have already been eclipsed by the 'performativity' principle, so that all knowledge is reduced to a series of mini-games in which the system's enhanced performance is always the main criterion for legitimacy. Critics have identified the repressed narrative driving Lyotard's excellent study as 'the dystopian prospect of a global private monopoly of information' (Jameson 1984a, xx) or 'the métarécit of the dissolution of métarécits' (Rosso 1987).

CHAPTER 11

1 See also Domna Stanton, whose distrust for generic commentary appears odd beside her 'genderic' analysis (11) of male theorists of autobiography. In her reading, gender creates formal markings in autobiographical theory.
2 'Dire la verité sur soi, se constituer comme un subjet plein – c'est un imaginaire. L'autobiographie a beau être impossible, ça ne l'empeche nullement d'exister' (Lejeune 1986, 31; 'Telling the truth about the self, constituting the self as complete subject – it is a fantasy. In spite of the fact that autobiography is impossible, this in no way prevents it from existing' 131-2).

3 On de Man's past, see Jon Wiener, 'Deconstructing Paul de Man,' *The Nation* (9 Jan. 1988: 22–4.
4 See also Isobel M. Findlay, 'Intimations of Accountability in the Discourse of Paul de Man,' *English Studies in Canada* 18:1 (March 1992): 59–81.
5 'This novel is autobiographical in form but not in fact. My family, neighbors and friends did not serve as models' (*Lives of Girls and Women*). 'This book, though not about my parents, is dedicated to them' (*The Story of Bobby O'Malley*). For a good account of the relations between Munro's life and text, see Robert Thacker, '"So Shocking a Verdict in Real Life": Autobiography in Alice Munro's Stories,' in Stich 153–61.
6 The title apparently (and appropriately) belongs to another, Arthur Rimbaud. See Scobie 127. Lejeune means to raise the problem that the first person in any narrative is an assumed role. Especially in using quotations, we speak the word of another, and to some extent all language is a form of quotation (as Roland Barthes has argued in 'La Mort de l'auteur'). As soon as we speak, therefore, we take the position of another. In this respect we might notice the pervasive theatrical metaphors throughout Munro's *Lives of Girls and Women*. Lejeune departs from Barthes by stressing the full ambidexterity of the motto: 'Dès que j'écris, en effet, je partage les désirs et les illusions des autobiographes, et je ne suis sûrement pas prêt à y renoncer. Je dis tout haut: "Je est un autre," et tout bas peut-être j'ajoute: "mais comme c'est dommage!"' (1986, 32–3; 'As soon as I write, as a matter of fact, I share the desires and illusions of autobiographers, and I am surely not ready to renounce them. I say outloud: "I is someone else," and in a whisper perhaps I add: "but what a shame!"' 133).
7 Lejeune also explains how autobiography functions to restore roots, especially to an urban middle class (213).
8 My echo of Marxian discourse in the word 'base' (with its implication of superstructure) is intentional: the mimetic focus in autobiographical scatology, including post-modern versions, is strongly circumstantial. The explanation that I offer, however, is not completely determined by an economic mode of production, but predicated on the text's reproduction of the cultural body-images that we have seen in Chapters 1 to 10, of which economic production is one facet.
9 Augustine's case is more complex than the use to which I am putting him. In Book Four of *De Doctrina Christiana* Augustine's desire for a natural, unadorned beauty suggests that the metaphor of the body can cut through rhetoric. Although Spengemann is quite right to call the

narrator of the *Confessiones* transcendent, autobiography was an alternative to even more formal and transcendent modes of rhetorical expression.
10 Despite recent and justifiable attacks on 'thematic' reading (Goldie), there is no such thing as a 'bounded' theme, no such thing as a trope that is purely textual. Scatology shows this more clearly than something like 'light imagery' can, but I suspect that within every thematic is a theory of representation.
11 Her anxiety of influence is not fully distinct from what Gilbert and Gubar call 'the anxiety of authorship' – the feeling that origins, shapes, sequences, and inheritances of the alphabet militate against a woman's writing (Gilbert and Gubar 41) – since Uncle Craig's self-important and ridiculously overdetailed record-keeping is a hyperbolic parody of the objective tendencies in historiography. If the female autobiographer tends to mistrust biological identity and yet initially to assert identity rather than subvert it (Stanton 15; C. Burke 108), such gestures owe something to the traditional exclusion of women from the symbolic order and to the determination of women by a patronymic alphabet (Gilbert and Gubar).
12 The body that will not rot is a staple of saints' lives, as Dunstan the hagiographer would know, and the topos reaches self-conscious expression in Dostoevsky's *The Brothers Karamazov* and Cohen's *Beautiful Losers*.
13 Of the videotape, Bobby says, 'My father was there and not there, an animated relic' (179). Although Bobby repudiates only the priesthood and not Catholicism, the scatological destruction of relics is a traditional technique of religious repudiation. See Chapter 10.
14 See James J. Preston, 'Purification,' *Encyclopedia of Religion*. The Rabelaisian analogy is quoted in Chapter 10; for other discussions, see Martin Pops, 'The Metamorphoses of Shit' 52; Kenneth Burke, 'Ritual Drama as Hub' 131-2; and *The Story of Bobby O'Malley* 165. Douglas emphasizes how confession can often cancel the pollution caused in the breaking of taboos. This symbolic tradition allows Arthur Kroker to reinterpret past autobiographies: speaking of Augustine, Kroker says that 'guilt offers the promise of a final peace through the mechanism of "confession," or shall we say "evacuation"' (46).

CHAPTER 12

1 'Le plaisir du texte, c'est ce moment où mon corps va suivre ses propres idées – car mon corps n'a pas les mêmes idées que moi' (1973, 30; 'The

pleasure of the text is that moment when my body pursues its own ideas – for my body does not have the same ideas that I do' 17).

2 Habermas reads post-modernism as a neoconservative movement. Jameson quite rightly questions the populist rhetoric of post-modernism and, with Eagleton and Foley, criticizes the connections between post-modernism and advanced monopoly capitalism. Foley adds that post-modernism promotes 'the fetishization of textuality' and thus 'mediates the extreme abstractions of a society in which all human functions are rendered equivalent' (18). Such a dismissal seems curiously unself-conscious about the marketing of texts (including *Telling the Truth: The Theory and Practice of Documentary Fiction*), and not fully conversant with how post-modern texts de-nature economic structures. See Chapter 7, especially the account of Gibson's work.

3 Jameson contrasts 'hermeneutical' readings, 'in which the work in its inert, objectal form is taken as a clue or a symptom for some vaster reality,' with post-modern art, which confronts the 'viewer' with 'all the contingency of some inexplicable natural object' (1991, 8). The unremarked sliding of Jameson's prose from 'reading' to 'viewer' is instructive: Jameson's contrast between depth and surface functions certainly works when one compares Van Gogh to Warhol, but not when one addresses Pynchon (whom Jameson very briefly mentions) or Canadian post-modernists.

4 Writing is a simulacrum; so, no doubt, is speech. When writing was a recent and elite technology the apocryphal writer of the first-century AD Book of Enoch said, 'Men were not created for this that they should confirm their faith ... with pen and ink' (1 Enoch, trans. M.A. Knibb, *The Aprocryphal Old Testament*, ed. H.F.D. Sparks, Oxford, 1984, 69:10). Lao Tzu, in fourth-century BC China, went further: 'Bring it about that the people will return to the use of the knotted rope' (*Tao Te Ching*, trans. D.C. Lau, Harmondworth, 1963, 80.193b). Socrates warned that writing would 'implant forgetfulness' in men's souls and that they would call things to remembrance 'no longer within themselves, but by means of external marks' (Plato, *Phaedrus*, trans. R. Hackforth, *The Collected Dialogues of Plato*, ed. Edith Hamilton and Huntington Cairns, Princeton, 1961, 520). See also Hutcheon on scepticism about the 'real' in simulacra theory (1988, 229).

5 Never completely broken up. Although Rooke emphasizes process against a completed world, he also contributes to the fetishizing of Shakespeare because parody needs the original 'central' text in order to gain a reading. A novel quoting the classic name of 'Shakespeare' in the

title has a better chance of being noticed by the Governor General's Award judges (those proxies for monarchs and classics). The parodic imitation employed in the text thus gets (and got) not only a 'classic' reading but, in 1982, a Governor General's Award. 'Even in mocking terms, parody reinforces; in formal terms, it inscribes the mocked conventions onto itself, thereby guaranteeing their continued existence' (Hutcheon 1985, 75). To this we could add: guaranteeing not only the continued existence of the conventions, but also the continued existence of the new text.

6 This corresponds partially with Hutcheon's comment on the politics of parody: 'Ambivalence set up between conservative repetition and revolutionary difference is part of the very paradoxical essence of parody' (Hutcheon 1985, 77).

7 This is perhaps what dismays Kaspar Schopp (whose name is the Old English word for poet) in *Antichthon*. Lost in Rome he sees a sewer, 'a feculent pool' (294), and he recoils in horror from this version of Giordano Bruno's natural Avernus. Judith Thompson's play *White Biting Dog* is another instance in which the nauseous specifics of matter destroy a materialist as much as a transcendent epistemology. From the beginning a transcendent lexis – God, prophecy, salvation, communion – orbits the unseen figure of a white dog; this alphabetic inversion does not subvert the transcendent (in Bakhtin's sense), but combines it explosively with a vocabulary and action which is bodily in the extreme: Pony eats and vomits the meat of the dachshunds that Cape stored in the freezer. There are no materialist consolations: Lomia, who can hear her food digesting (84), says, 'I love being inside my six layers of skin ... I feel ... like sewage' (68).

8 The closet meeting between theoretical and practical disembodiments occurs in *Prochain épisode*. Jailed, judicially separated from the objects of his desire, the narrator understands very clearly how writing defers. He substitutes words for his body: the words make an endless parabola towards the object, but the narrator is under no delusions that he is acting, doing, loving, excreting, dying when he writes. Yet even he speaks as if scatology is primary: 'Rien n'empêche le déprimé politique de conférer une coleration esthétique à cette sécrétion verbeuse' (26; 'Nothing prevents a depressed and politically-aware man from attributing aesthetic values to the verbal secretion' 22).

9 'Les banques des données ... sont la "nature" pour l'homme postmoderne' (Lyotard 84–5; 'Data banks ... are "nature" for postmodern man' 51).

222 Notes to pages 171–8

10 See *15 Canadian Poets x 2* where Bowering makes a similar metonymic reduction in 'Summer Solstice':

   shit, it comes
   & goes, it goes, thru us pretending we are
   not some more, shit

11 On the absence of rationalist paradigms, see Nancy E. Bjerring, 'Deconstructing the "Desert of Facts": Detection and Antidetection in Coming through Slaughter' 325–38. Bjerring's reading is quite convincing, but strangely celebratory of Buddy's anti-rational silence at the end of the novel: the reader discovers that Buddy is being sodomized by the attendants in the mental hospital, though Buddy himself does not seem to understand what is happening. This is good?
12 Compare August Strindberg's *A Dream Play* in which a gilded castle rises out of stable-muck.
13 See also Sandra Djwa's critique that F. lacks depth ('Leonard Cohen: Black Romantic' in Gnarowski 94–105).
14 Dennis Lee criticizes Cohen for adding an anti-climax by adding Part 3. Lee's 'savage fields' invite the explosion of past cosmologies but Lee's call for revolution in *Savage Fields* (Toronto: Anansi, 1977) and elsewhere is elegantly and very civilly put. For a critique of the 'pseudo-historical and anti-hierarchical pretense' that accepts equally 'all acts of self-creativity,' see Fekete 59–60. Fekete does not name Bataille, but almost certainly has him in mind.
15 For Jameson such scepticism goes too far. He criticizes Bob Perelman's poem 'China' because it provides, without so declaring, captions for the pictures of a missing book. For Jameson, E.L. Doctorow's *Ragtime* similarly verifies our confinement in Plato's cave: 'If there is any realism left here, it is a "realism" which springs from the shock of grasping that confinement and of realizing that, for whatever peculiar reasons, we seem condemned to seek the historical past through our own pop images and stereotypes about that past, which itself remains forever out of reach' (1982, 118). In his nostalgia for direct, if non-realist, signification Jameson relies for his metaphors on the source of dialectic and the concept of mimesis: the movement from the tribal encyclopedia or *doxa* to a conception of literature in which the receiver does not dramatically re-enact the story but stands outside of it and *interprets* it as the sign of something else (though not yet as politics).

16 For Norman O. Brown's famous thesis about Luther and depth commentary upon the bodily meaning of grace, see *Life against Death: The Psychoanalytic Meaning of History*.
17 'I dirtied on my beads' predicts a host of late-twentieth-century artistic practices, such as Andres Serrano's plastic crucifix soaking in his own urine ('Piss Christ' 1989), a work that led to American congressional attacks on the National Endowment for the Arts. In another work Serrano dipped a 'Christ' in milk because everyone seemed to want a pure Christ. See Tom Matthews, 'Fine Art or Foul,' *Newsweek* 116:1, 2 July 1990: 46–50.
18 'When language and the body are placed side by side, the weightlessness of any language that has lost its referential aspirations becomes especially noticeable' (Scarry 1988, xxii). I am conscious that my study cannot, finally, address the 'unpresentable' and that I have purposely taken Bataille (and perhaps Lyotard and Cohen) too literally. Someone like Kristeva allows Bataille a broader scope: 'Comment rendre visible ce qui n'est pas visible du fait qu'aucun code, convention, contrat, identité ne le supporte ... Nous ne nous débarrasserons jamais du refoulement, tant que nous parlons ... La "métaphore" comme trope poétique n'est plus de mise, avec son cortège d'idéalisation et de mystère' (1983, 342–3; 'How can one make visible that which is not visible because no code, convention, contract, or identity holds it up? ... As long as we speak, we shall never get rid of repression ... "Metaphor" as poetic figure is out of place along with its retinue of idealizations and mysteries' 1987, 366–7). I have taken Bataille and Cohen at their metaphors rather than at the feeling which they want to say precedes the metaphor.
19 For this reason Elias distrusted both 'isolationist dualism' – or human sciences set against the natural sciences, the human mind as a distinct entity within an organic container – and 'reductionist monism': behaviourism, ethology, sociobiology, in which human behaviour is explained as the product of biological urges (Mennell 202).
20 The refusal to express, so well expressed, is of course another sort of depth commentary with its own historical resources.
21 For additional references to Cohen's drug use, see L.S. Dorman and C.L. Rawlins, *Leonard Cohen: Prophet of the Heart* (New York: Omnibus, 1990) 134, 199; and Ian Pearson, 'Growing Old Disgracefully,' *Saturday Night* March 1993: 76.

Note to page 182

EPILOGUE

1 The clash of metaphors between an Atwood narrator who speaks of 'the obscure base note of ancient throwup and pee' (*Cat's Eye* 16) and a Mitchell narrator who speaks of 'urine's high soprano' (*The Vanishing Point* 6) is therefore not surprising.

Works Cited

Adams, Robert M. 'Review of *The Civilizing Process.*' *Times Literary Supplement* 15 Sept. 1978: 1015.
Agrippa, Henricus Cornelius. *De incertitudine et vanitate scientiarum et artium atque excellentia verbi dei declamatio (Of the Vanitie and Uncertaintie of Artes and Sciences)*. Trans. James Sanford (1569). In *Christopher Marlowe's Doctor Faustus: A 1604-Version Edition*. Ed. Michael Keefer. Peterborough: Broadview P, 1991.
Ahenakew, Edward. 'Cree Trickster Tales.' *Journal of American Folklore* 42 (1929): 309–53.
Aquin, Hubert. *Prochain épisode*. Montréal: Cercle du Livre de France, 1965; Trans. Penny Williams. Toronto: McClelland and Stewart, 1967.
Aquinas, Thomas. *Summa Contra Gentiles (On the Truth of the Catholic Faith)*. Trans. Charles J. O'Neil. Garden City, N.Y.: Hanover House, 1957.
– *Summa Theologiae (St Thomas Aquinas on Politics and Ethics)*. Ed. and trans. Paul E. Sigmund. New York: Norton, 1988.
Armstrong, Pat, and Hugh Armstrong. *The Double Ghetto: Canadian Women and Their Segregated Work*. Toronto: McClelland and Stewart, 1978; rev. ed. 1984.
Atwood, Margaret. *Bodily Harm*. Toronto: McClelland and Stewart, 1981.
– *Cat's Eye*. Toronto: Bantam, 1988.
– *The Handmaid's Tale*. Toronto: McClelland and Stewart, 1985.
– *Selected Poems*. Toronto: Oxford UP, 1976.
– 'Witches' (1980). *Second Words: Selected Critical Prose*. Toronto: Anansi, 1982, 329–33.
Atwood, Margaret, and Robert Weaver, eds. *The Oxford Book of Canadian Short Stories*. Toronto: Oxford UP, 1986.

Auerbach, Erich. *Mimesis; dargestellte Wirklichkeit in der abendländischen Literatur.* Bern: A. Francke, 1946; *Mimesis: The Representation of Reality in Western Literature.* Trans. Willard Trask. Garden City, N.Y.: Doubleday, 1953.
Augustine. *Confessiones (Confessions).* Trans. Edward B. Pusey. New York: P.F. Collier, 1909.
– *De Doctrina Christiana (On Christian Doctrine).* Trans. D.W. Robertson, Jr. New York: Bobbs Merrill, 1958.
– *De Trinitate (On the Trinity).* Trans. A.W. Haddan. Rev. W.G.T. Shedd. *Basic Writings of Saint Augustine.* Ed. Whitney J. Oates. New York: Random House, 1948.
Babcock, Barbara, ed. *The Reversible World: Symbolic Inversion in Art and Society.* Ithaca, N.Y.: Cornell UP, 1978.
Bader, Rudolf. 'Frederick Philip Grove and Naturalism Reconsidered.' *Gaining Ground: European Critics on Canadian Literature.* Ed. R. Kroetsch and Reingard M. Nischick. Edmonton: NeWest, 1985, 222–33.
Bakhtin, M.M. *The Dialogic Imagination: Four Essays.* Trans. Michael Holquist and Caryl Emerson. Austin: U of Texas P, 1981.
– *Rabelais and His World.* Trans. Helen Iswolsky. Bloomington, Ind.: Indiana UP, 1984.
Barker, Francis. *The Tremulous Private Body.* London: Methuen, 1984.
Barthes, Roland. 'La mort de l'auteur' (1968). *Le bruissement de la langue.* Paris: Seuil, 1984; 'The Death of the Author.' Trans. Richard Howard. *Contemporary Critical Theory.* Ed. Dan Latimer. New York: Harcourt Brace Jovanovich, 1989, 53–9.
– *Mythologies.* Paris: Seuil, 1957; Trans. Annette Lavers. London: Paladin, 1973.
– *Le plaisir du texte.* Paris: Seuil, 1973; *The Pleasure of the Text.* Trans. Richard Miller. New York: Hill and Wang, 1975.
Bataille, Georges. *Oeuvres complètes.* Vols. 1 and 2. Ed. Michel Foucault. Paris: Gallimard, 1970.
– *Visions of Excess: Selected Writings, 1927–1939.* Ed., trans., and intro. Allan Stoekl. Minneapolis: U of Minnesota P, 1985.
Baudrillard, Jean. *A l'ombre des majorités silencieuses.* Paris: Denoël/Gonthier, 1982.
– *Jean Baudrillard: Selected Writings.* Ed. and trans. Mark Poster. Stanford: Stanford UP, 1988.
– *La societé de consommation.* Paris: Denoël, 1986.
– *Oublier Foucault.* Paris: Galilée, 1977; 'Forgetting Foucault.' Trans. Nicole Dufresne. *Humanities in Society* 3:1 (Winter 1980): 87–111.

Benveniste, Émile. *Problèmes de linguistique generale*. Paris: Gallimard, 1966; *Problems in General Linguistics*. Trans. Mary Elizabeth Meek. Coral Gables, Fla.: U of Miami P, 1971.
Bernal, J.D. *The World, the Flesh, and the Devil*. Bloomington, Ind.: Indiana UP, 1929.
Bjerring, Nancy E. 'Deconstructing the "Desert of Facts": Detection and Antidetection in *Coming through Slaughter*.' *English Studies in Canada* 16:3 (Sept. 1990): 325–38.
Bottomley, Frank. *Attitudes to the Body in Western Christendom*. London: Lepus, 1979.
Bourke, John G. *Scatological Rites of All Nations* (1891). New York: Johnson Reprint, 1968.
Bowering, George. *Burning Water*. Toronto: General Publishing, 1980.
– 'Modernism Could Not Last Forever.' *The Mask in Place*. Winnipeg: Turnstone, 1982.
Bradbury, Malcolm, and James McFarlane. 'The Name and Nature of Modernism.' *Modernism: 1890–1930*. Eds. Bradbury and McFarlane. Harmondsworth, Middlesex: Penguin, 1976.
Breton, Raymond. 'West Indian, Chinese and European Ethnic Groups in Toronto: Perceptions of Problems and Resources.' *Two Nations, Many Cultures: Ethnic Groups in Canada*. Ed. Jean Leonard Elliot. Scarborough: Prentice-Hall, 1983.
Brooke, Christopher. *The Monastic World, 1000–1300*. London: Paul Elek, 1974.
Brooke, Frances. *The History of Emily Montague* (1769). Toronto: McClelland and Stewart, 1961.
Brown, Jennifer S.H., and Robert Brightman. *'Orders of the Dreamed': George Nelson on Cree and Northern Ojibway Religion and Myth* (1823). Winnipeg: U of Manitoba P, 1988.
Brown, N.O. *Life against Death: The Psychoanalytic Meaning of History*. New York: Vintage, 1959.
Buckler, Ernest. *The Mountain and the Valley*. Toronto: McClelland and Stewart, 1952.
Bukatman, Scott. 'The Cybernetic (City) State: Terminal Space becomes Phenomenal.' *Journal of the Fantastic in the Arts* 2:2 (Summer 1989): 43–63.
Bullough, Vern L. 'Review of *The Civilizing Process*.' *American Historical Review* 84 (April 1979): 444.
Burke, Kenneth. 'Ritual Drama as Hub.' *Terms for Order*. Ed. Stanley Edgar Hyman. Bloomington, Ind.: Indiana UP, 1964.

Burke, Peter. *Popular Culture in Early Modern Europe*. London: Harper and Row, 1978.
Calinescu, Matei. 'Introductory Remarks: Postmodernism, the Mimetic and Theatrical Fallacies.' *Exploring Postmodernism*. Ed. Matei Calinescu and Douwe Fokkema. Amsterdam: John Benjamins, 1987, 3–16.
Callaghan, Morley. *More Joy in Heaven*. Toronto: McClelland and Stewart, 1937.
– *Such Is My Beloved*. Toronto: McClelland and Stewart, 1934.
Cartier, Jacques. *Jacques Cartier [Voyages]*. Ed. Marcel Trudel. Montreal: Fides, 1968.
Cavendish, Richard. *A History of Witchcraft*. London: Weidenfeld and Nicolson, 1977.
Céline, Louis-Ferdinand. *Entretiens avec le professeur Y*. Paris: Gallimard, 1955.
– *Mort a Crédit. Romans*. Paris: Gallimard, 1962.
Certeau, Michel de. *Arts de faire (The Practice of Everyday Life)*. Trans. Steven F. Rendall. Los Angeles: U of California P, 1984.
Cixous, Hélène. 'Le rire de la Méduse.' *L'arc* 61 (1975): 39–54; 'The Laugh of the Medusa.' *New French Feminisims: An Anthology*. Ed. Elaine Marks and Isabelle de Courtivron. New York: Schocken, 1980, 245–64.
– 'Tancrede continue' (1983). *Entre l'écriture*. Paris: Des Femmes, 1986; 'Tancredi Continues.' *Writing Differences: Readings from the Seminar of Hélène Cixous*. Ed. and trans. Susan Sellers. New York: St. Martin's, 1988.
Clatworthy, Stewart, and Harvey Stevens. *An Overview of the Housing Conditions of Registered Indians in Canada*. Ottawa: Indian and Northern Affairs Canada, 1987.
Clement, Wallace. *Class, Power and Property: Essays on Canadian Society*. Toronto: Methuen, 1983.
Cluett, Robert. *Canadian Prose Style: A Preliminary Stylistic Analysis*. Toronto: ECW Press, 1990.
Cohen, Leonard. *Beautiful Losers*. Toronto: McClelland and Stewart, 1966.
Cohen, Ralph. 'History and Genre.' *New Literary History* 17:2 (Winter 1986): 203–19.
Corbin, Alain. *Le miasme et la jonquille (The Foul and the Fragrant: Odor and the French Social Imagination)*. Cambridge, Mass.: Harvard UP, 1986.
Cosman, Madeleine Pelner. *Fabulous Feasts: Medieval Cookery and Ceremony*. New York: George Braziller, 1976.

Craig, Alec. *The Banned Books of England and Other Countries*. London: George Allen and Unwin, 1962.
Craig, Terrence. *Racial Attitudes in English-Canadian Fiction, 1905–1980*. Waterloo: Wilfrid Laurier UP, 1987.
Culler, Jonathan. *Structuralist Poetics*. Ithaca, N.Y.: Cornell UP, 1975.
Culleton, Beatrice. *In Search of April Raintree*. Winnipeg: Pemmican, 1983.
Davies, Robertson. *The Enthusiasms of Robertson Davies*. Ed. Judith Skelton Grant. Toronto: McClelland and Stewart, 1979.
– *Fifth Business*. Markham, Ont.: Penguin, 1970.
– *The Lyre of Orpheus*. New York: Penguin, 1988.
– *The Manticore*. Markham, Ont.: Penguin, 1973.
– 'On Stephen Leacock' (1957). *Masks of Fiction*. Ed. A.J.M. Smith. Toronto: McClelland and Stewart, 1961.
– *The Rebel Angels*. New York: Penguin, 1981.
– *A Voice from the Attic*. Toronto: McClelland and Stewart, 1960.
– *What's Bred in the Bone*. New York: Penguin, 1985.
– *World of Wonders*. Markham, Ont.: Penguin, 1975.
Davis, Murray S. *Smut: Erotic Reality/Obscene Ideology*. Chicago: U of Chicago P, 1983.
Davis, Natalie Zemon. *Society and Culture in Early Modern France*. Stanford: Stanford UP, 1975.
Dell, Floyd. *Love in the Machine Age*. New York: Farrar and Rinehart, 1930.
Della Casa, Giovanni. *Galateo*. Trans. Konrad Eisenbichler and Kenneth R. Bartlett. Toronto: Centre for Reformation and Renaissance Studies, 1986.
De Man, Paul. 'Autobiography as De-facement.' *Modern Language Notes* 94:5 (Dec. 1979): 919–30.
De Mille, James. *The Dodge Club, or, Italy in MDCCCLIX* (1869). Sackville, N.B.: Mount Allison Bell Library, 1981.
– *A Strange Manuscript Found in a Copper Cylinder* (1880). Toronto: McClelland and Stewart, 1969.
Derrida, Jacques. 'La loi du genre' ('The Law of Genre'). Trans. Avital Ronell. *Glyph: Textual Studies*. Ed. Samuel Weber. Baltimore: Johns Hopkins UP, 1980, 177–229.
– *La vérité en peinture*. Paris: Flammarion, 1978; *The Truth in Painting*. Trans. Geoff Bennington and Ian MacLeod. Chicago: U of Chicago P, 1987.
Descartes, René. *The Essential Descartes*. Trans. Elizabeth S. Haldane and G.R.T. Ross. Ed. Margaret D. Wilson. New York: New American Library, 1969.

- 'Méditations:' *Oeuvres et Lettres*. Ed. André Bridoux. Paris: Gallimard, 1953.
Douglas, Mary. *Purity and Danger: An Analysis of Concepts of Pollution and Taboo*. London: Routledge and Kegan Paul, 1966.
Eagleton, Terry. 'Capitalism, Modernism and Postmodernism.' *New Left Review* 152 (July/August 1985): 60–73.
Eco, Umberto. 'The Influence of Roman Jacobson on the Development of Semiotics.' *Classics of Semiotics*. Ed. Martin Krampen et al. New York: Plenum, 1987.
- *Il nome della rosa (The Name of the Rose)*. Trans. William Weaver. New York: Harcourt Brace Jovanovich, 1983.
- *Postscript to 'The Name of the Rose.'* Trans. William Weaver. New York: Harcourt Brace Jovanovich, 1984.
Elias, Norbert. *Über den Prozess der Zivilisation*. Basel: Haus zum Falken, 1939; *The Civilizing Process: The History of Manners*. Trans. Edmund Jephcott. Oxford: Basil Blackwell, 1978.
Ellis, Havelock. *Studies in the Psychology of Sex*, Vol. II, Part 1. New York: Random House, 1936.
Engen, Trygg. 'Children's Sense of Smell.' *Clinical Measurement of Taste and Smell*. Ed. Herbert L. Meiselman and Richard S. Rivilin. New York: Macmillan, 1986, 318–23.
Enzensberger, Christian. *Grosserer Versuch über den Schmutz* (1968); *Smut: An Anatomy of Dirt*. Trans. Sandra Morris. New York: Seabury, 1972.
Erasmus. *De civilitate morum puerilium (On Good Manners for Boys)*. *Collected Works of Erasmus*, Vol. 3. Ed. J.K. Sowards. Toronto: U of Toronto P, 1985.
- *Encomium Moriae (Praise of Folly)*. Trans. Betty Radice. Harmondsworth, Middlesex: Penguin, 1971.
Ewen, Stuart. *Captains of Consciousness: Advertising and the Social Roots of Consumer Culture*. New York: McGraw-Hill, 1976.
Fekete, John. 'Literature and Politics/Literary Politics.' *Dalhousie Review* 66:1–2 (Spring/Summer 1986): 45–86.
Findley, Timothy. *Famous Last Words*. Markham, Ont.: Penguin, 1981.
- *Not Wanted on the Voyage*. Markham, Ont.: Penguin, 1984.
- *The Telling of Lies*. Markham, Ont.: Penguin, 1986.
Fisher, Seymour. 'Body Image.' *International Encyclopedia of the Social Sciences*. Ed. David L. Sills. New York: Macmillan, 1968.
Fleming, Joyce Dudney. 'Field Report: The State of the Apes.' *Anthropology: Contemporary Perspectives*. Ed. David E.K. Hunter and Phillip Whitten. Toronto: Little, Brown and Co., 1982, 96–103.

Fletcher, John, and Malcolm Bradbury. 'The Introverted Novel.' *Modernism: 1890–1930.* Eds. Malcolm Bradbury and James McFarlane. Harmondsworth, Middlesex: Penguin, 1976.
Foley, Barbara. *Telling the Truth: The Theory and Practice of Documentary Fiction.* Ithaca, N.Y.: Cornell UP, 1986.
Ford, Charlotte. *Charlotte Ford's Book of Modern Manners.* New York: Simon and Schuster, 1980.
Foucault, Michel. *Folie et déraison; histoire de la folie.* Paris: Plon, 1961; *Madness and Civilization.* Trans. Richard Howard. New York: Random House, 1965.
– *Histoire de la sexualité: la volonté de savoir.* Paris: Gallimard, 1976; *The History of Sexuality: Vol. 1, An Introduction.* Trans. Robert Hurley. New York: Random House, 1978.
– *Surveiller et punir: naissance de la prison.* Paris: Gallimard, 1975; *Discipline and Punish: The Birth of the Prison. The Foucault Reader.* Ed. Paul Rabinow. Trans. Alan Sheridan. New York: Pantheon, 1984.
Fraser, Sylvia. *Pandora.* Toronto: McClelland and Stewart, 1972.
Freud, Sigmund. *Aus der Geschichte einer infantilen Neurose* (1914; *From the History of an Infantile Neurosis*). *Gesammelte Werke.* Vol. 12. London: Imago, 1947; *Standard Edition of the Complete Psychological Works.* Trans. and ed. James Strachey. London: Hogarth, 1953, Vol. 12.
– *Charakter und Analerotik* (1908; *Character and Anal Eroticism*). *SE*, Vol. 9.
– *Das Medusenhaupt* (1940 [1922]; *Medusa's Head*). *SE*, Vol. 18.
– *Das Unbehagen in der Kultur* (1930; *Civilization and Its Discontents*). Trans. James Strachey. New York: Norton, 1961.
– *Drei Abhandlungen zur Sexualtheorie* (1905; *Three Essays on the Theory of Sexuality*). *SE*, Vol. 7.
– *Ein Traum als Beweismittel* (1913 [1912]; *An Evidential Dream*). *SE*, Vol. 12.
– *Jenseits des Lustprinzips* (1920; *Beyond the Pleasure Principle*). *SE*, Vol. 18.
– *Neue Folge der Vorlesungen zur Einführung in die Psychoanalyse* (1933 [1932]; *New Introductory Lectures on Psychoanalysis*). *SE*, Vol. 22.
– *Psychoanalytische Bemerkungen über einen autobiographisch beschriebenen Fall von Paranoia (Dementia paranoides)* (1911; *Psycho-Analytic Notes on an Autobiographical Account of a Case of Paranoia [Dementia Praecox]* [The Case of Schreber]). *SE*, Vol. 12.
– *Totem und Tabu* (1913). Frankfurt am Main: Fischer, 1956; *Totem and Taboo. The Basic Writings of Sigmund Freud.* Ed. and trans. A.A. Brill. New York: Random House, 1938.

- *Träume im Folklore* (1957 [1911]; Dreams in Folklore). *SE*, Vol. 12.
- *Über infantile sexualtheorien* (1908; On the Sexual Theories of Children). *SE*, Vol. 9.
- *Über Triebumsetzungen, insbesondere der Analerotik* (1917; On the Transformations of Instinct as Exemplified in Anal Eroticism). *SE*, Vol. 17.

Frye, Northrop. *Anatomy of Criticism*. Princeton, N.J.: Princeton UP, 1957.
- 'Conclusion.' *Literary History of Canada*. Ed. Carl F. Klinck et al. Toronto: U of Toronto P, 1965.

Gallop, Jane, and Carolyn G. Burke. 'Psychoanalysis and Feminism in France.' *The Future of Difference*. Ed. Hester Eisenstein and Alice Jardine. New Brunswick, N.J.: Rutgers UP, 1985, 106-21.

Geddes, Gary, ed. *15 Canadian Poets x 2*. Toronto: Oxford UP, 1988.

Gibson, William. *Count Zero*. New York: Ace, 1986.
- *Neuromancer*. New York: Ace, 1984.

Gilbert, Sandra Caruso Mortola, and Susan Dreyfuss Davis Gubar. 'Ceremonies of the Alphabet: Female Grandmatologies and the Female Authorgraph.' *The Female Autograph*. Ed. Domna C. Stanton. Chicago: U of Chicago P, 1984.

Gillan, Patricia. 'Therapeutic Uses of Obscenity.' *Censorship and Obscenity*. Ed. Rajeev Dhavan and Christie Davies. London: Martin Robertson, 1978, 127-47.

Gnarowski, Michael, ed. *Leonard Cohen: The Artist and His Critics*. Toronto: McGraw-Hill, 1976.

Godard, Barbara. 'Robertson Davies' Dialogic Imagination.' *Essays on Canadian Writing* 34 (Spring 1987): 64-80.

Godfrey, Dave. *The New Ancestors*. Toronto: McClelland and Stewart, 1970.
- Untitled letter in *Man Deserves Man: CUSO in Developing Countries*. Ed. Bill McWhinney and Dave Godfrey. Toronto: Ryerson P, 1968.

Goldie, Terry. *Fear and Temptation: The Image of the Indigene in Canadian, Australian and New Zealand Literatures*. Kingston: McGill-Queen's UP, 1989.
- 'Getting It Right: The Image of Indigenous Peoples in Canadian Fiction in the Eighties.' *English Studies in Canada* 14:1 (March 1988): 64-81.

Gordon, Charles W. (as Ralph Connor). *To Him That Hath: A Novel of the West of Today*. New York: George H. Doran, 1921.

Grant, Damian. *Realism*. London: Methuen, 1970.

Grant, George. 'In Defense of North America.' *A Passion for Identity: Introduction to Canadian Studies*. Ed. Eli Mandel and David Taras. Toronto: Methuen, 1987.

Greenstein, Michael. *Third Solitudes: Tradition and Discontinuity in Jewish-Canadian Literature.* Kingston: McGill-Queen's UP, 1989.
Grove, Frederick Philip. *A Search for America.* Toronto: McClelland and Stewart, 1927.
– *Settlers of the Marsh.* Toronto: McClelland and Stewart, 1925.
Gunn, James, ed. *The New Encyclopedia of Science Fiction.* New York: Viking, 1988.
Guthrie, R. Dale. *Body Hotspots: The Anatomy of Human Social Organs and Behavior.* New York: Van Nostrand Reinhold, 1976.
Habermas, Jürgen. 'Modernity – An Incomplete Project.' Trans. Selya Ben-Habib. *Postmodern Culture.* Ed. Hal Foster. London: Pluto, 1983, 3–15.
Haliburton, Thomas. *The Clockmaker.* Toronto: McClelland and Stewart, 1958.
Harpham, Geoffrey Galt. 'Conversion and the Language of Autobiography.' *Studies in Autobiography.* Ed. James Olney. New York: Oxford UP, 1988, 42–50.
Harris, Michael. 'Leonard Cohen: The Poet as Hero' (interview). *Leonard Cohen: The Artist and His Critics.* Ed. Michael Gnarowski. Toronto: McGraw-Hill, 1976, 46–56.
Harvey, Elizabeth D. 'Property, Digestion, and Intertext in Robertson Davies' *The Rebel Angels.*' *English Studies in Canada* 16:1 (March 1990): 91–106.
Heidenreich, Rosmarin. *The Postwar Novel in Canada: Narrative Patterns and Reader Response.* Waterloo: Wilfrid Laurier UP, 1989.
Heine, Heinrich. *Works of Prose.* Ed. Hermann Kesten. Trans. E.B. Ashton. New York: L.B. Fischer, 1943.
Heinzelman, Kurt. *The Economics of the Imagination.* Amherst: U of Massachusetts P, 1980.
Hermand, Jost. *Stänker und Weismacher.* Stuttgart: J.B. Metzleresche Verlagsbuchhandlung, 1971.
Highway, Tomson. *Dry Lips Oughta Move to Kapuskasing.* Saskatoon: Fifth House, 1989.
– *The Rez Sisters.* Saskatoon: Fifth House, 1988.
Hine, Daryl. *The Prince of Darkness and Co.* London: Abelard-Schuman, 1961.
Hodgins, Jack. *The Invention of the World.* Scarborough, Ont.: Macmillan, 1977.
Holquist, Michael. 'Introduction.' *The Dialogic Imagination* (M.M. Bakhtin). Austin: U of Texas P, 1981.
Hooker, Richard. *Of the Laws of Ecclesiastical Polity*, Vol. 1. Ed. Georges Edelen. Cambridge, Mass.: Belknap, 1977.

Howells, Coral Ann. 'Worlds Alongside: Contradictory Discourses in the Fiction of Alice Munro and Margaret Atwood.' *Gaining Ground*, 121–136.
Hughes, David R., and Evelyn Kallen, 'The Persistence of Systems of Ethnic Stratification' (1974). *Canada: A Sociological Profile*, 3rd ed. Ed. W.E. Mann and Les Wheatcroft. Toronto: Copp Clark, 1976.
Hutcheon, Linda. *The Canadian Postmodern: A Study of English-Canadian Fiction*. Toronto: Oxford UP, 1988a.
– *A Poetics of Postmodernism: History, Theory, Fiction*. London: Routledge, 1988b.
– *The Politics of Postmodernism*. London, Routledge, 1989.
– *A Theory of Parody: The Teachings of Twentieth Century Art Forms*. London: Methuen, 1985.
Huxley, Francis. *The Way of the Sacred*. London: Bloomsbury, 1989.
James, E.O. *Seasonal Feasts and Festivals*. London: Thames and Hudson, 1961.
Jameson, Fredric. 'Foreword' (1984a). *The Postmodern Condition*, vii–xxi.
– 'Of Islands and Trenches: Neutralization and the Production of Utopian Discourse' (1977). *Ideologies of Theory: Essays, 1971–1986*, Vol. 2. Minneapolis: U of Minneapolis P, 1988, 75–101.
– 'Pleasure: A Political Issue' (1983). *The Ideologies of Theory*, Vol. 2, 61–74.
– *The Political Unconscious*. Ithaca, N.Y.: Cornell UP, 1981.
– 'The Politics of Theory: Ideological Positions in the Postmodernism Debate' (1984b). *Contemporary Critical Theory*, 369–83.
– 'Postmodernism and Consumer Society' (1982). *Postmodern Culture*, 111–25.
– *Postmodernism, or, The Cultural Logic of Late Capitalism*. Durham: Duke UP, 1991.
Jarry, Alfred. *Ubu Roi*. Trans. Cyril Connolly and Simon Watson Taylor. London: Methuen, 1968.
Johnston, Wayne. *The Story of Bobby O'Malley*. Ottawa: Oberon, 1985.
Jung, Carl. *Antwort auf Hiob (Answer to Job)*. *Psychology and Religion: East and West*, 2nd ed. Trans. R.F.C. Hull. Princeton, N.J.: Princeton UP, 1969.
– *Psychologie und Alchemie*. Ed. Dieter Baumann et al. Freiburg: Walter, 1972; *Individual Dream Symbolism in Relation to Alchemy*. *The Portable Jung*. Ed. Joseph Campbell. Trans. R.F.C. Hull. New York: Viking, 1971.
Kayser, Wolfgang. *Das Groteske, seine Gestaltung in Malerei und Dichtung*. Oldenburg: G. Stalling, 1957; *The Grotesque in Art and*

Literature. Trans. Ulrich Weisstein. Bloomington, Ind.: Indiana UP, 1963.
Kinsella, W.P. *Shoeless Joe.* New York: Ballantine, 1982.
Kira, Alexander. *The Bathroom*, 2nd ed. New York: Viking, 1976.
Klein, A.M. *The Second Scroll.* Toronto: McClelland and Stewart, 1951.
Kristeva, Julia. 'Bataille solaire, ou le texte coupable.' *Histoires d'amour.* Paris: Denoël, 1983, 341–6; 'Bataille and the Sun, or the Guilty Text.' *Tales of Love.* Trans. Leon S. Roudiez. New York: Columbia UP, 1987.
– 'Mémoire.' *L'infini* 1 (1983): 39–54; 'My Memory's Hyperbole.' *The Female Autograph: Theory and Practice of Autobiography from the Tenth to the Twentieth Century.* Ed. Domna C. Stanton. Chicago: U of Chicago P, 1984, 219–35.
– *Pouvoirs de l'horreur.* Paris: Seuil, 1980; *Powers of Horror: An Essay on Abjection.* Trans. Leon S. Roudiez. New York: Columbia UP, 1982.
Kroetsch, Robert. *Alibi.* Toronto: General, 1983.
– *Badlands.* Toronto: General, 1975.
Kroker, Arthur, and David Cook. *The Postmodern Condition: Excremental Culture and Hyper-Aesthetics.* New York: St. Martin's P, 1986.
– *Technology and the Canadian Mind: Innis/McLuhan/Grant.* Montreal: New World Perspectives, 1984.
Lacan, Jacques. *Le Séminaire de Jacques Lacan*, Vol. 2. Ed. Jacques-Alain Miller. Paris: Seuil, 1978; *The Seminar of Jacques Lacan* (1953–4). Ed. Jacques-Alain Miller. Trans. Sylvanna Tomaselli. New York: W.W. Norton, 1988.
Ladoo, Harold Sonny. *No Pain Like This Body.* Toronto: Anansi, 1972.
– *Yesterdays.* Toronto: Anansi, 1974.
Laurence, Margaret. *The Diviners.* Toronto: Bantam, 1974.
– *A Jest of God.* Toronto: McClelland and Stewart, 1966.
– *The Stone Angel.* Toronto: McClelland and Stewart, 1964.
Leacock, Stephen. *My Discovery of England* (1921). Toronto: McClelland and Stewart, 1961.
– *Sunshine Sketches of a Little Town* (1912). Toronto: McClelland and Stewart, 1931.
Lee, Jae Num. *Swift and Scatalogical Satire.* Albuquerque: U of New Mexico P, 1971.
Lejeune, Philippe. *Je est un autre: L'autobiographie, de la littérature aux médias.* Paris: Seuil, 1980.
– *Le Pacte Autobiographique.* Paris: Seuil, 1975.
– *Moi Aussi.* Paris: Seuil, 1986.
– *On Autobiography.* Ed. Paul John Eakin. Trans. Katherine Leary. Minneapolis: U of Minnesota P, 1989.

Lévi-Strauss, Claude. *La pensée sauvage*. Paris: Plon, 1962; *The Savage Mind*. Trans. George Weidenfeld. London: Weidenfeld and Nicolson, 1966.
- *Tristes tropiques*. Paris: Plon, 1955; Trans. John and Doreen Weightman. New York: Simon and Schuster, 1974.

Limon, John. *The Place of Fiction in the Time of Science: A Disciplinary History of American Writing*. New York: Cambridge UP, 1990.

Linden, Eugene. *Apes, Men, and Language*. New York: E.P. Dutton, 1974.

Lowry, Malcolm. *Under the Volcano*. Harmondsworth, Middlesex: Penguin, 1947.

Luhmann, Niklas. *Rechtssoziologie* (1972; *A Sociological Theory of Law*). Trans. Elizabeth King and Martin Albrow. London: Routledge and Kegan Paul, 1985.

Lumsden, Susan. 'Leonard Cohen Wants the Unconditional Leadership of the World,' in Gnarowski, ed., 69–73.

Luther, Martin. *D. Martin Luther Werke: Tischreden* (1913). Weimar: Hermann Böhlaus Nachfolger, 1967; *Table Talk. Luther's Works*, Vol. 54. Ed. and trans. Theodore G. Tappert. Philadelphia: Fortress, 1967.

Lyotard, Jean-François. *La Condition Postmoderne*. Paris: Les Editions de Minuit, 1979; *The Postmodern Condition*. Trans. Geoff Bennington and Brian Massumi. Minneapolis: U of Minnesota P, 1984.
- 'Réponse à la question: qu'est-ce que le postmoderne?' *Critique* 37:419 (April 1982): 357–67.

MacLennan, Hugh. *Two Solitudes*. Toronto: Macmillan, 1945.

Manuel, Frank, and Fritzie Manuel. *Utopian Thought in the Western World*. Cambridge, Mass.: Belknap, 1979.

Marchak, M. Patricia. *Ideological Perspectives on Canada*, 2nd ed. Toronto: McGraw-Hill Ryerson, 1981.

Marks, Geoffrey, and William K. Beatty. *Epidemics*. New York: Charles Scribner's Sons, 1976.

Marlyn, John. *Under the Ribs of Death*. Toronto: McClelland and Stewart, 1957.

Martin, Judith. *Miss Manners' Guide to Rearing Perfect Children*. New York: Atheneum, 1984.

Matthews, Robin. *Canadian Literature*. Toronto: Steel Rail, 1978.

McFarland, David, ed. *The Oxford Companion to Animal Behavior*. Oxford: Oxford UP, 1987.

McGrew, Roderick E. *Encyclopedia of Medical History*. New York: McGraw-Hill, 1985.

McKeon, Michael. *The Origins of the English Novel, 1600–1740*. Baltimore: Johns Hopkins UP, 1987.
McLuhan, Marshall. 'Canada: the Borderline Case.' *The Canadian Imagination: Dimensions of a Literary Culture*. Ed. David Staines. Cambridge, Mass.: Harvard UP, 1977.
– *The Gutenberg Galaxy: The Making of Typographic Man*. New York: Signet, 1962.
– *Letters of Marshall McLuhan*. Ed. Matie Molinaro, Corinne McLuhan, William Toye. Toronto: Oxford UP, 1987.
– *Understanding Media: The Extensions of Man*. New York: Signet, 1964.
McMullen, Lorraine. 'Women in Grove's Novels.' *The Grove Symposium*. Ed. John Nause. Ottawa: U of Ottawa P, 1974.
Mennell, Stephen. *Norbert Elias: Civilization and the Human Self-Image*. Oxford: Blackwell, 1989.
Miller, James. *The Passion of Michel Foucault*. New York: Simon and Schuster, 1993.
Miller, Llewellyn. *The Encyclopedia of Etiquette*. New York: Crown, 1967.
Mistry, Rohinton. 'Squatter' (1987). *An Anthology of Canadian Literature in English*, rev. and abridged. Ed. Russell Brown, Donna Bennett, and Nathalie Cooke. Toronto: Oxford UP, 1990.
Mitchell, W.O. *The Vanishing Point*. Toronto: McClelland and Stewart, 1973.
– *Who Has Seen the Wind?* Toronto: Macmillan, 1947.
Monk, Patricia. 'Somatotyping, Scatomancy, and Sophia: The Relation of Body and Soul in the Novels of Robertson Davies.' *English Studies in Canada* 12:1 (March 1986): 79–100.
Montaigne, Michel de. *Essais*. Paris: Gallimard, 1950; *Essays*. Trans. John Florio (1603). New York: Random House, n.d.
Moodie, Susanna. *Mark Hurdlestone; or, the Two Brothers*. New York: Dewitt and Davenport, n.d.
– *Roughing It in the Bush*, 2nd ed. (1852). Toronto: McClelland and Stewart, 1989.
– *Susanna Moodie: Letters of a Lifetime*. Ed. Carl Ballstadt, Elizabeth Hopkins, and Michael Peterman. Toronto: U of Toronto P, 1985.
Moore, Barrington, Jr. *Privacy: Studies in Social and Cultural History*. Armonk, N.Y.: M.E. Sharpe, 1984.
Moore, Brian. *Black Robe*. Toronto: McClelland and Stewart, 1985.
– *The Luck of Ginger Coffey*. Toronto: McClelland and Stewart, 1960.
Mowat, Farley. *People of the Deer*. New York: Pyramid, 1952.

Mullen, Barbara D., and Kerry Anne McGinn. *The Ostomy Book*. Palo Alto: Bull, 1980.
Munro, Alice. *Lives of Girls and Women*. New York: Signet, 1971.
- *The Progress of Love*. Toronto: McClelland and Stewart, 1986.
- *Who Do You Think You Are?* Toronto: Macmillan, 1978.
Naylor, R.T. *Canada in the European Age: 1453-1919*. Vancouver: New Star Books, 1987.
Nietzsche, Friedrich. *Also Sprach Zarathustra. Friedrich Nietzsche: Werke in Drei Banden*. München: Carl Hanser Verlag, 1960; *Thus Spoke Zarathustra*. Trans. R.J. Hollingdale. Harmondsworth, Middlesex: Penguin, 1961.
- *Die Geburt der Tragödie. Werke; The Birth of Tragedy from the Spirit of Music*. Trans. Francis Golffing. Garden City, N.Y.: Doubleday, 1956.
Novak, Maximillian E. ''Gulliver's Travels* and the Picaresque Voyage: Some Reflections on the Hazards of Genre Criticism.' *The Genres of Gulliver's Travels*. Ed. Frederick N. Smith. Newark: U of Delaware P, 1990, 23-38.
O'Faolain, Julia, and Lauro Martines, eds. *Not in God's Image: Women in History from the Greeks to the Victorians*. New York: Harper and Row, 1973.
O'Hagan, Howard. *The School-Marm Tree*. Vancouver: Talonbooks, 1977.
- *Tay John*. Toronto: McClelland and Stewart, 1939.
Ondaatje, Michael. *The Collected Works of Billy the Kid: Left-Handed Poems*. Toronto: Anansi, 1970.
- *Coming through Slaughter*. Toronto: Anansi, 1976.
- *The English Patient*. Toronto: Random House, 1992.
- *Running in the Family*. Toronto: General Publishing, 1982.
Onians, Richard Broxton. *The Origins of European Thought about the body, the mind, the soul, the world, time, and fate: new interpretations of Greek, Roman, and kindred evidence, also of some basic Jewish and Christian beliefs*. Cambridge: Cambridge UP, 1954.
Ostenso, Martha. *Wild Geese* (1925). Toronto: McClelland and Stewart, 1989.
Pache, Walter. '"The Fiction Makes Us Real": Aspects of Postmodernism in Canada.' *Gaining Ground*, 64-78.
Pachter, Henry M. *Magic into Science: The Story of Paracelsus*. New York: Henry Shuman, 1951.
Palmer, Howard. 'Mosaic versus Melting Pot?: Immigration and Ethnicity in Canada and the United States.' *A Passion for Identity: Introduction to Canadian Studies*. Ed. Eli Mandel and David Taras. Toronto: Methuen, 1987.

Paracelsus. *The Hermetic and Alchemical Writings*, Vol. 2. Ed. Arthur Edward Waite. Berkeley: Shambhala, 1976.
Partridge, Eric. *A Dictionary of Slang and Unconventional English*, Vol. 2. London: Routledge and Kegan Paul, 1961.
Paz, Octavio. *Conjunctions and Disjunctions*. Trans. Helen R. Lane. New York: Viking, 1969.
Perry-Jenkins, Maureen, and Karen Folk. 'Class, Couples, and Conflict: Effects of the Division of Labour on Assessments of Marriage in Dual-Earner Families.' *Journal of Marriage and the Family* 56:1 (Feb. 1994): 165–80.
Peyser, C.S. 'William Herbert Sheldon.' *Concise Encyclopedia of Psychology*. Ed. Raymond J. Corsini. New York: Wiley, 1987.
Pineo, Peter C., and John Porter. 'Ethnic Origins and Occupational Attainment.' *Ascription and Achievement: Studies in Mobility and Status Attainment in Canada*. Ed. Monica Boyd et al. Ottawa: Carleton UP, 1985.
Pops, Martin. 'The Metamorphoses of Shit.' *Salmagundi* 56 (Spring 1982): 26–61.
Porter, John. *The Vertical Mosaic: An Analysis of Social Class and Power in Canada*. Toronto: U of Toronto P, 1965.
Porush, David. 'Cybernauts in Cyberspace: William Gibson's *Neuromancer*.' *Aliens: The Anthropology of Science Fiction*. Ed. George E. Slusser and Eric S. Rabkin. Edwardsville, Ill.: Southern Illinois UP, 1987, 168–78.
– 'Cybernetic Fiction and Postmodern Science.' *New Literary History* 20:2 (Winter 1989): 373–96.
Post, Elizabeth L. *Emily Post's Etiquette*. New York: Harper and Row, 1984.
Preston, James J. 'Purification.' *Encyclopedia of Religion*. Ed. Mircea Eliade et al. New York: Macmillan, 1987.
Pudney, John. *The Smallest Room*. London: Michael Joseph, 1954.
Rabelais, François. *Oeuvres Complètes*. Paris: Gallimard, 1955; *The Histories of Gargantua and Pantagruel*. Trans. J.M. Cohen. Harmondsworth, Middlesex: Penguin, 1955.
Ramcharan, Subhas. *Racism: Nonwhites in Canada*. Toronto: Butterworths, 1982.
Rawcliffe, D.H. *Occult and Supernatural Phenomena*. New York: Dover, 1952.
Richardson, John. *Wacousta* (1832). Ed. Douglas Cronk. Ottawa: Carleton UP, 1990.

Richler, Mordecai. *The Apprenticeship of Duddy Kravitz.* Harmondsworth, Middlesex: Penguin, 1959.
- *Jacob Two-Two Meets the Hooded Fang.* New York: Bantam, 1975.
- *Joshua Then and Now.* Toronto: McClelland and Stewart, 1980.
- *St Urbain's Horseman.* Toronto: Bantam, 1966.
- *Solomon Gursky Was Here.* Harmondsworth, Middlesex: Penguin, 1989.
- *Son of a Smaller Hero.* Toronto: McClelland and Stewart, 1955.
Rooke, Leon. *Shakespeare's Dog.* Toronto: General Publishing, 1981.
Rosebury, Theodor. *Life on Man.* New York: Viking, 1969.
Rosenberg, Stuart. E. *The Jewish Community in Canada.* Toronto: McClelland and Stewart, 1970.
Ross, Sinclair. *As For Me and My House.* Toronto: McClelland and Stewart, 1941.
Rosso, Stefano. 'Postmodern Italy: Notes on the "Crisis of Reason," "Weak Thought," and *The Name of the Rose.*' *Exploring Postmodernism.* Eds. Matei Calinescu and Douwe Fokkema. Amsterdam: John Benjamin, 1987, 79–92.
Roy, Gabrielle. *La petite poule d'eau* (1951). Montréal: Beauchemin, 1970; *Where Nests the Water Hen.* Trans. Harry L. Binsse. Toronto: McClelland and Stewart, 1951.
Rudwin, Maximilian. *The Devil in Language and Literature.* New York: AMS Press, 1931.
Said, Edward W. 'Opponents, Audiences, Constituencies and Community.' *Postmodern Culture,* 135–59.
- *The World, the Text and the Critic.* Cambridge, Mass.: Harvard UP, 1983.
Scarry, Elaine. *The Body in Pain: The Making and Unmaking of the World.* New York: Oxford UP, 1985.
- 'Introduction.' *Literature and the Body: Essays on Populations and Persons.* Baltimore: Johns Hopkins UP, 1988.
Schlatter, Richard B. *The Social Ideas of Religious Leaders, 1660–1688.* London: Oxford UP, 1940.
Schneidau, Herbert N. *Sacred Discontent: The Bible and Western Tradition.* Baton Rouge: Louisiana State UP, 1976.
Schweickart, Patrocinio P. 'Reading Ourselves: Toward a Feminist Theory of Reading.' *Speaking of Gender.* Ed. Elaine Showalter. New York: Routledge, 1989, 17–44.
Schwenger, Peter. 'The Masculine Mode.' *Speaking of Gender,* 101–112.
Scobie, Stephen. *Signature Event Cantext.* Edmonton: NeWest, 1989.
Scott, Chris. *Antichthon.* Dunvegan, Ont.: Quadrant, 1982.

Seigal, Jerrold. 'Review of *The Civilizing Process.*' *Journal of Modern History* 51 (March 1979): 123–6.
Shell, Marc. *The Economy of Literature.* Baltimore: Johns Hopkins UP, 1978.
Showalter, Elaine. 'Introduction: The Rise of Gender.' *Speaking of Gender,* 1–13.
Smart, Elizabeth. *The Assumption of Rogues and Rascals.* London: Granada, 1978.
– *By Grand Central Station I Sat Down and Wept.* New York: Panther, 1945.
Smith, Anthony. *The Body.* New York: Walker and Co., 1968.
Spariosu, Mihai. 'Allegory, Hermeneutics, and Postmodernism.' *Exploring Postmodernism,* 59–78.
Spengemann, William C. *The Forms of Autobiography: Episodes from the History of a Literary Genre.* New Haven: Yale UP, 1980.
Spiro, Solomon J. *Tapestry for Design: Judaic Allusions in* The Second Scroll *and* The Collected Poems of A.M. Klein. Vancouver: U of British Columbia P, 1984.
Stallybrass, Peter, and Allon White. *The Politics and Poetics of Transgression.* Ithaca, N.Y.: Cornell UP, 1986.
Stanton, Domna C. ed. *The Female Autograph: Theory and Practice of Autobiography from the Tenth to the Twentieth Century.* Chicago: U of Chicago P, 1984.
Stern, Harold S. 'The Ethics of the Clean and the Unclean.' *Judaism* 6 (1957): 319–27.
Stich, K.P. 'Introduction.' *Reflections: Autobiography and Canadian Literature.* Ottawa: U of Ottawa P, 1988, ix–xii.
Stimpson, Catherine. 'Are the Differences Spreading? Feminist Criticism and Postmodernism.' *English Studies in Canada* 15:4 (Dec. 1989): 364–82.
Stoekl, Allan. 'Introduction.' *Georges Bataille's Visions of Excess: Selected Writings, 1927–1939.* Ed. Allan Stoekl. Minneapolis: U of Minnesota P, 1985.
Such, Peter. *Riverrun.* Toronto: Clarke, Irwin, 1973.
– 'The Short Life and Sudden Death of Harold Ladoo.' *Saturday Night* 89 (May 1974): 36.
Süskind, Patrick. *Das Parfüm.* Zürich: Diogenes, 1985; *Perfume.* Trans. John E. Woods. New York: Alfred A. Knopf, 1986.
Sutherland, John. *Offensive Literature: Decensorship in Britain, 1960–1982.* Totown, N.J.: Barnes and Noble, 1982.

Sweatman, Margaret. *Fox.* Winnipeg: Turnstone, 1991.
Swift, Jonathan. *Jonathan Swift: A Selection of His Works.* Ed. Philip Pinkus. Toronto: Macmillan, 1965.
- *'A Tale of a Tub' with Other Early Works, 1696–1707.* Ed. Herbert Davis. Oxford: Basil Blackwell, 1939.
Tatum, Stephen. *Inventing Billy the Kid: Visions of the Outlaw in America, 1881–1981.* Albuquerque: U of New Mexico P, 1982.
Thomas, Audrey. *Latakia.* Vancouver: Talonbooks, 1979.
- *Mrs Blood.* Vancouver: Talonbooks, 1975.
Thomas, Keith. *Man and the Natural World.* New York: Pantheon, 1983.
Thompson, Judith. *White Biting Dog.* Toronto: Playwrights, 1984.
Thompson, Philip. *The Grotesque.* London: Methuen, 1972.
Tillich, Paul. *The Protestant Era.* Trans. James Luther Adams. Chicago: U of Chicago P, 1948.
Todorov, Tzvetan. *Introduction à la littérature fantastique (The Fantastic: A Structural Approach to a Literary Genre).* Trans. Richard Howard. Ithaca, N.Y.: Cornell UP, 1975.
Turner, Bryan S. *The Body and Society: Explorations in Social Theory.* Oxford: Basil Blackwell, 1984.
Twigg, Alan. *For Openers: Conversations with 24 Canadian Writers.* Madeira Park, B.C.: Harbour Publishing, 1981.
Vanderbilt, Amy. *The Amy Vanderbilt Complete Book of Etiquette.* Rev. and expanded by Letitia Baldrige. Garden City, N.Y.: Doubleday, 1978.
Vico, Giambattista. *Principii di una scienza nuova intorno alla natura delle nazioni; The New Science,* rev. trans. of the 3rd ed. (1744). Trans. Thomas Goddard Bergin and Max Harold Fisch. Ithaca, N.Y.: Cornell UP, 1968.
Vigarello, Georges. *Le Propre et le sale: l'hygiene du corps depuis le Moyen Age.* Paris: Seuil, 1985; *Concepts of Cleanliness: Changing Attitudes in France since the Middle Ages.* Trans. Jean Birrell. Cambridge: Cambridge UP, 1988.
Vogt, A.E. van. *The World of Null-A.* New York: Berkley, 1945.
Walker, Benjamin. *The Encyclopedia of Esoteric Man.* London: Routledge and Kegan Paul, 1977.
Watson, Sheila. *The Double Hook.* Toronto: McClelland and Stewart, 1959.
Weber, Max. *The Protestant Ethic and the Spirit of Capitalism.* New York: Scribner's, 1958.
Welsford, Enid. *The Fool: His Social and Literary History.* London: Faber and Faber, 1935.

Wiebe, Rudy. *The Temptations of Big Bear.* Toronto: McClelland and Stewart, 1973.
Williams, David. 'After Post-modernism.' *Trace: Prairie Writers on Writing.* Ed. Birk Sproxton. Winnipeg: Turnstone, 1986.
- *The Burning Wood.* Toronto: Anansi, 1975.
- *Confessional Fictions: A Portrait of the Artist in the Canadian Novel.* Toronto: U of Toronto P, 1991.
- 'The Confessions of a Self-Made Man: Forms of Autobiography in *Fifth Business.*' *Journal of Canadian Studies* 24:1 (Spring 1989): 81–102.
- *Eye of the Father.* Toronto: Anansi, 1985.
- '"Looking into a Void": The Clash of Realism and Modernism in *As For Me and My House.*' *Canadiana: Studies in Canadian Literature.* Ed. Jorn Carlsen and Knud Larsen Aarhus. Denmark: Canadian Studies Conference, U of Aarhus, 1984, 25–42.
- *The River Horsemen.* Toronto: Anansi, 1981.
Wilson, Ethel. *Swamp Angel.* Toronto: McClelland and Stewart, 1954.
Winnett, Susan. 'Coming Unstrung: Men, Women, Narrative, and Principles of Pleasure.' *PMLA* 105:3 (May 1990): 505–18.
Wiseman, Adele. *The Sacrifice.* Toronto: General, 1956.
Woodcock, George. 'Don't Ever Ask for the True Story; or, Second Thoughts on Autobiography.' *Essays on Canadian Writing* 29 (Summer 1984): 16.
Wright, Lawrence. *Clean and Decent: The Fascinating History of the Bathroom and the Water Closet.* London: Routledge and Kegan Paul, 1960.
Wyke, Clement H. 'Harold Ladoo's Alternate Worlds: Canada and Carib Island.' *Canadian Literature* 95 (Winter 1982): 39–49.
Ziolkowski, Jan M. 'The Form and Spirit of Beast Fable.' *Bestia* 2 (May 1990): 4–18.

Index

Abelard, Peter, 211
Adorno, Theodor, 70
aging, 20
Agrippa, Henricus Cornelius: *De incertitudine et vanitate scientiarum et artium*, 96
alchemy, 96, 109, 132–3
allegory, 71–3, 78–9, 83–4, 169, 187, 203, 217
angelism, 92–3
animals, 6, 8–9, 22–4, 31, 34–5, 42, 64, 70, 82, 118, 120–3, 132, 137, 140, 158–60, 166, 168, 170, 172, 175, 185, 188, 190, 192–6, 198, 211–12, 221; and language, 10, 42, 190
anorexia, 76
anus, 23–4, 62, 64, 106, 131, 165, 173, 205, 207, 213, 215; anal eroticism, 12, 56, 65, 77, 81, 91, 117, 139, 172; anal retention, 49, 116, 125, 157
Aquin, Hubert: *Prochain épisode*, 200, 221
Aquinas, Thomas, 116, 211; *Summa Contra Gentiles*, 121; *Summa Theologiae*, 100, 121

Aristotle, 105
Armstrong, Pat and Hugh, 103
Atwood, Margaret, 27, 29, 100, 110, 116, 134, 183, 195, 212–13; *Bodily Harm*, 28, 43, 57, 74, 88–9, 185; *Cat's Eye*, 28–30, 43, 86, 94–5, 112–14, 117–18, 211–12, 224; *Edible Woman, The*, 19, 30, 43, 47–8, 60, 72, 76–8, 112, 204, 212; *Handmaid's Tale, The*, 72, 111–12, 117, 123, 127, 211
Auerbach, Erich, 11, 135, 201
Augustine, 106, 135, 163; *Confessiones*, 121, 152, 154, 218–19; *De Doctrina Christiana*, 10–11; *De Trinitate*, 121
Austin, J.L., 146
autobiography, 51–2, 54–5, 144–5, 147–61, 163, 166, 175, 179–80, 217–19; omniscience in, 159–61

Babcock, Barbara, 216
Bacon, Francis, 94, 216
Bakhtin, Mikhail, 11, 37, 50, 75–6, 78, 96, 109, 116, 138, 144, 160, 166, 175–6, 187, 190, 202, 204, 211–12, 215–16, 221

Index

Barker, Francis, 11, 49, 77, 189, 197–8
Barlaeus, Caspar, 197–8
Barth, John: *Giles Goat Boy*, 105, 166
Barthes, Roland, 163, 170, 172, 175, 218–20
Bataille, Georges, 23, 138–9, 145, 163, 165, 169–70, 177, 184, 192, 205–6, 216, 222–3
bathrooms, 20, 22–3, 28, 32–5, 44–5, 50, 58, 64, 72–4, 80, 101, 105, 111, 120–1, 127, 153, 156–7, 175, 189, 195; architecture, 18–19, 25–8; cleaning of, 27, 50, 73, 103–4, 111; wheelchair, 47. *See also* manners
Baudrillard, Jean, 81, 163, 170, 172, 179, 204–5
Beckett, Samuel, 11, 164; *All That Fall*, 133, 191
Benedict of Nursia, Saint, 192
Benveniste, Émile, 149
Bergiani, 198
Bernal, J.D., 191, 208
Bernardus Silvestris, 192
Bible, 66–7, 118–21, 123–4, 126, 132–4, 136, 165–7, 185, 189, 201, 212, 214, 216
bile, 91
Bjerring, Nancy, 222
blood, 8, 61–3, 84, 101, 108, 112, 118, 125–6, 138, 201, 209–10
body, 24, 28, 30–1, 46, 50, 56, 60, 63, 66, 75, 81, 86, 98, 112, 115, 120, 123–4, 129, 137, 143, 170, 178–9, 197–8, 205, 209, 211–13, 218–20, 223; designer body, 94, 170, 176, 179, 205; disembodiment, 91–6, 120–1, 139–40, 169–71, 175–6, 185–6, 193, 208; filthy, 9, 27, 48, 68, 76, 92–4, 96, 102–3, 108, 113, 116, 120, 126, 131, 135, 151–2, 155, 158–9, 166, 171–3, 176, 183, 188, 194, 204; and power, 71–2, 76–8, 83–4, 111; and texts, 5, 7–8, 11, 71, 107, 117, 139–40, 144–5, 149–50, 153, 155, 158–61, 164–6, 168–9, 173–4, 176, 179–85, 210, 218–19, 221, 223; transcendence, 31, 107–8, 135, 152, 156–7, 167–8, 173, 192, 219; unitary, 131. *See also* blood; excrement; farting; hygiene; mucous; semen; soul; spitting; sweat; tears; urine
Borden, Robert, 76
Bordieau, Pierre, 6
Bosch, Heironymus, 205
Bourke, John G., 85–6
Bowering, George, 91, 163, 222; *Burning Water*, 36, 65–6, 95–6, 98
Bradbury, Malcolm, 164
Breton, Raymond, 58
Brontë, Emily: *Wuthering Heights*, 205
Brooke, Frances: *History of Emily Montague, The*, 12, 26, 124, 193
Brown, Norman O., 64, 79, 205
Buckler, Ernest, 29; *Mountain and the Valley, The*, 27, 30–1, 194
Bukatman, Scott, 93
Burke, Carolyn, 219

Caen, Roger, 106
Calinescu, Matei, 145
Callaghan, Morley: *More Joy in Heaven*, 48; *Such Is My Beloved*, 12, 43, 47–8, 124
Canada, 49, 56, 62, 118, 164;

Centennial, 25–6; CUSO, 74; eastern, 19, 33, 195; free trade, 80; Governor General's Award, 221; immigrants, 17–18, 44–5, 53–6, 59, 70, 199–200; Kingston Penitentiary, 86; Manitoba, 32, 53–4; Newfoundland, 61; Northwest Rebellion, 67, 201; Nova Scotia, 83; Ontario, 26; Quebec, 72, 86, 184, 200, 202; western, 19, 25–6, 33, 75, 198; Winnipeg General Strike, 53–4
carnival, 37–8, 51
Cartier, Jacques, 12
Catherine of Sienna, Saint, 139
Céline, Louis-Ferdinand, 63, 181–2, 210
Certeau, Michel de, 8, 52, 179, 198
Chadwick, E., 87
childhood, 4, 6, 21, 23, 159; sexual abuse, 110, 132; toilet training, 78, 91, 167–8, 207
Chilo, 197
Christianity, 48, 59, 62–3, 66–7, 105–6, 110, 113, 115–40, 160, 164–5, 167–9, 183, 189, 201, 210, 219, 223; Anglican, 74, 126, 131; Catholic, 77, 89–90, 119, 121–2, 128–9, 135, 138, 154–6, 219; Christology, 121, 128, 133–5, 198, 214, 223; death of God, 119; devil, 121–2, 130, 167–8, 213; Fundamentalist, 66, 117–18; Gnostic, 120–1, 128–9, 139, 169–70, 212, 214; Protestant, 115–18, 121–5, 131–2, 137, 201, 211–13; United Church, 131
city, 26–34, 195
civility. *See* manners
civilization, 62, 64; 'origins,' 21–4, 37, 57, 60, 65, 82, 159, 172–3, 189, 192–4; 'overcivilization,' 32–3, 36, 48, 84, 91, 100–3, 110–11, 113–14; and writing, 68
civilized self, 4, 18–24, 27, 31, 47, 55, 59, 71, 84, 93, 113, 139, 151–2, 158–9, 168, 172–3, 182–3, 190, 193–4, 204, 222; commodity self, 76–7, 204; parodies of, 34–8, 188; religious self, 116–17, 123, 134; secular self, 154–5; and women, 100–3, 209. *See also* manners
Cixous, Hélène, 107, 165–6, 182
Clarkson, Adrienne, 180
class, 18, 41–53, 55, 86–7, 104, 109, 179, 183, 188, 193, 196–8, 206, 218
cleanliness. *See* hygiene
Clement of Alexandria: *Stromata*, 128
Cluett, Robert, 114, 135, 191, 197
Cohen, Leonard, 65, 91, 117, 138, 145, 179–80; *Beautiful Losers*, 37, 58, 60, 77, 93–4, 138–40, 145, 150, 175–80, 185, 219, 222–3
Cohen, Ralph, 143–4
colonialism, 46, 57–60, 73–5, 85–8, 135
Connor, Ralph (Charles W. Gordon): *To Him That Hath*, 185
Corbin, Alain, 51, 198, 208
Cornell, Joseph, 171–2
country, 8, 25–33, 193–4
Craig, Terrence, 54, 68–9
Cromwell, Oliver, 211
Culler, Jonathan, 144
Culleton, Beatrice: *In Search of April Raintree*, 202

Davies, Robertson, 29, 51–2, 116,

150, 183, 195; *Fifth Business*, 43, 72, 130, 155, 215, 219; *Lyre of Orpheus, The*, 22, 48–9, 103, 109, 197, 215; *Manticore, The*, 131, 157–9; *Rebel Angels, The*, 22–3, 79, 88–9, 96–8, 108–9, 132–3, 197, 215; *What's Bred in the Bone*, 32–3, 46, 132, 159–61; *World of Wonders*, 8, 26, 132, 152, 186–7
Da Vinci, Leonardo, 192
Davis, Murray, 184, 195
Davis, Natalie Zemon, 51, 83, 107
dead matter, 9–10, 65, 106, 153–5, 159–60, 165, 168, 183, 214, 219; 'heterogeneous' matter, 169–79, 183, 206, 221
deconstruction, 68, 143–6, 148, 151–2, 161, 169–71
Dell, Floyd, 207
Della Casa, Giovanni: *Galateo*, 3, 190
De Man, Paul, 148–9, 163
De Mille, James: *Dodge Club, The*, 86, 206; *Strange Manuscript Found in a Copper Cylinder, A*, 12, 18
Derrida, Jacques, 9, 119, 143–6, 212
Descartes, René, 10, 36, 184
Détienne, Marcel, 179
dialogism. *See* language
diarrhoea, 61, 70
digestion. *See* food
disease, 45, 89–90, 215; bacteriology, 4, 86–7, 206–8; cholera, 86–7, 90, 206; diabetes, 96; penicillin, 97; polio, 86; renal malaria, 70; urine and feces as symptoms, 96
Dobson, Matthew, 96

Doctorow, E.L.: *Ragtime*, 222
Dostoevsky, Fyodor: *Brothers Karamazov, The*, 128, 219
Douglas, Mary, 9, 24, 42, 44, 55, 58, 64, 106, 120, 140, 143, 165, 196, 207, 210, 219

Eagleton, Terry, 107, 163, 167, 220
Eakin, John Paul, 148
eating. *See* food; manners
Eco, Umberto, 190, 211; *nome della rosa, Il*, 116
economy, 71, 76–84, 101, 146, 203–6, 218, 220; and abstraction, 78; agriculture, 28; consumerism, 28, 76–8, 112–13, 196–7; money, 78–9, 124, 133, 204–5
Elias, Norbert, 4–7, 24, 41–2, 101, 179, 189–90, 206, 208, 223
Eliot, T.S., 70, 151, 203, 214
Ellis, Havelock, 8
Emerson, Ralph Waldo, 27, 194
Encyclopedia of Etiquette, The, 6
enema, 131, 157
Enoch, Book of, 220
Enzensberger, Christian, 18, 76, 90, 186
Erasmus, 188; *De civilitate morum puerilium*, 6, 13, 167; *Encomium Moriae*, 213
etiquette. *See* manners
euphemism. *See* language
Europe, 49, 62; bathrooms, 18
Ewen, Stuart, 76, 196
excrement, excretion, 3, 8–10, 12, 23–4, 35, 37–8, 44–5, 47, 50, 55, 57–9, 61–2, 64–6, 73, 87, 90–1, 96–7, 116, 120, 127–9, 132, 148, 150–1, 157–8, 165–6, 171, 173, 177, 186, 190–2, 195–6, 206, 208,

213, 215–16, 222; abject foetus, 106; bomari, 23, 88, 109; constipation, 91, 105, 134, 138, 176, 178, 209; and 'creaturalness,' 137; measurement of, 97; and monetary exchange, 78–80, 133, 205–6; and primitivism, 65, 201; retention of, 101; and signification, 159
existentialism, 62–4, 90, 153

farting, 6, 22, 31, 34, 36, 121, 131–2, 159, 195, 198, 206, 213
fasting, 37, 176
Fekete, John, 70, 222
festa stultorum, 118, 212
filth-cure, 28, 88, 97, 132, 208
Findley, Timothy, 116, 134; *Famous Last Words*, 35–6, 43, 84, 119–20, 168–9; *Not Wanted on the Voyage*, 43, 46–7, 84, 118–20, 127, 167–8, 174, 196; *Telling of Lies, The*, 47, 157–8, 168
Fletcher, John, 164
Foley, Barbara, 71, 144, 163, 182, 203, 217, 220
food, 45, 59–60, 76, 87, 97, 121, 128, 137–9, 196, 200–1, 207–9, 213–14, 221
Ford, Charlotte: *Charlotte Ford's Book of Modern Manners*, 6, 35, 190, 211
Fortunatus, 209
Foucault, Michel, 5–6, 71–2, 77, 123, 152, 170–1, 182, 185
Francis of Assisi, Saint, 192
Fraser, Sylvia, 111; *Pandora*, 110
Frazer, James, 24, 88
Freud, Sigmund, 4, 7, 23, 32, 62, 65, 78–80, 91, 102, 105–7, 116–18,
122–5, 134, 148, 154, 157, 172, 182, 190, 196, 204–6, 210–11, 214
Frye, Northrop, 144, 173, 190

garbage. *See* pollution
Genette, Gérard, 149–50
genre, 9, 12, 61, 119, 143–6, 163, 174, 187–8, 194, 217
Ghana, 57, 72–4, 204
Gibson, William, 12, 91, 94, 183, 208; *Count Zero*, 77–8, 81, 92–3, 170–2; *Neuromancer*, 37, 78, 92–3, 170–1
Gilbert, Sandra, 107, 219
Godard, Barbara, 48, 197
Godfrey, Dave, 73–4, 88, 203–4; *New Ancestors, The*, 47, 57–8, 72–4, 87, 108
Goldie, Terry, 60, 64, 219
Gordon, Charles W. *See* Ralph Connor
Grant, Damian, 45
Grant, George, 9, 91, 116
Graves, Robert, 22, 138
Greenstein, Michael, 68–9, 140
Gregory the Great (Pope), 192
Grove, Frederick Philip, 45, 148; *Search for America, A*, 45–6, 79, 157; *Settlers of the Marsh*, 102, 210
Gubar, Susan, 107, 219

Habermas, Jürgen, 163, 220
Haliburton, Thomas, 183; *Clockmaker, The*, 12, 26, 83, 101, 193, 205–6
handicaps, 32, 46–7, 95, 134, 159
Harpham, Geoffrey, 154
Harrington, John, 34, 122, 192
Harvey, Elizabeth, 97

Harvey, William, 97, 209
Hawking, Stephen, 95, 208
Highway, Tomson, 69; *Dry Lips Oughta Move to Kapuskasing*, 202; *Rez Sisters, The*, 202
Hinduism, 58-9, 88-9, 126-7, 196, 214
Hine, Daryl: *Prince of Darkness & Co., The*, 22, 138
Hippocrates, 215
Hodgins, Jack, 29; *Invention of the World, The*, 20, 26, 182
Hooker, Richard, 140, 166
Howells, Coral Ann, 182
humours, 86, 100, 105, 207, 215
Hutcheon, Linda, 138, 163-5, 169-70, 175, 209-10, 214, 221
hygiene, 12, 24, 42, 55, 76, 87-91, 113, 117, 155, 169, 185, 200, 204, 206; and immigrants, 45, 53-4; and social control, 44, 86, 100-1; washing, 30, 58, 86-7, 94, 103, 131, 136, 159-60, 188, 192, 199, 211. *See also* manners

Imagism, 70, 84, 164, 203
immigration. *See* Canada
India, 58
Iser, Wolfgang, 50
Islam, 108, 210
Israel, 69

Jacobson, Roman, 144
Jameson, Fredric, 11, 71-2, 144, 163, 176, 217, 220, 222
Jarry, Alfred, 11
Jerome (Saint), 106, 192
Johnston, Wayne, 91, 116; *Story of Bobby O'Malley, The*, 43, 46, 79, 89-90, 102-3, 112, 129-30, 152-7, 218-19

Jones, D.G., 195
Joyce, James, 11, 198, 210; *Ulysses*, 181, 214
Judaism, 105, 115, 119-20, 135-7, 140, 165, 167, 189, 207-8, 215-16
Jung, Carl, 133, 159, 172, 214

Kayser, Wolfgang, 13, 191
King, William Lyon Mackenzie, 56
Kinsella, W.P.: *Shoeless Joe*, 116, 187-8
Klein, A.M., 68, 71, 117, 202-3; *Second Scroll, The*, 43, 69-70, 75, 139-40
Krafft-Ebing, R.V., 191
Kristeva, Julia, 18, 24, 55, 93, 101, 107-8, 119-20, 139, 165, 178, 183-5, 189, 195, 204, 210, 223
Kroetsch, Robert, 209; *Alibi*, 172-3; *Badlands*, 172
Kroker, Arthur, 12, 77, 94, 145, 163-5, 170, 205, 219

Lacan, Jacques, 7, 100
Ladoo, Harold Sonny, 29, 58, 88, 116, 150-1; *No Pain Like This Body*, 88-9, 108, 126; *Yesterdays*, 21, 35-7, 58-9, 74, 79, 126-7, 149-1, 198, 200
Lampman, Archibald, 195
language, 10, 49, 68, 100, 113-14, 135, 139, 145-6, 154, 164, 181-8, 191, 193, 216, 223; bowdlerism, 124; deictic markers, 9, 149, 218; dialogism, 48, 65, 116, 125, 130, 156, 197, 217; euphemism, 48, 117-19, 124-5, 129, 136, 186, 189-90, 195; expletives, levels of formality, 6, 9-10, 19, 28, 49, 101, 124, 134, 136, 138, 157, 171, 181-2, 185, 190, 211, 213-14;

graffiti, 82, 118–20; and social structure, 9, 49. *See also* obscenity; scatology; taboo
Lao Tzu: *Tao Te Ching*, 220
latrines. *See* bathrooms
Laurence, Margaret, 12, 29, 116, 135, 183; *Diviners, The*, 19–20, 29, 32, 52, 62, 72, 133–4, 185, 191, 195; *Jest of God, A*, 46, 106, 134; *Stone Angel, The*, 19, 31–2, 79, 134, 158, 191
law, 5–6, 186. *See also* obscenity; politics
Lawrence, D.H., 11; *Lady Chatterley's Lover*, 12, 181
Layton, Irving, 182, 215–16
Leacock, Stephen, 199–200; *My Discovery of England*, 49
Lee, Dennis, 222
Lee, Jae Num, 216
Lejeune, Philippe, 51–2, 148–9, 161, 163, 217–18
Lennep, D.J. van, 107
Lévi-Strauss, Claude, 24, 192–3
liberal humanism, 128–30, 136, 168, 188, 209
lice, 44–5, 55, 60, 63
Li Po, 84
Literary Garland, The, 207
Lowry, Malcolm: *Under the Volcano*, 74–5, 95, 149
Luhmann, Niklas, 5–6
Luther, Martin, 121–2, 125, 132, 137–8, 178, 213, 215
Lyotard, Jean-François, 92, 145, 163, 170–1, 178, 217, 221, 223

MacLennan, Hugh: *Two Solitudes*, 72, 76, 81, 184; *Voices in Time*, 97
Maimonides, Moses, 88, 207–8

manners, 3–8, 12–13, 33, 41, 43, 47, 62, 101, 149, 152, 172, 183, 188, 190, 213–14; bathroom, 4, 6–7, 12, 18, 23, 59, 101, 189, 192–3. *See also* civilized self; hygiene; urine
Mantegna, Andrea, 198
manure, 9, 26–7, 102, 105, 137, 193, 206, 208
marginality, 9–10, 26–7, 42, 52, 55, 59, 62, 68–70, 118–19, 166, 198, 202
Marlyn, John: *Under the Ribs of Death*, 53–4
Martin, Judith, 188; *Miss Manners' Guide to Rearing Perfect Children*, 7, 183, 214
materialism, 11, 80–1, 84, 116–20, 125, 127, 128–30, 133, 135–7, 139–40, 144, 154–5, 167, 169, 174, 188, 190–1, 193, 203, 212, 221; medical materialism, 88, 207–8, 216
Mather, Cotton, 90, 123, 213
Maximilian I (King of Mexico), 75
McFarlane, James, 164
McKeon, Michael, 30, 46, 81, 83, 116, 137, 144, 187–8, 194, 196–7, 216
McLuhan, Marshall, 92, 144, 181, 191, 195, 198
McMullen, Lorraine, 102
Melville, Herman: *Moby Dick*, 86, 206
Mennell, Stephen, 190, 196
menstruation, 63, 84, 87, 102, 108, 111–12, 119, 125–6, 210
Mexico, 74–5
miasma, 85–7, 206
milk teeth, 128
Miller, James: *Passion of Michel Foucault, The*, 5

Milton, John, 189
mimesis, 70–2, 80–1, 83–4, 117, 139, 143–5, 148–51, 156, 159–61, 163, 166–7, 170–2, 174, 178, 182–3, 186–8, 211, 217–18, 222–3
Mistry, Rohinton, 54, 59–60
Mitchell, W.O., 68; *Vanishing Point, The*, 21–2, 64, 90–1, 117, 191, 224; *Who Has Seen the Wind*, 26
modernism, 82, 125, 163–4, 172, 182, 194, 214
Monk, Patricia, 97–8
Montaigne, Michel de, 98, 184
Moodie, Susanna, 18, 86–7, 195, 206; *Mark Hurdlestone*, 12, 43, 79, 86–7, 101, 124, 205, 207; *Roughing It in the Bush*, 12, 17–18, 26, 86, 193
Moore, Brian, 54, 76, 116; *Black Robe*, 54, 62, 65, 68, 72, 79, 134–5, 206, 215; *Luck of Ginger Coffey, The*, 21, 44–5, 54, 75
Moore, Samuel, 86
More, Thomas, 10
Mowat, Farley, 60–1; *People of the Deer*, 60–1
mucous, 8, 33, 48, 62, 154, 167, 198
Mulroney, Brian, 70
Munro, Alice, 29, 149, 183; *Lives of Girls and Women*, 13, 19, 27, 29, 43, 50–1, 110–11, 131, 152–3, 209, 218–19; *Progress of Love, The*, 110, 208; *Who Do You Think You Are?*, 18, 29, 32, 46, 52, 110–11, 149
Mussolini, Benito, 84

Natives, 54–5, 60–8, 72, 90–1, 96, 106, 135; Algonkian, 62, 206; Beothuk, 61; Blackfoot, 202; Cree, 62–4, 66–9, 191, 202; Ihalmiùt, 60–1; Iroquois, 65, 177–8, 201; Laguna, 202; Ojibway, 69; Ottawa, 201; and religion, 64–5, 67–8, 137; Winnebago, 201. *See also* Trickster
neocolonialism, 74
Nietzsche, Friedrich, 119, 121; *Also Sprach Zarathustra*, 137
Nkrumah, Kwame, 73, 204
Novak, Maximillian, 144

obscenity, 48, 62, 64, 107, 109, 121, 138–9, 184–6, 214, 216; censorship, 7, 13, 107, 151, 185–6, 189, 197–8. *See also* law; taboo
odour, 3, 11, 33, 35, 43, 57, 60–2, 78, 81, 86–7, 118, 166, 168–9, 191, 193, 202, 206
O'Hagan, Howard, 29; *School-Marm Tree, The*, 33, 101; *Tay John*, 12, 187
Ondaatje, Michael, 82, 172, 183, 210; *Collected Works of Billy the Kid, The: Left-Handed Poems*, 11, 81–3, 150, 173–5; *Coming through Slaughter*, 11, 43, 46, 82, 173–5, 222; *English Patient, The*, 84; *Running in the Family*, 82–3, 158, 174–5, 188
Orangeism, 62
Ostenso, Martha, 12, 29; *Wild Geese*, 20, 26–7, 29, 102, 193
ovaries, 104–5, 112

Pache, Walter, 163
Palmer, Howard, 54, 56
panopticism. *See* surveillance
Paracelsus, 96, 193, 215

parody, 30, 34–8, 65–8, 77, 125, 127–8, 133–4, 146, 150, 160, 165–7, 171–2, 176–7, 185, 188, 194, 212, 214, 219–21
Pasteur, Louis, 4, 86, 206, 208
Paz, Octavio, 81
Pepys, Samuel, 197–8
Perelman, Bob, 222
Pineo, Peter, 53, 193, 198
Pisan, Christine de, 210
Platner, Ernst, 86
Plato, 81, 138, 165, 187, 215, 220, 222
politics, 37–8, 41–2, 51, 69, 71–8, 81–4, 123, 135, 195, 202–4, 206, 221; authority, 37, 48–9, 52, 72, 80–1, 83, 127–8, 138, 158–9, 165–6, 170–1, 197; British empire, 56, 59–60, 73–5, 84, 113, 199–200, 204; democracy, 18, 44–6, 72, 75–6, 168, 176, 204; fascism, 55, 84, 168–9, 199, 202, 206; Marxism, 73–4, 116, 179, 203, 218; monarchy, 75, 166, 204, 221; revolution 47, 73–4
pollution, 10, 53, 77, 108, 111–14, 144, 153, 157, 187, 206; environmental, 21, 87, 90–1, 192, 208; garbage, 43, 48, 52, 56, 75, 93, 133–4, 158, 165, 171–2, 195, 215; religious, 9, 58, 63, 87–8, 106, 108, 115, 117, 119–21, 126–7, 136, 139, 165, 177–8, 207–8, 210, 216, 219; and repetition 184–5, 187. *See also* taboo
Pope, Alexander, 200
Porter, John, 42, 53, 193, 198, 202
Porush, David, 93, 95, 170
Post, Emily: *Emily Post's Etiquette*, 6, 214

post-colonialism, 36, 74–5
post-modernism, 12, 98, 145, 150, 163–80, 194, 203, 217, 219–23; and the body, 165–6, 171–80, 219–20; death of the author, 163, 170, 172, 209, 218; indeterminacy, 174, 184; *mise en abîme*, 118; simulation, 77, 92–3, 120, 145, 169–70, 176–8, 217, 220
Poulet, Georges, 50
Pound, Ezra, 70, 168–9, 198, 203
Pownall, David: *Masterclass*, 13
Pratt, E.J., 212; *Brébeuf and His Brethren*, 60, 201
primitivism, 18, 36–7, 46, 65, 88, 138, 151
privacy, 12, 20, 35, 47, 49, 71–2, 148
progressive narrative, 46, 50, 54, 76, 197
psychoanalysis, 4–5, 10, 24, 55, 79, 91, 100, 106–7, 116–17, 122–4, 138–9, 155, 158–61, 179, 184
Pynchon, Thomas, 220; *Crying of Lot 49, The*, 166, 171

Rabelais, 140, 157; *Gargantua*, 129–30, 135; *Pantagruel*, 96, 122, 195, 202, 211
race, 44, 53–70, 80, 104, 186, 193, 198–202; Anglo-conformity, 56, 199; Canadian government policy, 54, 70; colour, 54, 57, Eastern Europeans, 53–4, 199–200; 'implied' Canadian, 59–60; Jews, 55–7, 68–70, 177–8, 199, 202; West Indians, 58; Zionism, 68–70. *See also* Natives
Radin, Paul, 201
Ramcharan, Subhas, 55

rationality, 10, 23, 88, 131, 156, 160, 165–6, 173–4, 209–10, 216, 222
realism, 11, 31–2, 36, 50, 91, 93, 124, 133–5, 137, 148, 164, 168, 170–1, 174, 176, 182–3, 188, 193–4, 222. See also mimesis
reception theory, 50, 100, 144, 209, 222
religion, 24, 115–40, 211–17, 221. See also Christianity; Hinduism; Islam; Judaism; Natives (and religion)
Rembrandt Harmensz van Rijn, 197–8
repression, 4–7, 9–10, 12–13, 18, 22–3, 36–7, 48, 56, 59, 62, 64, 66, 77, 81–2, 106–7, 122–4, 128, 132, 134, 139, 154, 156, 158, 188, 194, 223; incitement to speak, 77, 151, 182; and language, 46, 182, 186; lifting of, 34, 155; and literature, 19, 28, 31–2, 52, 150. See also obscenity
reversible world, 51, 166–7, 216
Ricardo, David, 78
Richardson, John: *Wacousta*, 60–1, 101, 200–1
Richler, Mordecai, 12, 29, 33, 52, 80, 116, 183, 202; *Apprenticeship of Duddy Kravitz, The*, 26, 44, 47, 50, 70, 78, 80–1, 83, 88, 95, 185–6; *Jacob Two-Two Meets the Hooded Fang*, 189; *Joshua Then and Now*, 33–4, 48, 56–7, 68, 87, 135–6, 186, 200; *Solomon Gursky Was Here*, 43, 51, 55–6, 137; *Son of a Smaller Hero*, 20, 34, 43–4; *St Urbain's Horseman*, 3, 21, 38, 44, 46, 55–7, 68–9, 75, 136
Riffaterre, Michel, 165
Rimbaud, Arthur, 218
romance, 32, 61, 187–8, 194, 197, 205, 211
Rooke, Leon, 117, 169; *Shakespeare's Dog*, 34–5, 139–40, 166–8, 174, 183, 220–1
Rorty, Richard, 165
Ross, Sinclair: *As For Me and My House*, 124–5, 191, 214
Rosso, Stefano, 217
Roy, Gabrielle, 29; *petite poule d'eau, La*, 8, 29, 60, 195
Rushdie, Salman: *Midnight's Children*, 11

Said, Edward, 11, 190
saliva. See spitting
Santorius, S., 97
satire, 12, 44, 47, 55–7, 60, 64, 83, 89, 96, 111, 136, 138, 201, 211, 213, 216
Saussure, Ferdinand de, 144
Scarry, Elaine, 11, 191, 212, 223
scatology, 12, 26–7, 30–2, 37, 42–3, 45, 47, 49, 50, 55–8, 60–2, 64, 76, 94, 111, 113, 119–20, 157–8, 206–7, 219; and aesthetics, 13, 36, 68–70, 84, 93, 104, 119, 135, 143, 159, 161, 166, 171, 173, 184–8, 219; as epistemology, 127, 139, 155, 168, 185, 188, 216, 221, 223; and ethnography, 64, 68; as naturalizer, 83, 90, 130, 133, 168–9, 171, 174, 188; and parody, 65–8; scatomancy, 97, 134, 173; scatophagy, 96–7, 129–30, 139,

151, 173, 177, 212; and signification, 137, 163, 165, 173-4, 182, 184; and social structure, 50, 143, 151, 216
scepticism, 34-8, 51, 58, 64, 68, 133, 154-5, 163, 167, 178-9, 186, 188, 194
Schweickart, Patrocinio, 100, 113, 209
Schwenger, Peter, 209
science, 23, 27, 85-98, 124, 133, 150, 190, 206-9, 215, 223. See also disease; technology
science fiction, 92-3, 171
Scott, Chris, 116, 183; *Antichthon* 127-9, 221
semen, 65, 112, 215
Serrano, Andres, 223
sewers, sewage, 25-7, 64, 86, 153-5, 174, 195, 206-7, 221
Shakespeare, William, 166
shaman, 67-8
Sheldon, W.H., 97, 132-3
Shell, Marc, 71, 79
Shklovsky, Viktor, 144
Showalter, Elaine, 100-1
Silko, Leslie Marmon, 202
slang. *See* language (expletives)
Smart, Elizabeth, 108, 210; *Assumption of Rogues and Rascals, The,* 103, 105, 157; *By Grand Central Station I Sat Down and Wept,* 103-5
smegma, 131
smell. *See* odour
Smith, Robertson, 24
Snow, John, 87
sodomy, 8, 12, 74, 108, 121, 126-7, 132, 152, 173, 187, 222

somatotyping, 97
soul, 12, 54, 123-4, 128, 135, 139-40, 167, 184, 211-12, 215-16
Spariosu, Mihai, 145, 217
speech act theory, 171-2, 180
Spengemann, William, 150, 154, 218-19
Spiro, Solomon, 70
spitting, saliva, 9, 45, 92, 121, 128, 131-2, 195, 206, 214-15
Sri Lanka, 82
Stallybrass, Peter, 6, 37-8, 41-2, 51, 76, 85-7, 196
Stanton, Domna, 217, 219
Stercus, 193
Stich, K.P., 148-9, 209
Stimpson, Catherine, 209
Stoekl, Allan, 206
Strindberg, August: *A Dream Play,* 222
Such, Peter: *Riverrun,* 61-2
surveillance, 5-6, 19, 111, 154-5, 158
Süskind, Patrick: *Das Parfüm,* 5, 182, 207
sweat, 61, 125
Sweatman, Margaret: *Fox,* 53-4
Swedenborg, Emmanuel, 194
Swift, Jonathan, 83, 109, 200; 'A Discourse Concerning the Mechanical Operation of the Spirit,' 97; *Gulliver's Travels,* 96

taboo 6-7, 42, 45, 59-60, 108, 120, 144-6, 151, 165, 193, 196, 210-11, 213-14, 216; and class, 51; and silence, 6-8. *See also* pollution
Tacitus, 11

Tatum, Stephen, 174
tears, 128, 168, 172, 201
technology, 23, 37, 77, 91–4, 96, 171, 208
Tertullian, 106
Thomas, Audrey, 29, 112; *Latakia*, 21–2, 103–4; *Mrs Blood*, 8, 21, 31, 108, 125–6, 214
Thompson, Judith: *White Biting Dog*, 191, 221
Thompson, Philip, 166
Tillich, Paul, 137, 186
Todorov, Tzvetan, 144
toilets. *See* bathrooms
Traill, Catharine Parr, 32
translation, 63, 123–4
Trickster, 21, 64–5, 67–8, 164, 201–2
Trinidad, 36, 58, 88, 126–7
Trotula, 210
Turner, Bryan, 76

unconscious, 7, 52, 81, 112, 129, 131, 133, 179, 206
underwear, 9, 113–14, 118, 169
United States, 81–2, 205–6
urine, urination, 6, 27, 31, 35, 37, 44, 47, 56–7, 65, 78, 80, 82, 93–6, 121, 123, 132, 153, 158, 166, 168, 173–4, 177, 190, 193, 199, 205, 216, 223, 224; as antiseptic, 88–9; retention of, 101, 111, 155; as territorial marking, 70, 82, 174; Texas catheter, 92; and virginity, 102, 209

Valcourt, Bernard, 70
Valentinus, 121, 128
Vanderbilt, Amy: *Amy Vanderbilt Complete Book of Etiquette, The*, 6
Van Gogh, Vincent, 220
Van Leewenhoek, Anthony, 215
Vespasian, 205
Vico, Giambattista, 143
Vietnam, 82
Vigarello, Georges, 18
virtual reality, 78, 92–5, 170–2
Vogt, A.E. van, 12
vomit, 36, 61, 68–70, 139, 156, 166–7, 174, 200, 221, 224

Walker, Benjamin, 10
Walker, Edward, 204
Warhol, Andy, 220
washing. *See* hygiene
Watson, Sheila: *Double Hook, The*, 164
Watt, Ian, 211
Weber, Max, 115–16, 205, 211
Webster, Mary, 123
Welch, James: *Winter in the Blood*, 202
welfare, 43
Wellhausen, Julius, 118
White, Allon, 6, 37–8, 41–2, 51, 76, 85–7, 196
White, Hayden, 144
Wiebe, Rudy, 65–6; *Temptations of Big Bear, The*, 61–4, 201
Wikkramasinha, Lakdasa, 82
Williams, David, 54–5, 76, 116; *Burning Wood, The*, 55, 66–7, 135; *Eye of the Father*, 44, 50, 55, 108, 134–5, 157; *River Horsemen, The*, 12, 55, 67–8, 75, 106, 135, 149
Williams, Raymond, 193

Wilson, Ethel, 27, 29; *Swamp Angel*, 28
Winnett, Susan, 108
Wiseman, Adele: *Sacrifice, The*, 53
witches, 106, 121, 123, 213
women, 19, 42, 63-4, 78, 99-114, 125-6, 202, 205, 209-11, 213; abortion, 108, 112; childbirth, 101, 105-7, 112, 153, 157, 209; female writing, 104-5, 107, 165-6, 210, 217, 219; housework, 103-4; mothers, 49, 93, 210
Woodcock, George, 54
Wordsworth, William, 185
Wyke, Clement, 200

Zola, Émile, 98